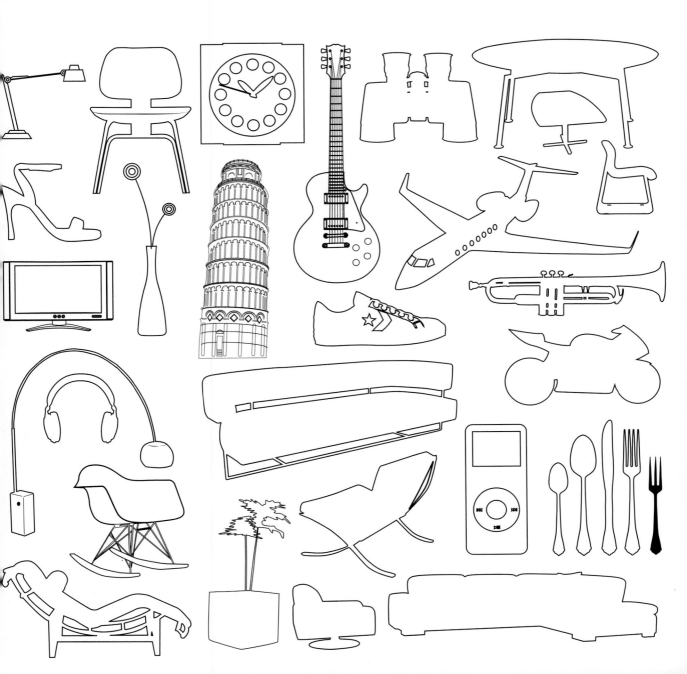

beautiful

an introduction to

—

robert clay

thing
design

Oxford · New York

English edition
First published in 2009 by
Berg
Editorial offices:
First Floor, Angel Court, 81 St Clements Street, Oxford OX4 1AW, UK
175 Fifth Avenue, New York, NY 10010, USA

Berg is the imprint of Oxford International Publishers Ltd.

Library of Congress Cataloging-in-Publication Data
A catalogue record for this book is available from the Library of Congress.

British Library Cataloguing-in-Publication Data
A catalogue record for this book is available from the British Library.

ISBN   978 1 84788 264 6 (Cloth)
          978 1 84788 263 9 (Paper)

Design by Chris Bromley.
Printed by the MPG Books Group in the UK

www.bergpublishers.com

contents

To the beautiful Ava

acknowledgements

─────

I would like to thank:

- Tristan Palmer, Editorial Director, Berg Publishers
- Centre for Enterprise, University of Teesside
- Marek Reichman, Director of Design, Aston Martin Lagonda Ltd
- Sean Hughes, Creative Director, Philips Design, Hong Kong
- Tony Castro, Director, Tony Castro Naval Architects and Yacht Designers, Southampton
- Jamie Billing and Tracy Cordingley, Technical/Creative Design Directors, Alte Design Ltd, UK

Thanks also to the many companies and individuals, too numerous to list here, who contributed information and images of their designs.

introduction

———

design, art and technology

The word *design* means different things to different people depending on where they sit on the design spectrum – a spectrum with art placed at one end and technology at the other. One thing they all have in common however is composition – the assembling of different elements in order to express thoughts and emotions (in the case of the artist) or to solve a particular technical problem (in the case of the engineer). Of course much design is a blend of art and design and belongs somewhere away from either end of the spectrum; for example the fashion designer is concerned with the visual and sensual qualities of textile materials and the style and fit of a garment on a person, as well as technical issues to do with manufacturing and production. Most people would place fashion designers towards the 'art' end of the spectrum, however, with engineers placed more towards the technology end – although the products of the civil engineer, a bridge design for example, have a large impact on the visual environment and should therefore also be considered an art form. Perhaps the works of the architect and the industrial (product) designer belong smack in the middle of the art/ design spectrum – each has to balance visual elegance with engineering and materials technology (as well as user requirements). Of course all artists and designers also have to consider the constraints of cost of their creations.

In many countries the choice of a scientific or technical career while still at school often rules out the further study of art and, although some improvements in some curricula have taken place in recent years, the importance of the *visual* often merely receives lip service or is missed out altogether. This is a tragedy for the individual as well as society. In many towns and cities throughout the so-called developed world we find ourselves surrounded by much that is of poor visual quality, whether this be the buildings and environment or, on a smaller scale, furniture and product designs. We seem content to put up with poorly planned town spaces and transport systems. Any high street looks like any other high street in any other town and it is often instructive to look up above the plastic shop signs to see the original architecture left unmasked. Many of these built environments have probably ended up in a bit of a mess because visual education in many countries has concentrated on art at the expense of architecture and design. Wonderful as the fine arts are, we neglect the man-made visual environment and artefact at our peril.

One of the aims of this book is an attempt to highlight the relationships between art and technology, why each depends on the other and how these relationships can impact on our emotional wellbeing. The education of engineering students in many universities hardly ever includes issues of beauty, or even the end users' requirements of the machine they are designing. To be fair, however, the thing they are designing might only have a small functional part to play in the larger machine (although parts of machines can be beautiful too!). This is also true of the relationship between the structural engineer and the architect; technology is not the enemy of art – both are necessary to achieve the goals of physical elegance and spiritual reward in design. There has always been some confusion about the different roles of the architect/designer and the engineer, so it's worth making a distinction here. Although there is considerable overlap between these disciplines, the main difference between the architect/designer and the engineer is their different *starting points* – the architect/designer usually starts by considering the requirements of the end users of their designs (where beauty is only one consideration) and then works towards the employment of technology in order to solve problems. The engineer on the other hand usually starts (and ends) with a technical problem, although the solution can sometimes affect the end user's experiences – for example designing a more compact car engine/transmission system in order to enable greater passenger space and comfort. This, of course, also has implications for the appearance of the car. All design activity (apart from certain solitary crafts) is a team effort in any case and the greater the shared understanding and empathy between the different disciplines of each team member, the greater will be the chances of producing a better design solution.

We would all surely prefer to live in pleasant surroundings and occupy a well designed, visually satisfying and solidly built house. The furniture, domestic appliances and the myriad of other manufactured objects we surround ourselves with, are chosen largely on visual and emotional criteria. For example what were the main reasons, besides cost, for choosing your last car or set of tableware? Shape, form, detail, colour, texture, tactile properties, and ease of use – all of these properties of objects have some role to play besides cost. Even dyed-in-the-wool engineers make visual and emotional choices when it comes to exchanging their old car for a new model. A sensually pleasing product can also improve our performance – the human factors guru Donald Norman states that: '... we now have evidence that aesthetically pleasing objects enable you to work better' – and that 'products and systems that make you feel good are easier to deal with and produce more harmonious results'.[1]

The young in modern society have a particularly strong appetite for the visual – loosely termed 'fashion' – and this can include a multitude of manufactured artefacts, anything from clothing to the particular MP3 player or scooter they choose to buy. Design is a huge wealth creating industry in which any developed or developing nation needs to maintain a stake.

Some knowledge of the history of design is vital to an understanding of where we are in the scheme of things today. To understand the reasons why a particular product or building was designed in a particular 'style' – one needs to be aware of the social, economic, technological and aesthetic forces prevailing at the time. Design develops over time – contemporary design is the way it is because of an evolutionary process of thought and an acceptance of new ways of doing things. Nineteenth-century thinkers such as William Morris and John Ruskin hated the idea of the mass manufacture of products by machines – they thought that true beauty could only be brought about by individual craftsmen making a particular design by hand tools alone. They maintained that there was a certain quality about individually crafted products, each one being slightly different from the next, that would be lost in making things by unthinking and unfeeling machines (a view not necessarily shared by their Arts and Crafts contemporaries in mainland Europe). Morris and Ruskin's socialist ideal of making good design available to all was self-defeating, however – the irony being that many hand-crafted products were extremely expensive and could not be produced in sufficient quantities and at a price the ordinary person could afford. Nowadays we take for granted machine-made products, many of which we consider beautiful (the 'machine aesthetic') – the fact that there are many identical products doesn't seem to matter in the slightest to most of us. There has, however, been a resurgence of interest in the crafts in recent years. Although we appreciate the machine-made artefact, we also sometimes take pleasure in the uniqueness of the 'one off'.

Design is constantly changing and history can only teach us so much about what to do next, however. In this context we should not be teaching design history as an end in itself but as a means to an end. The designer and forecaster Kevin McCullagh says: 'One might also argue that a successful contextual education should feed students' creativity. If creativity is the connection of previously unrelated ideas/concepts, then a well-stocked mind with a knowledge framework on which to hang new ideas would seem a positive asset.'[2]

Design is a multidisciplinary subject and the visual element cannot be separated out from other related areas such as; the historical, contextual, technical and the practical. Visual education can sometimes be a somewhat hit-and-miss affair and it can take a long time for an individual to acquire sufficient knowledge and visual skills in order to become a competent practising designer. Of course it is impossible to become a good designer from simply reading books – and it is also impossible to formally *teach* students how to design beautiful things. However those new (or new-ish) to the subject would hopefully benefit from a resource that, at the outset, helps them to make the necessary connections between different elements, understand basic concepts and illuminate certain well-known principles that might otherwise be trusted to luck.

Most people are attracted to the study of design because they are interested in beauty, among other things such as problem solving and inventing new products. But beauty is not simply concerned with how things look; the underlying structures of buildings and objects can also be beautiful in an abstract sense. For example, a bridge structure has to withstand many different and changing (dynamic) forces and therefore its design should aim at resisting these forces through the simplest arrangement of its forms, for the sake of efficiency and economy (just as nature does a lot with very little). Designing a suspension bridge requires considerable knowledge and expertise in mathematics, materials science and engineering to counteract such forces, and yet these 'non-artistic' constraints almost (in a sense) automatically produce a most beautiful and graceful object. This can also be seen in boat and aeroplane design where the shape of an object is largely determined by the load it has to carry, the medium it travels through and its performance requirements (for example, speed). Again these constraints can produce beautiful forms even without any artistic intervention. It might seem then that beauty is a by-product of evolution, whether natural or technological, but in being impressed with bridges and aeroplanes we seem to sense the underlying beauty of their structure, perhaps analogous to a person's beauty being an indicator of underlying good health. But this puts beauty in the driving seat – we are attracted to beautiful people and objects and this is usually the thing we first notice about them. Whichever does come first, beauty or function, beauty is suffused throughout all fields of design and this book attempts to introduce the subject in the sense that beauty is a doorway into discussing *all* design. Everything is inextricably connected to everything else.

Although simplicity is a fundamental aim when designing things, like the bridge example above, this does not always produce a beautiful object. Achieving a simple-yet-elegant solution is what we are after and many designers prefer to use the word 'elegance' instead of 'beauty' (or 'aesthetically pleasing') when talking about a good example, or the high efficiency, of a particular design solution. There are potentially many different solutions to a particular design problem or set of constraints but the most elegant solutions are those that use fewer materials, are unfussy and yet do a better job compared to their more complicated rivals. Elaboration does not necessarily equal sophistication. The modernist architect Mies van der Rohe encapsulated this in his phrase 'less is more' – a motto that has been abused ever since but one that we should take in the spirit in which it was meant, that is, we should seek simplicity, not in a crude sense but rather to *beautifully* get the maximum out of the minimum. This way lies elegance. Although (often conflicting) constraints can be sometimes cause us difficulties when designing things, constraints can also *help* us to come up with a design proposal. Conversely the fewer constraints we are faced with can make life even more difficult – the dreaded 'open brief'. This is particularly acute where fashion is a factor, as in the case of car styling for example (where different car designs often share identical and well engineered platforms); the same technical specification can result in two completely different styles of car by two different manufacturers (or brands), one ugly and the other beautiful. This is where function meets art and where logic and words begin to fail.

evolution, culture and beauty

From early childhood onwards we are all profoundly affected by our surroundings, the natural and built environments have the capacity to lift or dampen our spirits – particular environments can make us feel happy, gloomy or even fearful. Buildings, spaces, trees and greenery, the sunlight and weather – all interact with the human condition. We are all products of the sun and earth and it's no wonder that our emotions are affected by our surroundings, interpreted through our senses; we

are an integral part of the planet and its life and studies of the affects of environments on human emotions and health are numerous.[3]

George Ferguson, a past president of Britain's Royal Institute of British Architects (RIBA), maintained that good architecture is an issue that concerns a country's mental health as well as its architectural heritage and proposed setting up an 'X list' of awful buildings that should be demolished.

Scientists have argued that our ability to appreciate beauty is entirely a product of evolutionary adaptation. For example the beauty of apple blossom in the spring is simply a sign that there will be plenty to eat this summer, therefore giving rise to a feeling of pleasure. Also colour vision helps us to determine whether or not the fruit is ripe enough to eat. A physically beautiful person is a sign of good health and fertility and therefore beauty is obviously a very powerful factor in the mating stakes. We are also attracted to a beautiful person because beauty is the opposite of disease or injury – a diseased person might not be such a good bet in the interests of survival and reproduction. The philosopher Elaine Scarry proposes that when we see beauty we have an inherent desire to reproduce it and that, by mating with a beautiful individual, we will produce beautiful (and therefore healthy) children.[4]

Scarry also believes that we have a natural wish to reproduce beauty in many other forms, for example through photographs or paintings of a particular landscape or sunset. Human beings, and perhaps most animal species, are impressed by particularly beautiful examples of their own kind – every animal seeks the ideal mate for himself or herself. Of course other attributes are advantageous, for example some male species of Australian and New Guinea bower-bird try to attract their mate with demonstrations of building skills, first constructing elaborate bowers or 'display stages' from twigs and grasses on which to strut their stuff in the hope of attracting a female.[5] These well-maintained bowers are often decorated with shells, small pebbles and flowers (which are replaced when starting to fade) and are sometimes even 'painted' with the juice from coloured berries. A particularly elegant and well decorated bower seems to get the most attention from the females (who build a separate nest in which to raise their young). The bower-bird's antics would seem to indicate an innate sense of beauty somewhat akin to our own – perhaps human architects and designers are, at base, trying to attract the attention of the opposite sex too!

Geoffrey Miller[6] believes that the ancient practice of body painting began as a way of attracting sexual partners – it makes evolutionary sense to pick the best body decorator. As well as choosing someone who looks good, you are also selecting valuable genetic endowments for any children you may have; genes for assets such as dexterity, creativity, conscientiousness and resourcefulness (because the ochre dye necessary for body painting can be hard to find). These are traits for survival as well as artistry. In the animal world the male peacock attempts to attract the female peahen through his huge and colourful tail display. Carrying around such a large and heavy tail however has disadvantages for survival, making the bird more vulnerable to attack by predators. However the fact that the male peacock copes with this encumbrance is actually a sign of *good* survival skills, demonstrating high levels of strength and fitness. Among humans the possession of a high level of skill at tool making also demonstrates desirable traits. Many stone-age hand axes have been found that are highly symmetrical in three dimensions – even though symmetry is not strictly

necessary for the tool to be a good cutter. Steven Mithen suggests that these especially fine and aesthetically pleasing hand-axes – the 'sexy hand-axe' – might have been made primarily to impress the opposite sex.[7]

Evolution has produced many different creatures whose behaviour patterns include building and shaping things from inanimate objects and natural materials. The bird's nest has its human equivalent in the dwellings and objects that we design and use, although humans continue to develop and improve designs whereas nests and cobwebs have remained essentially the same for millennia. The humble bicycle started off as a wooden-framed structure that allowed you to walk whilst sitting down and its design has evolved over the years as advances in materials technology have affected its construction, and today many bicycles are supreme examples of elegant design (though some bicycles are more elegant than others!). Indeed cycling is now a much more efficient means of getting around than walking and scientists maintain that the bicycle is as much a product of evolution as is an animal. The evolutionary biologist Richard Dawkins maintains that when an animal's genes have an effect on inanimate objects outside its own body, for example producing a nest, cobweb or a bicycle, this is still brought about by evolution. Dawkins calls this effect the 'extended phenotype'.[8]

Evolution can no doubt explain the basis for recognizing beauty as an aid to survival and reproduction and the 'Ultra-Darwinists' would say that that is all there is to it. However, we continue to take an interest in beauty long after our survival needs have been met, although this may simply be due to us being unable to switch off survival's drive, akin to eating too much long after our bodily requirements have been met simply for pleasure or comfort. Whatever the reason, this continued interest in beauty is true of any culture, although different cultures have different notions of beauty, indicating that there is a significant *learned* element in addition to those driven by survival instincts. The neuroscientist Professor Vilayanur S. Ramachandran, Director of the Centre for Brain and Cognition at the University of California, suggests that universal aesthetic principles do exist.[9] That perhaps 90 per cent of the variance in art is driven by cultural diversity but the remaining 10 per cent is governed by universal laws that are common to all brains. This is analogous to humans being 'wired' for language at birth, but the particular language an individual learns is dependent on the culture he or she is born into.

Culture, then, started where evolution 'left off', carrying on and developing notions of beauty long after beauty served any practical purpose in our lives. Steven Rose argues that there is much more to life than can be explained by biological determinism alone – the arrangement of genes cannot determine what happens to an individual in the course of his or her life; the influence of others on thought, the particular culture the individual is born into or the interests and ambitions of a person.[10]

The resulting society of individuals is therefore much more significant and meaningful than merely the sum of its genes. The cultural equivalent of the role of genes in biological evolution has been dubbed 'memes' – though cultural evolution happens much more rapidly.[11]

Therefore intellectual endeavour, including notions of beauty in whatever form, should no longer be regarded simply as a product of survival behaviour but must also be considered as a significant force in the universe in its own right. Beauty aside, this abstract force of intellect has, through our ideas and inventions, already had a physical affect on the geography, biology and climate of our planet.

comparisons with other forms of beauty

There are of course forms of beauty other than the visual to be found in all walks of life, for example scientific or mathematical beauty. Mendeleyev's Periodic Table of Elements – strict sequential steps of atomic weights each describing or predicting a new element – or Einstein's famously simple equation $E = MC^2$ describing the equivalence of energy and mass (Einstein himself maintained that a good theory should possess beauty) – and these insights into the structures of the universe are rightly regarded as sublime by most of us. Such theories contain very powerful truths and possess an abstract beauty or elegance that appeals to the reasoning and imaginative mind. However, many significant mathematical formulas are 'untidy'; for example, Pi is not a nice round whole number but it nevertheless appeals to the intellect as an important abstract mathematical tool.

In contrast, musical beauty seems to bypass reasoning completely and directly affects the emotions. Some would argue that, because of this, music is the highest of all the arts. This might be due to the suggestion that music has its origins in a form of 'musical' or tonal communication uttered by *Homo sapiens*' ancestors (prior to the development of 'proper' language) in order to communicate with each other and also express emotions.[12]

Even the domestic dog knows the mood of its owner by the tone of his voice. So it is likely that 'music' existed even before words and is therefore already deeply embedded in our emotional brains. We all know that babies are more likely to go to sleep when sung to, rather than talked at. Scientists tell us that music is a uniquely human trait and that even birdsong is not music – the sounds that birds make are only particular calls or signals to other birds, to attract a mate or defend a territory for example. However, if one definition of music is that sounds can express and communicate emotions, then birdsong may indeed be a primitive form of music – analogous to the sounds made by our human ancestors – birds can certainly express and communicate emotions to other birds: even we humans can sense their alarm through their agitated calls when a cat comes too close for comfort. We also sometimes think we can detect a melody in a blackbird's 'song', but this is only putting our interpretation onto something – the blackbird doesn't tap its feet.

Interestingly, mathematics, music, drama and dance can all be written down as a set of instructions or guidelines, but it is only through the eyes, ears, mind and emotions of the observer that a true appreciation of these types of beauty is experienced. Words are therefore inadequate to describe the experience of beauty – to quote Philip Rawson:[13] 'and that is why spokesmen for the arts always claim, quite rightly, to be operating beyond the reach of ordinary, utilitarian communication. That is also why the resolutely inartistic can never understand the point of art.'

The physicist Brian Ridley[14] suggests that we use the term 'magical truth' to describe non-material human forces – art, poetry, music, literature or even an individual's personality, charisma or creativity. Ridley does not mean magic in the sense of black magic or the supernatural – rather, that non-material human forces are magical forces in the sense that they are non-mechanical and therefore indescribable by science. The experience of beauty then is a magic truth, belonging: 'purely to the human world of sensibility'. Ridley goes on to say that magical truth and scientific truth are complementary – mathematics can describe the universe but its beauty is experienced only in the mind.

judging beauty

There have been many attempts by philosophers, past and present, to define beauty. The British philosopher and art critic Clive Bell (1881–1964) stated that: 'any system of aesthetics which pretends to be based on some objective truth is palpably ridiculous as not to be worth discussing' – meaning that beauty is entirely subjective in nature and is experienced by everyone on his or her own terms.[15]

Aesthetics is the name given to the philosophy (or academic study) of beauty, which attempts to objectively describe beauty (and issues of taste) through language, and explain the causes and the experience of beauty as felt, through the written word, although some philosophers say that this is impossible (for example Wittgenstein). The eighteenth century German philosopher Immanuel Kant, however, proposed that objects can be judged beautiful when they satisfy a disinterested desire – one that doesn't involve personal interests or needs. Thus Kant maintained that judgements of beauty are nothing to do with personal taste but are universal.

Artists and architects of the Italian Renaissance believed that the human form was the basis of beauty, and that buildings and that structures should be designed with human proportions in mind – 'man is the measure of all things'. Certainly all buildings before and since the Renaissance have been designed around human proportions – we all have to use them – but we still get ugly buildings. You will need to make up your own mind on these issues, the main theoretical arguments are set out in 'theory boxes' towards the ends of the chapters of this book. However this is not a book about the philosophy of beauty per se but rather an introduction to design in terms of *integrating* the practical, historical and contextual issues – subjects that are often taught as separate entities but are nevertheless all essential to becoming a good designer – a designer capable of realizing beautiful holistic solutions to a variety of new problems.

The perception of beauty produces an immediate internal *sensation* in the observer in response to some external object or event. This sensation is certainly felt but is subjective in nature and difficult or impossible to put into words. For our purposes here then, it is probably useful if we replace the word 'sensation' with 'judgement' when attempting to discuss beauty. We could say that to experience beauty requires a *judgement* on the part of the individual. Is a particular building or poem better or worse than another other building or poem? Is this person more beautiful compared to this other person? If all human beings were suddenly wiped out there would be no one left to make these kinds of judgements – so logically 'beauty' would cease to exist, although some philosophers might disagree. So where does all this get the budding design student? If there are no measurable properties to beauty how does one set about

learning to construct beautiful things? (Although beauty is only one aspect of art and design.) This is fraught with difficulty – most people can appreciate physical beauty but fewer will have the ability to create it. This is an often painful struggle and one of the reasons for writing this book was an attempt to provide an introduction, or a set of 'handles', to help students grasp concepts of accepted wisdom and design logic that might assist in judging beauty in their chosen vocation, as well as providing them with some conceptual tools that will hopefully help to compose that thing some have called 'visual music'. The first thing to accept is the realization that the world and time in which the student finds him or herself is part of a process – the history of art, design, science and human endeavour in general is a continually evolving process – our current values have been shaped over previous times and our contribution will effect the direction of 'future history'.

Our notions of beauty are therefore constantly evolving. No doubt there will be beautiful new buildings as well as ugly new buildings. How will we decide which is which? To help us with these

Fig 1 Bugatti Type 35. 1925. Technology dates but beauty doesn't.

issues we should seek the opinions of those individuals in society who specialize in making such judgements – artists, designers, architects, historians, composers, writers, tutors and critics. Such people have studied their subjects in depth over a long period of time and have a body of knowledge and experience to bring to bear on issues of beauty and taste. Even these people argue with each other however, but argument is a healthy sign. One could say that consulting these 'judges of beauty' is analogous to the role of judges in law, to whom we look for guidance in matters of justice and punishment, although even there we find differences in opinion and sentencing. Perhaps one measure of beauty at least does lie in the field of science and technology. The materials, technologies and aspirations of past generations have always led to particular outstanding designs – for example, Bugatti's T35 racing car of 1924 (Figure 1). Further, what goes into making a particularly beautiful design is often very subtle. For example, the Parthenon in Athens built nearly 2,500 years ago is deliberately distorted to make it 'look right'. If looked at carefully, similar distortions and swellings can also be detected on a smaller scale in product designs generally and today's car designs in particular. Deciding which car to buy involves a judgement of contemporary sculpture by the purchaser, whether they are consciously artistic or not. For this reason car design is included in 'sculptural properties of everyday objects' in Chapter 3.

Certain structures and objects, like the ones mentioned above, remain classics of beauty today, even though technically they were surpassed years ago. This does not mean that we cannot appreciate their inherent beauty and the skill of the designers – just as we can appreciate the beauty of today's products. Time does not diminish their elegance – technology dates but beauty does not. However we may not be able to fully understand the significance and beauty of past designs and works of art – we would need to learn about the cultural values, beliefs and symbolic meanings of the people who produced a particular work in a particular period. Although design history is essential reading for design students, books on their own are ultimately of limited practical help in learning to be a good designer. You will need to talk to like-minded people, experiment, try to solve a variety of design problems, and make mistakes; there is no substitute for experience.

As noted earlier, there is a lot more to design than just visual attributes; for example how easy is it for the user to understand and operate a domestic appliance (the man–machine interface)? How reliable is it? How well does it perform its tasks? Is it easy to maintain? What materials and manufacturing processes are used in a particular product's design? What forces does a structure have to resist? The list goes on and there are many books written on these related subjects. Although all of these factors have a strong bearing on the visual outcome of the design, what seems to be missing for anyone learning about design is help with the intellectual challenge of reconciling these different aspects of design into visually elegant whole solutions. Design is a holistic enterprise; no one ingredient can be separated out; beauty cannot be tacked on after the functional problems have been solved.

chapter one

---

on taste

chapter outline

The particular culture an individual is brought up in has inescapable influences on that person's preferences. The beliefs, symbols and ways of doing things in a particular culture are deeply ingrained in its people and these things can sometimes seem very strange to outsiders. Taste, fashion and design are inextricably linked together and it is very difficult to discuss one of these in isolation, also current fashions change over time, which complicates things even further. Taste in furnishings and clothing, for example, can provide clues about an individual's status in society; the particular socio-economic group that he or she belongs to and can even provide an indication of that person's set of personal values. Therefore, as Stephen Bayley said, taste is not so much about the appearance of things, but more about the ideas that give rise to them.

Good taste should not be confused with excess or luxury – it is better to design excellent everyday products than conjure up some highly decorated, gold plated and expensive confection. The art historian Kenneth Clark said that splendour is anyway dehumanizing, and a certain sense of limitation seems to be a condition of good taste in any society. Certainly Plato thought so. The incorporation of decoration and ornament in design is a considerable bone of contention among designers. How much and in what style? Should decoration be dispensed with altogether? Pure modernists eschew decoration of any kind, whereas designers of the Arts and Crafts movement in the late nineteenth century positively celebrated rich pattern, colour and ornament. Many modernist architects and designers would argue however that good design has nothing to do with issues of taste and that designing things can be approached entirely objectively.

We are sometimes shocked by a new building or artefact, therefore we need education and intellectual tools to help us make sense of new situations and solve new problems as they arise. Technological developments, especially, have always affected the direction and appearance of designs. For example the introduction of the straight steel beam began to replace stone and iron arches and buildings at the start of the twentieth century, giving rise to the skyscraper, and developments in plastics revolutionized much of product designs throughout the twentieth century. Some people, however, actually prefer the designs (and art) of the past but this still involves making judgements about what was good and bad about past design and therefore still requires an educated eye.

There is no simple or quick way to gain an understanding of design theories and issues of taste and to acquire a reasonable body of knowledge of the rich and varied history of design – this is a never-ending occupation. However, this chapter attempts to provide a succinct introduction to these issues and offer notions of good design that have emerged over the years. These may help illustrate some of the reasons for different designs and styles evolving over time but, as Sir Terence Conran has pointed out, whatever your design philosophy, '*style* is no substitute for *substance*'.

the culture trap

Those of us trained under the ethos of modernism in the early to middle period of the twentieth century were pretty sure what good design was in terms of visual elegance and its relation to function. The Western tradition of modernism, with its origins in the Bauhaus of the 1920s and elsewhere, stated that beauty (in a nutshell) lies in a 'pared down' elegance, decoration of any kind is superfluous and form should be dictated by function alone (Figure 2). Thus generations of designers were taught in the main by modernists who tended to think that designing things could be approached entirely objectively and judgements about what constituted good design did not rely on issues of taste to do with art and culture. Function and user requirements of products and buildings were nearly all that mattered and these things could almost be measured. Beauty would almost automatically flow from such elegant logic – anyone who took a different view must be either misguided or simply old fashioned.

Over the intervening years, however, these rather rigid ideas about design and elegance were subject to growing criticism about the often soulless nature of modernist architecture and product designs. These post-modernists maintained that the human spirit is not sustained by meeting functional needs alone and ideas about ornament, decoration and historical references began to re-emerge. Postmodernists accepted that points of view other than modernism's ideals could be just as valid; that different societies with different values, histories and traditions all have equal rights to a visual culture different to that of mainstream Western thinking. Modernism, for all its elegant logic, is only one point of view,

Fig 2 Modernism – Mies Van Der Rohe's Illinois Institute of Technology, Chicago. Crown building, 1956.

although to many it remains the most important and influential design movement of the twentieth century – immeasurably more significant than the 'passing fads' (though wonderful fads) of some other Western movements such as Art Nouveau, Art Deco, Futurism and Expressionism, which many observers regard as interesting fashions at best, and theatrical nonsense at worst, though these ideas did help brighten up the architectural landscape in the face of often 'brutalist' designs. Modernism's influence will, however, continue to be of major significance, constantly evolving and mutating in the future as the power of the computer is increasingly exploited to enable the creation of much more complex, intelligent and humane structures.

Every society throughout history has had its own ideas as to what is 'best' in terms of visual elegance. The most obvious example of this is the variety of people's dress and fashion in different countries. Fashion in a particular culture also changes over time, which makes judgements about elegance even more difficult to make. Even today's car industry is as much about fashion as it is about engineering. What might be regarded as elegant in Eastern cultures, for example, may look strange at first to our Western eyes and vice versa. Different visual signals and symbols mean different things in different societies in different historical periods. The same is true whether considering dress, architecture or product design. How, then, are we to make any sense of this diversity in time and culture and come up with universal guidelines for achieving visual elegance? This is impossible. Concepts of beauty are fluid and ever changing with the different values and perceptions of people over time and location. However, an attempt at constructing a defining statement that covers this diversity could be made as follows, which might help us to nail down a starting point: 'Wherever

a culture or society strongly believes in a set of values – whether in the form of mythical gods, the afterlife, Christianity, Zen Buddhism, science, technology or the arts – the best products of these societies are usually very impressive to any observer from any culture.'

This is along the lines of Kant's concept of 'purposiveness' – that an object should have been created for a purpose, even though future generations may not know what that purpose is or was. Examples could include the Parthenon, Tutankhamun's burial mask, St Peter's Cathedral in Rome, the Concorde supersonic airliner, or tensile structures like the Millennium Dome in London. As previously noted, time does not diminish their beauty even though the technology used to create them may be dated.

beliefs and symbols

It is impossible, then, to be completely objective about design when we are brought up in a particular society with its own cultural traditions and values. Every society uses symbols that are important to them, which to an observer from another society or time may be completely meaningless. We probably don't entirely understand the artist's use of symbolism in the form, details and colour of early tribal masks, yet many of these carvings impress us with their expressive power. Therefore, the same work of art can have different meanings over time to different audiences.

The traditional Japanese garden often employs metaphors – a rock can be used to represent a person, animal or spirit, a 'stream' of pebbles can represent flowing water, occasionally crossed by 'stepping stones' of larger flat topped rocks. Sometimes garden designs are based on old fables and stories. Shintoism, the original

Fig 3 Japanese Zen Rock Garden. Rocks create ripples in smooth flowing waters.

religion of Japan, is grounded in the worship of nature, spirits and ancestors. It says that mankind must honour and live in harmony with nature – thus the Japanese garden provides an oasis of tranquillity in which to contemplate the universe. To the uninitiated Western eye, none of these meanings will be immediately apparent, but this does not stop us from enjoying the peaceful beauty of the Japanese garden (Figure 3).

Traditional Chinese architecture uses symbols that have great significance within their own society – but these wouldn't mean very much to the outsider, however striking a particular building might be. The dragon and phoenix are symbols of emperors and gods in Chinese culture and are therefore used as the main decorative features on palaces and also some houses. Colour is important too; palaces are often painted in yellows and greens, because these are regarded as the noblest of all colours, and the dragon and phoenix are

usually painted red or gold on a green background. Further, certain numbers have special significance – even numbers are regarded as female (or *yin*) and odd numbers are male (or *yang*). The number nine is especially significant – this is the largest odd number under ten and regarded as the luckiest of all numbers – and is often to be found in Chinese architecture, such as nine columns, nine bays, or a building's proportions arranged in multiples of nine. In Thailand, however, the number nine is regarded as inauspicious, as it equals the number of openings in the human body. A traditional Chinese dwelling consists basically of a roof supported by posts, the walls serving no structural purpose. The widely projecting roof design provides shade in the summer as well as throwing off heavy rainwater in the wet season. The upturned corners on the roofs of some buildings and pagodas are designed to ward off evil spirits – an architectural gesture and a tricky place for a spirit to land upon. In Chinese folklore the lion was said to be the ninth son of the dragon and is therefore employed to guard royal palaces. Sometimes the number five was combined with the number nine in royal buildings, for example, the Great Hall of the Imperial Palace in Beijing is nine bays wide by five deep. The Imperial Palace's origins date from the Yuan dynasty (1271–1368). Emperor Yongle of the Ming dynasty had the palace enlarged to its present day size between 1406 and 1420, including the building of the Temple of Heaven (Figure 4), after he had transferred the capital from Nanjin to Beijing. The design of the Temple of Heaven (originally the Temple of Heaven and Earth) is based on elaborate symbolism and significant numbers. The buildings of the Temple are round 'like the sky', whereas the foundation buildings of the complex are flat, like the earth.

To Western eyes, the brightly coloured dragons and assorted mythical beasts adorning Chinese buildings can seem at first to be overtly ornamental. However, when travelling through these places you soon get used to it and usually end up enjoying the spectacle of these wonderfully expressive buildings. So much so that upon returning to the West much architecture seems rather boring by comparison – the face of modernism can often appear very austere to fresh eyes.

In recent years, however, many of the West's new buildings and designed objects are becoming much more fluid in their appearance, moving away from the severe box-like structures, minimalist products and the postmodern pastiche of recent times, becoming much more sculpturally expressive, owing their forms as much to art as technology. The explosion in computer power has made the design and manufacture of complex shapes and structures much easier and architects and designers are taking opportunities to exploit this. See, for example, Zaha Hadid's design for the Nuragic and Contemporary Art Museum at Cagliari in Sardinia, Italy (Figure 5). The Italian Futurists of the early twentieth century would no doubt have appreciated these forms – the Futurists celebrated the machine age and attempted to suggest both speed and power in their art, using 'expressionistic' forms that suggest movement in space. Some observers would anyway argue that nothing much is new and the 'isms' of today are just reworkings of ideas of past generations – a rather negative view and one that shouldn't stop us from enjoying the spectacle. Although we can't fail to be impressed by iconic architectural design and works of art from any culture, there is also huge scope for fun and self-expression in design, which often defies classification.

Fig 4 Temple of Heaven. Beijing. c.1420.

Fig 5 The expressive forms of the Nuragic and Contemporary Art Museum, Cagliari, Italy. By Zaha Hadid. Expected completion date: end of 2010.

so what is good taste?

What is 'taste' in the context of design? When we say that people have good taste in their choice of furnishings, for example, by what yardstick are we measuring this? Are there universal rules that distinguish between good and bad taste? Arguments about taste have been with us for a long time and, as noted previously, the particular culture an individual is brought up in has inescapable influences on that person's preferences. Taste, fashion and design are inextricably linked together and it is very difficult to discuss one of these in isolation. Current fashions change over time – when too many people like and use a particular design or style it no longer appears special, and soon something else takes its place. A person's taste in clothes is also an indicator (or symbol) for the particular strata in society that the individual belongs to – a set of values that signal a person's status in that society. For example a bank manager wouldn't normally wear jeans to work, despite their excellent hard-wearing qualities. As Stephen Bayley said in the foreword to his book on taste: 'taste is not so much about what things look like, as about the ideas that gave rise to them. Intention is the key to understanding taste; we must judge the spirit that informs an object or a gesture, rather than the form of the object or gesture itself, which is a matter of design.'[1]

Analogies with taste in designed objects have often been made with the *sense* of taste – the comparison of different foods on the palate. As individuals we certainly know which foods taste good and which foods we dislike. This obviously starts in early childhood but as we grow older and experience a wider variety of foods our palates become more educated and adept at discerning differences that are often very subtle. A connoisseur can even identify the grape, year and region of the world a particular wine originated from. This connoisseur's palate has been educated over a significant period of time, immersed in a particular culture of food and drink and thus has developed an *acquired* taste. A Western palate, however, may know nothing about the subtleties of Eastern food and vice versa. Therefore, an individual acquires the preferred tastes of the particular strata of the society to which he or she belongs. This same individual, however, may know nothing about good design. Unless educated in design, a person could not be expected to know much about the difference between good or inferior designs, other than the more obvious – for example, the comfort of a particular chair or the awfulness of a run-down inner city's visual and physical deprivation.

So a search for universal laws of good taste in design is fruitless: there are just too many variables across time and cultures. These variables include influences such as education, religion, symbolism and other cultural metaphors that can be meaningless to any society other than those that created them. Buildings and other artefacts have deeply engrained symbolic meanings to the people of a particular culture, but that is not to say we cannot find any beauty in another culture's symbols even though we do not fully understand their original meanings. Tarzan, to take an extreme example, suddenly brought out of the jungle for the first time, would not recognize the vast difference between a church steeple and a moon rocket ready for take off (although the 'programmed' part of his brain would probably recognize the significance of Jane's appearance!). As Donis A. Dondis says in her book on visual literacy: 'Just as some cultural groups eat things others would be sickened by, we have visual preferences ingrained in us.'[2] However, much common sense has been written about what constitutes good *design* (although this also has implications for taste). In the introduction

to his book[3] accompanying the exhibition *Taste, An Exhibition about Values in Design* held at the Victoria and Albert Museum in 1983, Stephen Bayley writes:

Although the actual style of any object might differ from age to age, those which are most admired by successive generations have certain qualities in common:

1. an intelligibility in their form, so that you can understand their purpose

2. a coherence and harmony between the form and the details

3. an appropriate choice of materials to the function

4. an intelligent equation between construction and purpose, so that the available technology is exploited to the full.

Bayley goes on to say that these principles are:

… all abstract and none is susceptible to one particular interpretation; they can find form in different designs and different styles, but each is controlled by the elements of refinement, restraint and sensitive discrimination. The principles of design are, in fact, The Rules of Taste. An understanding of Taste is a necessary part of any successful design and if it means anything at all it means something that can be put into one word … Taste is the same as manners.

In the same book, John Pile's chapter 'In Praise of Tasteless Products' looks at taste from another point of view:

… this is not to suggest that an individual may not come to like the things he has learned to choose. He almost surely will 'acquire a taste' through familiarity, if nothing else … When viewed in this

way, ideas of 'good taste' and 'bad,' or even 'high' and 'low,' begin to lose their meaning. To untangle this confusion we need to remind ourselves that arriving at a truly good design has nothing to do with taste. Most of us would settle for a definition something like the well-known three part (Vitruvian) formula that requires:

> 1. a thing must do its job, solve some real human problem, be useful and functional
>
> 2. it must also be well made of suitable materials, through application of well chosen structures and techniques
>
> 3. it must embody these technical qualities in form (shape, colour, and any other aspects one can sense) that clearly expresses its reality.

Although Bayley and Pile's requirements for good design are valid, taken out of context they seem to gloss over one of the major stumbling blocks that appear wherever design and art meet (or overlap). Decoration and ornament together constitute a considerable bone of contention among experts of taste in design and, although 'details' or 'other aspects' in Bayley and Pile's lists may take decoration into account, this issue causes much vexation among designers and public alike. Pure modernists eschew decoration of any kind, whereas designers of the Arts and Crafts movement positively celebrated rich pattern, colour and ornament. There are certainly superb examples of modernist interiors and furniture, as well as superb examples of richly decorated interiors and furniture. There are also extremely bad examples of both schools. This is where design and taste collide with fashion – the *Zeitgeist* of the day – one's point of view on *how much* decoration or detailing to use seems to depend on the period that one is born into. The Victorians' appetite for elaborate pattern and ornamentation in interior and furniture design was driven to some extent by

people's desire to show off their status and wealth in society. Because hand crafted items were very expensive to produce, the more finely detailed hand crafted objects you surrounded yourself with, the more you could impress your friends and neighbours. Bayley states that good taste however should not be confused with excess or luxury – it is better to design excellent everyday products than to conjure up some ghastly gold plated and expensive confection. As the art historian Kenneth Clark has said: 'Splendour is dehumanising, and a certain sense of limitation seems to be a condition of what we call good taste.'[4]

Plato certainly regarded luxury as a disease – the ostentatious display of luxury by leaders (and aristocrats or other high status individuals) can be offensive to the ordinary mass of people and was therefore regarded by Plato as dangerous to society. It was simply bad manners and could breed revolution once out of control. Plato's tutor Socrates didn't care about material possessions beyond simple food and shelter and endured considerable hardships without complaint. Apparently he didn't care much more for the life that he possessed either, choosing death rather than having his questionings about religion and government curtailed by the authorities (Plato suspected that Socrates wished to carry on his open questioning in the afterlife rather than be restricted in this one).

Later societies have had similar views on luxury. The Roman Emperor Hadrian lived modestly compared to his predecessors and this is one reason for his popularity, ruling as he did over a long period of a comparatively harmonious society in Rome. Of course standards of luxury move with the times – hot and cold running water, electricity and central heating were once regarded as luxuries even within living memory, and now we simply take these things as essential.

But the ostentatious 'showing off' of much greater luxuries than the norms of the day is still regarded as bad manners in many societies.

Augustus Welby Northmore Pugin was a major figure in nineteenth-century Gothic Revival architecture and design and an enthusiastic proponent of pattern design and ornament. His designs for Victorian churches as well as the Houses of Parliament in London (in collaboration with the architect Charles Barry) are some of the finest examples of decoration of the period (whatever you may feel about its necessity) and they are still much admired today by enthusiasts (Figure 6). Pugin's slogan 'Decorate construction, do not construct decoration' does nowadays, however, seem at odds with much of what he actually designed. Today most of us would not want a return to what appears as 'over-the-top' decorated interior designs and furniture but neither would most of us want minimalist and austere all-white interiors with severe and uncomfortable-looking furniture designs (however visually elegant). The Western mainstream ethos at the start of the twenty-first century seems to have become a softer more humane modernism, the inclusion of some colour and texture to delight the senses, and the use of expressive forms – a little visual music as opposed to bleak silence on the one hand or overwhelming noise on the other.

As we have seen, experts on the subject of taste and its relationship with design differ in their points of view, and this makes it even more difficult for the design novice to get a handle on things. Each of us has therefore to come to terms with these many shades of opinion, and arrive at our own conclusions for our own age and culture. Art and design are open-ended subjects: there is no one right answer for a given problem or set of circumstances and to many designers this is what makes the subject so endlessly fascinating.

At the end of the nineteenth century the American philosopher George Santayana had the following to say about taste (he was obviously entrapped in his own cultural notions of the day however – the 'savages' he refers to are homo-sapiens with the same brain/mind as ourselves):[5]

Fig 6 Overdecoration? Houses of Parliament, London. 1858. A. W. N. Pugin.

Taste, when it is spontaneous, always begins with the senses. Children and savages, as we are so often told, delight in bright and variegated colours; the simplest people appreciate the neatness of muslin curtains, shining varnish, and burnished pots. A rustic garden is a shallow patchwork of the liveliest flowers, without that reserve and repose which is given by spaces and masses. Noise and vivacity is all that childish music contains, and primitive songs add little more of form than what is required to compose a few monotonous cadences. These limitations are not to be regretted; they are proof of sincerity. Such simplicity is not the absence of taste, but the beginning of it.

To develop 'an eye' for good taste or good design (in a particular culture) therefore demands firstly a spontaneous interest in the subject, followed by a process of education over time which includes; exposure to examples of excellent design, making comparisons between these examples, arguing with other designers and artists, learning something of the history and philosophy of design and also the thoughts of past and contemporary designers, architects and artists, and attempting to design things for yourself and seeking criticism from others. There is no one right answer to a particular design problem; there is no one 'best' chair or design of a house (or best wine for that matter). There are as many examples of good design as there are bad examples; design is a subjective discipline, but a discipline nonetheless. To learn to discriminate between the good, ordinary and bad you need to study and preferably practise these things. There is, of course, room for personal preference *within* good design. Different architects will have different preferences among examples of good buildings but there is usually a general consensus about which buildings come under the good category and which are indifferent, bad, or pretentious – just as there is usually a general consensus among professional wine tasters about the quality of a particular wine. This process of education and experience helps us to make decisions about whether or not a new and original building or artefact is a genuine and honest attempt at quality, although to be truly successful a building should delight architects and critics but, more importantly, the end users of that building too.

Many modernist architects and designers would argue, however, that good design has nothing to do with issues of taste and that designing things (and solving problems) can be approached entirely objectively. In Bryan Appleyard's book *Richard Rogers*, he quotes the architect as saying:

Taste is the enemy of aesthetics … it is abstract, at best elegant and fashionable, it is always ephemeral, for it is not rooted in philosophy or even craftsmanship, being purely a product of the senses. As such it can always be challenged and is always superseded, for how can one judge whose taste is best … Good design on the other hand speaks to us across the ages.

Whether or not you agree that taste has a role to play in design, it is difficult to acquire 'good taste' or good design skills without undergoing years of visual education and having hands-on experience (a lifelong process) – if this were not the case there would be no need for the thousands of design courses in centres of learning around the world. Design is also not a static discipline; new ways of thinking, the introduction of new materials and technologies, the changing values and fashions in culture and societies, all influence the direction of design today and tomorrow. We are sometimes shocked by a new building or artefact, therefore we need education and intellectual tools to help us make sense of new situations and solve new problems as they arise. At this point it is probably worth quoting Stephen Bayley's simply stated requirements for good design: 'There is only one worthwhile definition of quality in design, and that is making the most of contemporary possibilities.'

learning and judgement

This book attempts to describe some concepts of visual beauty, or visual elegance, in words, ideas and pictures that are meaningful to students and that assist those students in their quest to become better designers. Learning can be a difficult process at the best of times. In subjective disciplines such as literature or art this can be particularly true as there do not seem to be many rules or facts (beyond the technical) to guide the student. Many problems faced by designers are new and unique, requiring good imaginative and creative skills. There is often no precedent to refer to for guidance, no one right answer. How do we know if the design proposal is a good one? Is it an elegant solution? We can only resort to providing good examples of existing particular pieces of work, explain and discuss as best we can why these are good examples.

Similar difficulties are faced by students and teachers in other disciplines. The late Richard Feynman was a Nobel prize-winning physicist based in the United States. In addition to his physics work, Feynman was also curious about art. His sister Arlene was a practising artist who had a special interest in calligraphy. The following quotation is taken from his autobiography[6] and may help to show that we are not alone in the struggle to understand and improve our visual skills:

She had the right paper, brushes and ink, and was practising calligraphy. She had bought a Chinese dictionary, to get a lot of other symbols. One time when I came to visit her, Arlene was practicing these things.

She says to herself, 'No. That one's wrong.'

So I, the 'great scientist', say, 'What do you mean, wrong? It's only a human convention. There's no law of nature which says how they're supposed to look; you can draw them any way you want.'

'I mean, artistically it's wrong. It's a question of balance, of how it feels.'

'But one way is just as good as another,' I protest.

'Here,' she says, and she hands me the brush. 'Make one yourself.'

So I made one, and I said, 'Wait a minute. Let me make another one – it's too blobby.' (I couldn't say why it was wrong, after all.)

'How do you know how blobby it's supposed to be?' she says.

I learned what she meant. There's a particular way you have to make the stroke for it to look good. An aesthetic thing has a certain set, a certain character, which I can't define. Because it couldn't be defined made me think there was nothing to it – and it's a fascination I've had for art ever since.

There are parallel problems with other forms of art too – for example, how do we teach someone to be a good poet or composer, and how would we measure these things? Those who attempt to measure works of art have already missed the point anyway.

getting a grip

In his book *Analysis of Beauty*, published in 1753, the painter and satirist William Hogarth arranged the elements that he considered important factors in the composition of visual beauty in art and design under chapter headings – for example, 'on fitness', 'on simplicity', 'on quantity', 'on variety' 'on symmetry', and outlined his reasoning with reference to the book's accompanying drawings and engravings. It is perhaps remarkable, given the developments in art and design in the intervening two-and-a-half centuries, how these issues are still relevant to today's architecture and product designs. Central to Hogarth's ideas about beauty was the serpentine line – or 'S' shape. He believed that because this flowing shape often appeared in nature (for example, in human long bones) man-made objects such as chair legs and vases would appear more graceful if they too were designed to follow this 'line of beauty'. For example in *The Country Dance* engraving shown in Figure 7 Hogarth rather amusingly contrasts the elegant forms and movements of the 'ideal' couple on the left against all the other graceless dancers in the scene in order to illustrate his idea that the

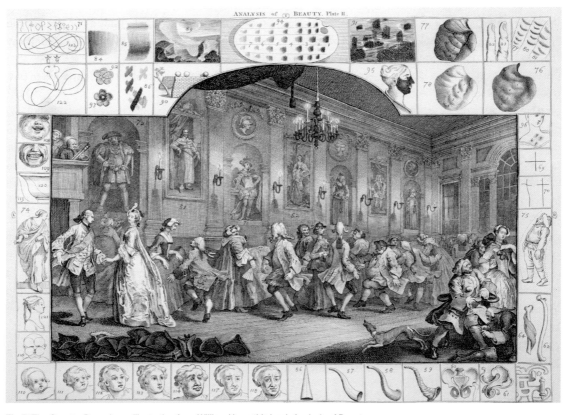

Fig 7 'The Country Dance' – an illustration from William Hogarth's book *Analysis of Beauty* of 1753, which compares the serpentine forms and movements of the 'ideal couple' on the left with the clumsy and graceless forms of the other dancers.

serpentine 'S' shape, form or line, is in fact the line of beauty. The diagram in the very top left-hand corner of the engraving shows drawn lines 'representing' the shapes of the dancers, where only the ideal couple reflect this line of beauty.

Hogarth's *Analysis of Beauty* may have influenced the Irish philosopher Edmund Burke's thinking when writing his famous treatise on the Sublime and Beautiful published four years later.[7] They agree about the contribution to beauty made by what Burke calls gradual variation: 'as perfectly beautiful bodies are not composed of angular parts, so their parts never continue long in the same line. They vary their direction every moment.' This tallies with Hogarth's line of beauty and his admiration for variety where: '… the eye hath this sort of enjoyment in winding walks, and serpentine rivers, and all sorts of objects whose forms … are composed principally of what I call, the waving and serpentine lines.' Nowadays, however, we regard Hogarth's ideal of the serpentine line as rather quaint and old fashioned – the human skeleton is the result of natural selection where function alone is the driving force. A straight table leg functions just as well as a curved one and is a lot easier to manufacture. We have come to appreciate machine-made components as being fit for their intended purpose and elegant in themselves; there is no functional need for curvature or elaborate feet – a table is not an animal.

Technological developments have always affected the direction and appearance of architecture and designs. For example the steel beam has replaced the stone arch in today's buildings, and developments in plastics revolutionized much product design throughout the twentieth century. Today's machines are much more efficient and intelligent than at any other time in history. Some people actually prefer the art and designs of the past, but this still involves making judgements about what was good and bad about past design, and therefore still requires an educated taste. In his classic book *The Story of Art*, Ernst Gombrich asserts that (unlike technology) art does not really develop in the sense of today's art being better or more beautiful than yesterday's. (Who could improve on Michelangelo's *David* for instance?) Instead, art simply changes with each successive generation as different things become more or less important in a particular culture (or in the mind of an individual). Of course beauty is only one aspect of art – art can also evoke emotions other than pleasure, such as sadness, anger, or even fear.

Like Hogarth, many artists, architects and designers since antiquity have tried to distil in words those elements, or ways of thinking, which make up the essence of good design, taste and beauty. There is, however, no simple or quick way to gain an understanding of design theories and acquire a reasonable body of knowledge of the rich and varied history of design – this is a lifetime's occupation. However, as a 'jump start' for students new to design it may be useful as an introduction to offer concepts of good design by resorting to mottos (or 'strap lines' in marketing speak) as notions of good design, which have emerged over the years. These clichés are very limited – and we should resist the tendency towards pigeonholing art and design – but sometimes they are useful as an aid to grasping ideas of good design. However, sometimes they are just amusing and sometimes they are completely useless. The accompanying pictures show related examples of products and buildings/interiors. They may help illustrate some of the reasons for different styles evolving over time but, as Sir Terence Conran has pointed out, whatever your design philosophy, '*style* is no substitute for *substance*'.

design clichés

1. Form Follows Function (Louis H Sullivan, American Architect, 1856–1924, and Tutor of Frank Lloyd Wright) This is a well-worn cliché and clarion call of the Modern Movement but is still usually a good starting point from which to begin designing anything. We can see this design thinking in nature. For example, the shape of a tree exploits the nature of the material it is made from, its first function being to remain standing up – the same shape in stone would collapse straight away. The substances that make up the human body – bones, muscle, etc. – have evolved into their particular body forms and these forms largely determine the shapes and sizes of the things we use – a kettle, bath or toilet – and the materials these objects are made from depend on the functions they themselves have to perform (this relates to 'truth to materials' below). So we start to learn about good shapes for different materials for particular functions intuitively from early childhood. But what is a good shape for reinforced concrete? This is a material that can be cast into almost any shape. It helps if the designer starts from the premise of function even though this can lead to unusual buildings, such as Frank Lloyd Wright's spiral design for the Guggenheim Museum in New York (Figure 8). Wright maintained that the shape of the museum was dictated by functional requirements: visitors could view the art on the wall whilst walking down the gradual incline of a spiral ramp uninterrupted by steps or doors, having first arrived at the top floor via an elevator.

In the age of the microchip, however, the function of many product designs can often be

Fig 8 Guggenheim Museum, New York. 1959. By Frank Lloyd Wright.

divorced from form, although miniature products will still need user-friendly keypads and screens in order to fit our eyes, ears and hands efficiently. In her book *The Substance of Style*, Virginia Postrel argues that the choice of a beautiful casing enclosing your computer might take preference over having the latest cutting-edge technology microchip inside – especially if you don't need the fastest processor in the world. We human beings also derive pleasure from our visual, aural and tactile senses – a house isn't just a machine for living in. In addition to helping us with our chores, good design has the capacity to provide us with delight in our everyday lives, and this delight is implicit in Donald Norman's three main aims for good product design; simplicity, versatility and pleasurability.

Fig 9 Interior of a Japanese inn. Elegance through carefully considered simplicity.

2. Less is More (Mies van der Rohe, German-born Architect, 1886–1969)

The 'less is more' ethos of modernism maintained that beauty lies in an understated elegance and that the aim of the designer should be to try to create solutions to problems via the most efficient means. If one component could do the job of two, or if non-functional parts could be dispensed with altogether (including 'superfluous' decoration), then form and detail should be dictated by function alone. That is not to say that the aim should be a crude simplicity – rather it should be a sophisticated simplicity. Many modernists admired traditional and modern Japanese interiors for this reason. Although the Japanese interior in Figure 9 may appear simple, great care has been taken in the choice of materials, finishes, textures, colours and proportions of its construction - designing apparently simple things can be a complicated business.

3. Less is a Bore (Robert Venturi, American Architect, b. 1925)

The middle and latter half of the twentieth century saw an increasing disillusionment with the Modern Movement's ethos of minimalist design. Although the aim of the modernists was the achievement of elegance through the reduction of superfluous elements, in the hands of inferior architects and planners this often resulted in crude and soulless buildings and spaces – and modernism became dubbed as the 'New Brutalism' by commentators. As a result architects and designers began to experiment again with ornament and colour, often borrowing motifs from the past and blending them into their new designs. In the forefront of this postmodern movement were the American architects Robert Venturi and Michael Graves. Postmodernism also influenced much product design of the period, a style that was particularly embraced by the Italian kitchen products manufacturer Alessi, who employed Michael Graves and others to design a variety of products and appliances, some of which are now regarded as design classics (Figure 10).

Many commentators, however, view postmodernism as 'entertainment' rather than 'design' and

Fig 10 Michael Graves postmodern Kettle for Alessi. 1985. Kettle with handle and small bird-shaped whistle in polyamide. Magnetic stainless steel bottom.

4. Form Expresses Function (Product Semantics) Running parallel to postmodernism's rejection of pure modernism in the 1980s was the idea that form should not just follow function but express it as well. In product design especially, the appearance and design of different appliances were converging to such an extent that, for example, a television set might be mistaken for a microwave oven. It became difficult to distinguish a radio receiver from a CD player. Controls of differing functions on the same appliance looked identical to each other, leaving the user unsure about exactly which ring on the cooking hob was switched on, for example. Taken to extremes this could obviously lead to dangerous situations as well as visual boredom. The expression of a product's function through form became known as 'product semantics' and several new designs appeared on the market in the 1980s, such as Philips' 'Roller Radio' and the prototype Elaine printer shown in Figure 11 – its forms expressing the flow of paper.

5 Form Follows Fashion ('Style Wears Out Quicker than Gears' – Ernest Elmo Calkins)
Although the Modern Movement supposedly had technological and functional reasons for its designs, other styles simply had fashion or 'art' as their rationale. These fashions nevertheless led to some outstanding works of art and design. For example, Art Nouveau (the new art) at the turn of the twentieth century took as its inspiration natural plant forms, a curvaceous swirling style famously pursued by Hector Guimard in his designs for the Paris Metro entrances and other buildings (Figure 12).

Art Deco in the 1920s and 1930s took geometry as its inspiration – the term 'Art Deco'

is therefore devoid of any deeper meaning – they maintain that designers should be attempting to design meaningful and elegant things with today's materials and technology, not borrowing motifs from the past as pretentious 'stick-on' symbols, taken out of their original context. On the other hand there should be room for entertainment and fun, we do not have to take ourselves so seriously all the time. In the 1980s the 'Memphis' group of designers led by the Italian designer Ettore Sottsass deliberately set out to provoke the design establishment with their ethos of 'anti-design' as a reaction against the cold logic of modernism. What might have turned out as ridiculous designs in less clever hands actually came to be regarded as cult objects. The Memphis group created products with highly decorated and colourful surfaces, often using materials, shapes and proportions in bizarre ways.

being (later) derived from the title of a 1925 exhibition in Paris: Exposition Internationale des Arts Décoratifs et Industriels Modernes. The fashion for Art Deco interiors was spread through the media of film, the style being adopted by Hollywood in the 1930s and 1940s. This period also saw the beginnings of the fad for 'streamlining' of products and vehicles, which reached its zenith in 1950s American automobile design (Figure 13). The tail fins and 'jet exhausts' of American cars could be described as 'constructed decoration' (see below) – but they had a certain expressive dynamic that nowadays we find rather amusing. The 1950s also saw the appearance of 'free form' designs in the UK, first exhibited at the 1951 Festival of Britain Exhibition in London, which took the form of curving lozenge shapes in furniture and pattern design, often in pastel colours. It could be argued that the 'high tech' trends in architecture and design of the 1970s and 1980s were driven as much by fashion as by engineering, for example, the 'inside out' Pompidou Centre in Paris (Figure 41 in Chapter 2) designed by Richard Rogers and Renzo Piano, and also the Lloyds building in the City of London.

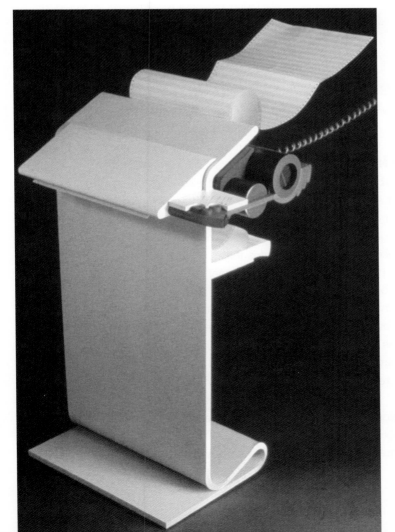

Fig 11 The Elaine Printer design expresses the flow of paper. c.1990.

Fig 12 Art Nouveau – Entrance Gate to the Domaine Berenger, Paris. 1898. Hector Guimard.

6 Decorate Construction, Do Not Construct Decoration (Structural Honesty) (Augustus W. N. Pugin, English Architect and Designer, 1812–52) A good example of how *not* to do this is the architectural folly. A sure giveaway to be seen on many buildings is the placing of columns on the façade of a building that do not actually support anything – this is constructed decoration writ large. The definition of the architectural folly is a building that does not have a purpose – such constructions were often built as ornaments in the surrounding grounds and gardens of grand houses and sometimes used to create vistas and focal points.

Jewellery design deserves special attention here as it is almost always entirely decorative. Perhaps the maxim 'form follows function' is redundant here? What function does a necklace perform, for example? How can we judge it as being 'fit for purpose'? As previously noted, the ancient art of body painting and decoration was a sign of dexterity, creativity and resourcefulness and these designs were good indicators for survival as well as artistry and were therefore important when it came to choosing a mate. These body decorations and artefacts were also indicators of a person's social standing in a society. Jewellery still performs this 'function' to some extent today, the extreme case being the Crown Jewels. Of course noble metals and gemstones (metallurgists refer to metals such as gold, silver and platinum, which are highly resistant to corrosion, as noble metals) have a monetary value due to their rarity and costly retrieval from the earth and have been used as a medium of exchange in trading for centuries. However, these materials are also highly valued for their inherent properties and beauty. According to Dan Cruickshank, the Egyptians valued gold: 'because it seemed evidence of the divine – it did not corrode so it spoke of eternity and its colour and sheen seemed of the sun'.[8]

You could also describe jewellery as 'art for art's sake' – we admire paintings and sculpture as being beautiful in themselves, especially in the case of non-figurative art where a particular work's terms of reference might bear no relation to things seen in the real world. So how then do we judge the difference between good and bad jewellery? Perhaps the first test we could apply is that of honesty – is the piece pretending to be something it isn't? There is nothing wrong with well-designed plastic jewellery but metal-coated plastic jewellery is usually a sham. Pugin's maxim 'decorate construction, do not construct decoration' should apply to jewellery design – body decoration should subtly enhance a person's appearance and should not be so prominent as to be the first thing we notice. As we have seen, many cultures regard overblown magnificence and opulence as contradicting beauty – ostentation and luxury therefore have nothing to do with good design and many high street jewellers' windows are full of expensive rubbish. Even if pieces are made of solid gold and set with precious stones, the designs often leave a lot to be desired – for example, a ghastly ostentatious watch such as a top of the range jewelled Rolex.

A wristwatch is a marriage of the useful with the decorative, and increasingly electronics and jewellery are converging as the technology becomes more miniaturized over time – you could say that mobile phones, electronic notepads, or MP3 players are as much jewellery accessories as are bracelets and necklaces. Jewellery, like clothing, is subject to fashion and our taste in jewellery design changes over time as new ideas influence future designs.

7. Fitness for Purpose The Anglepoise Lamp (Figure 14) was invented by the automotive engineer George Carwardine and first manufactured by Terry's Springs of Redditch in 1933. There now exist many forms of counterbalanced desk lamps but the Anglepoise is the original classic design, modified versions of which are still in production today. It allows the light source to be suspended anywhere above a desk (or the clamp version for the drawing board) and its enduring popularity demonstrates that it remains truly 'fit for purpose'. Donald Norman's three axioms of design – simplicity, versatility and pleasurability – are by no means easy to achieve but together could be described as attributes of 'fitness for purpose'.

Fig 13
'Streamlining'
– 1959 Cadillac
Series 62 Tail.

Fig 14 The function-led Anglepoise Lamp
design. 1933.

8. Colour Follows Function, *then* Fashion

Just about everyone has difficulties handling colour – for example, a small swatch of colour might look great until you paint a whole wall with it! Even though computers can nowadays easily render (and illuminate) a particular interior design colour scheme on a screen, we can still be surprised by the physical reality. A good place to start is to decide what function you want the colour to fulfil. Do you want a room to look larger or smaller, cooler or warmer, calming or stimulating? Surface texture also affects our perception of colour: compare a highly reflective glossy surface with a matt (or rough) finish in the same colour – the matt can sometimes look darker. Perhaps you want to increase the playful aspect of a particular product or alert people's attention to a source of potential danger. Products or clothes can be coloured to either stand out from the crowd or blend in. Yellow is probably the safest colour for a car – it is light in tone and therefore more easily noticeable at night or even in the snow, yet many people shy away from 'loud' colours, preferring more subtle tones. However, if every car had to be yellow by law, we would soon regard them as being nothing unusual and yellow cars would be absorbed into our culture.

In hot climates we sometimes prefer lighter coloured clothing, as these reflect more heat from the sun compared with darker colours. See Chapter 4 for more on colour.

9. Seek Simplicity, but Distrust It (Alfred North Whitehead, 1861–1947, English Mathematician and Philosopher)

Or alternatively – 'simplicity is the keynote of good design' – which means essentially the same thing and is also related to the 'less is more' cliché above. Again most designers prefer to use the word 'elegance' instead of 'simplicity' when talking about a particularly good

example or the efficiency of something. This also applies to other fields such as writing – an elegantly concise version of a piece of writing could be much shorter and yet more interesting. There are usually many different solutions to a particular design problem; the most elegant solutions would probably be those that used less materials, made one component do the work of two, were unfussy, and yet did a better job compared to their more complicated rivals – 'the paradox of reduction and enrichment'.

10. Truth to Materials (Attributed to John Ruskin – One of his Seven Lamps of Architecture 'The Lamp of Truth' – Often Quoted by A. W. N. Pugin)

This is an ethos beloved by designers of the Arts and Crafts Movement of the late nineteenth century, and also a reference to 'honest design' – the construction or structure of a design should remain obvious and not hidden away. For example the metal hinges and joints in Pugin's furniture designs were deliberately left exposed and these functional details also served as ornamentation in themselves. Truth to materials is a principle of modernists as well as Arts and Crafts designers – materials and manufacturing processes should be chosen for their suitability for the task they are required to perform and should not be used as a mere cosmetic device.

Ideally a material shouldn't pretend to be something else (for example, a chromium-plated plastic part masquerading as a polished stainless steel component, or a melamine worktop pretending to be grained wood). There is nothing inherently wrong with plastic or melamine – they each remain an excellent choice for many applications but pretending to be metal or real timber is dishonest. There are times, however, when you may want to bend the rules a little, the cosmetic treatment of a small part may be necessary to

Fig 15 Walt Disney Concert Hall, Los Angeles by Frank Gehry, 2003. Its form could be interpreted as suggesting musical movement – the sweep of the conductor's baton frozen in time and space.

maintain the overall harmony of a particular design.

11. Form Furthers Expression At the beginning of the twenty-first century, high-status or 'iconic' buildings are becoming as much pieces of public sculpture as they are architecture – but where does sculpture end and design begin and does it matter anyway? Maybe we should just simply enjoy these as 'visual concerts' and not try to fit them into pigeon-holes. Many have criticized iconic architecture as just 'showing off' by architects and their clients. These buildings will probably always remain out of mainstream design because of their one-off nature and the huge expense of building them.

Despite producing some unusually shaped buildings, Frank Gehry states that he actually starts with function – for example, the internal shapes of his Walt Disney concert hall (Figure 15) are largely determined by acoustic requirements. Gehry also likes to get deeply involved with the users of a proposed building so they can have their say in the design process before it is built.

12. Form Follows Emotion This was a phrase coined by Hartmut Esslinger, a designer with the Frog design consultancy in Germany. It conveys a recognition that the sensory side of our nature, sight, hearing, smell, touch, taste, is just as important to our quality of life as our rational side. As well as taking pleasure in colours, textures, sights and sounds, aesthetic feedback is fundamental to our understanding of the world we inhabit. Virginia Postrel quotes David Brown (former president of Pasadena's Art Center) as saying: 'We are by nature – by deep biological nature – visual, tactile creatures' and Postrel maintains that no other justification is necessary for pleasing our sensory and emotional natures.[9]

We cannot ignore our aesthetic sensibilities and emotions when choosing which house to live in, the clothes we wear or the car we drive. Manufacturers that do ignore this non-rational side of our nature are going to be left behind in the future.

The materials, design, tactile properties, colours and ease of use of Apple's iMac computer probably played a more important role than its technical specification in the minds of many consumers when it came to choosing which computer to buy, particularly in a field where any make of computer is sufficiently powerful and versatile enough for most people. Postrel envisions a future in which we will take beauty for granted – that beautiful buildings, environments and products will become the rule and not the exception, in a similar way that today we expect the plumbing and electric lighting to work whereas once this was a luxury for the wealthy few.

Fig 16 Crock-Pot with four-quart capacity. Designed by Michael Graves in 2000 for Target Stores and manufactured by Black & Decker.

Fig 17 'Go' furniture for indoor and/or outdoor use. By Ross Lovegrove, 2001.

case studies

Michael Graves Product Design

The American architect and designer Michael Graves, one of the founders of postmodernism, designs buildings, furniture and product designs that combine ease of use with a playfulness and wit. Many of his buildings and interiors are furnished with his own custom-made designs. Graves' product designs often border on zoomorphism – taking on the expression or 'stance' of living things. For example the tilted egg-shaped knob on the lid of the slow cooker in Figure 16 could be interpreted as a light-hearted gesture, perhaps an expectant 'looking up' at the user about to grip it. Also this and the other (temperature control) egg-shaped knob have a visual 'conversation' with each other every time the egg-shaped pointer is turned to a new position. The overall form of the cooker is an expression of a relaxed contentedness (akin in two dimensions to soft letterforms compared with other more straight-backed rectilinear characters).

Whether you prefer Graves' designs or mainstream domestic appliances depends on your taste, although particular examples from both categories may well be described as good design.

Ross Lovegrove Furniture Design – The 'Go' System

'GO' is a collection of multi-purpose chairs and tables designed for Bernhardt Design in the USA, making its first appearance in 2001 and later licensed to Danerka for the European market. The chair is manufactured from pressure die-cast magnesium, a material (weight for weight) much stronger than ordinary aluminium alloys and one that is more often found in vehicle and aeroplane components (for example, cast-magnesium car and motorcycle wheels). The tooling for pressure die casting is expensive but expected high sales figures for the collection justifies this initial risk as the cost can be spread over many units produced. The chair is available in different powder coated finishes (silver or white) and also offers a choice of seat materials – wood, upholstered fabric or leather and also a polycarbonate version that can be used outside (together with appropriate versions of the table). The sloping forms of the chair promote water run-off and quicker drying after rain and the chairs can be stacked together when not in use.

Lovegrove's interest in sculpture and the natural world has produced many organic product designs and furniture. The GO chair is almost skeletal – having strong bonelike shapes with no straight lines, akin to the human form and designed with careful thought given to the posture and comfort of the user. Lovegrove aims to marry human needs with progressive new technologies in order to produce everyday works of art that are a delight to behold and use – designs that will last and not be slaves to any particular passing fashion, and as far as possible make careful use of earth's resources.

There are of course other types of well designed good quality multipurpose furniture collections available, such as several elegant designs using teak, and it depends on our individual taste on which we prefer. Cost obviously comes into this but the cheapest of anything is often not the most economic – perhaps being more easily damaged or wearing out long before the more expensive design. There are however many examples of good designs that are also cheap.

Architecture and Interior Design in Thailand

The traditional Thai house is usually a plain affair with little or no decoration when compared with the country's religious architecture, which can be very ornate, rich in wood carvings and decoration – styles that have evolved over time, often borrowing and adapting various design influences from other parts of Asia, particularly China and India. Thailand's churches are, however, always recognizably 'Thai' due to a certain lightness of touch and delicate intricacy of ornament when compared to the often heavy approach of these other countries. The Chinese influence in ornamental decoration is especially notable in the use of porcelain fragments, colours and adornments and reached its zenith during the first half of the nineteenth century, especially in the homes of the wealthy.

Around the start of the twentieth century, traditionally ornate public architecture began to decline when the design of buildings became increasingly influenced by European styles, the spread of the Modern Movement and also to some extent the work of Frank Lloyd Wright in America and Japan. These changes had little impact on the design of the traditional Thai house, however, which could be already regarded as 'modernist' due its functional design perfectly fitting its purpose. A Thai house can have different features according to the culture, environment and climate of a particular region, however all houses tend to share the same basic construction. This consists of a one-storey dwelling on a raised platform supported by wooden posts, having an open ground-level area under the platform for ventilation and also protection from floods (most Thai people live and farm in low-lying areas). Wooden post construction is also more resistant to earthquakes than a stone building due to timber's inherent flexibility and resilience under dynamic shock loads. In some regional designs the posts are slanted inwards at a small angle to increase stability. Substantial wooden pins and pegs are used to join the posts and boards together as ordinary nails and screws would quickly corrode in the high humidity. This also makes the house easier to dismantle and move to a different location if necessary. The walls are usually prefabricated wooden panels that are hoisted and fixed into place and sometimes the external walls slope outwards towards the top, as in the northern region, or inwards as in the central region. The space under the house is used for various activities and for storing fishing boats, tools and agricultural equipment and the overall design perfectly fit the occupants' behaviour and everyday lives

Fig 18 Traditional House, Thailand. Achieving beauty through considered
use of natural materials and sound craftsmanship.

The houses are rectangular in plan and usually have three walls with one side left open. The roof is steeper in wetter regions to promote the faster run-off of water during the rainy season and has long overhanging eaves to throw the rain away from the house - as well as providing shade from the hot sun. Some roofs are curved – becoming steeper towards the ridge at the top and more horizontal towards the eaves – which have the effect of throwing rainwater even further away from the house, rather like a water-park chute. Roofing materials can be thatched using reeds or broad tung leaves, or tiled using wooden or unglazed ceramic tiles. There are no internal ceilings in the traditional house and the large roof space helps to keep the rooms cool in hot weather – warm air rises and escapes through vents placed under the eaves.

The wide covered veranda is used for eating and other family activities and is usually adjacent to the kitchen and bathroom. As a family expands, a second house is often built and connected to the existing one by the common veranda. The floors are usually wooden and the windows have shutters (for stormy weather) and bamboo drop-down blinds. The house and its rooms are usually quite plain, perhaps using small panels of fretwork under the windows (which also aid ventilation) or woven strips of wood and split bamboo for decoration to relieve the otherwise large 'blank' areas of planking making up the walls and partitions. The dwellings nevertheless still have that gentle beauty that we associate with Thailand itself. Who needs decoration anyway when the trees and palms just outside the window provide shapes, colour and shadows enough to please anyone – elegant curving and detailed natural forms that provide a counterpoint to the rectilinear forms of the building.

Bamboo was used in constructing early houses (and still is for low-income families or newly weds), but now the best houses use local teak in their construction and such a dwelling can last up to 200 years. In addition to these natural building materials, Thailand has a long tradition of ceramic and tile production and also handmade silks and cottons with which to furnish a house. A combination of natural local materials with intrinsic colours, logical design and good quality craftsmanship can together produce a beautifully simple and peaceful dwelling that is ideally suited to its environment and climate.

theory box

Plato and Aristotle (Fourth and Fifth Centuries BC)

Aesthetics is a branch of philosophy concerned with the perception and description of beauty and ugliness. Is beauty a quality of the object perceived or does it exist only in the mind of the observer? The Greek philosophers Plato (about 427 to 347 BC) and Aristotle (384 to 322 BC) believed that beauty was a distinct property of the physical world and that a beautiful object or place remained beautiful even if there was no one there to observe it. In other words the Parthenon in Athens, or a mountain peak, would remain beautiful even if human beings suddenly disappeared from the planet.

Plato believed that reality consisted of archetypes, or *Forms*, which lay outside the reach of all human perception. These perfect and eternal models (the 'really real') are the basis of all existence but the world and forms that we experience every day are only imitations of these models. Plato regarded the changing world around us as a poor, decaying copy of the original and that the role of the artist was to record the experienced world and its imperfect models. Thus the artist's work was itself a copy of a copy and therefore could never reach perfection – the artist might occasionally catch a *glimpse* of great beauty, for example, in a flower, but this would inevitably fade and could never hope to reach the eternal beauty of the original flower *Form* or model. Even geometric constructs such as the circle could never be reproduced perfectly – slight errors would always be present on closer inspection. Plato also regarded the arts as potentially dangerous to society – he thought that the works of painters, poets, composers and playwrights had a powerful influence on the moral character of the citizens (in his ideal *Republic*) and proposed that the arts should be strictly controlled. He even suggested banishing some types of artists and musicians from his *Republic* because he thought their work might encourage immorality or bad behaviour.

Plato also applied the notion of Eternal Forms to other aspects of life, for example, justice, but like the work of artists these could only be rough copies of the originals and remain approximations of the eternal ideal Forms. Plato believed that the mind or soul belongs to the world of eternal forms and the 'really real' in the next life, but our bodies are tied to the nature of our physical existence, and are bound to decay and die just like everything else in nature. Although Aristotle, like Plato, believed in the existence of rational unchanging Forms beyond our reach, his view of the experienced world was that everything in it aspired to these ideal Forms (without ever achieving it) – that the existing world was imperfect certainly – but that imitative artists could construct paintings and artefacts that actually *improved* on forms found in nature – 'art partly completes what nature cannot bring to a finish' – and therefore art can sometimes imitate the eternal ideal. The third century philosopher Plotinus took a similar view to Aristotle – that art can reveal the essence or form of an object with much greater clarity than that perceived through ordinary experience.

Cultural Semiotics (Twentieth Century)

Cultural semiotics is a branch of communication theory that investigates sign systems and symbolic methods of representation used to communicate abstract thoughts, ideas and emotions between individuals and groups. Semiotics can be applied to several disciplines including art, literature and sociology. In Roland Barthes' book *The Fashion System*, published in France in 1967, the author explores the relationship between the photographs of clothing and the accompanying text used in fashion magazines, for which he uses the terms 'image-clothing' and 'written garment'. Barthes is interested in the way that these visual and written 'sign systems' produce the abstract notion of fashion (or even myths). A garment has meanings beyond its physical reality – thus fashion is used as a sign or symbol of a person's status (or particular group to which a person belongs) in society. Another Frenchman, Pierre Bourdieu (1930–2002), proposed that there is such a thing as the 'sociology of taste' and that a person's upbringing and education naturally equips that person with his or her own inheritance of 'cultural capital'. Two of his main categories of cultural capital are *high* and *popular* aesthetics.

High Aesthetic

This term refers to those individuals in a particular society perceived as having high levels of cultural capital, and therefore always coming from families in the upper echelons of society who already value the arts, learning, literature and travel and who are not opposed to experiment or the *avant garde* in the arts. Such preferences and certain behavioural traits are passed on in families automatically and are taken for granted by the next generation. These groups generally prefer form over function.

Popular Aesthetic

This term refers to those 'ordinary' individuals in the same society whose outlook is 'based on a continuity between art and life' and do not like experimentation or challenges to 'common sense', who instead favour logic and order in the arts. These individuals fear change and potential exposure through social blunder. Generally preferring function over form.

Bourdieu is interested in the way these structures of taste are used to maintain 'social borders' by reinforcing social distinctions. He proposes that although a person's cultural capital can be increased through education, a particular person's cultural capital will never reach the level of those born into the elite. These are very French notions and are regarded as somewhat old fashioned nowadays.

chapter two

—

design evolution

chapter outline

The relationship between human beings and shelter is fundamental to survival and therefore architecture would seem to be a good starting point from which to consider design evolution. A particular building's function and visual aesthetics are strongly related to the human form and scale, for example, determining the minimum ceiling height and the proportions of doors. This relationship has, of course, been a fundamental principle since human dwellings and artefacts first appeared. This became a particular focal point for artists and architects during the Italian Renaissance, who attempted to relate the human form to geometry and apply this to buildings as well as town planning.

In the first half of the twentieth century one of the founders of the Modern Movement, Le Corbusier, attempted to further quantify human proportions as an aid to designing buildings and objects. As useful as these and other more recently collated anthropometric data are to designers, such information only gets us so far however, a building or a telephone may indeed be designed with the human form in mind – but we still get ugly buildings and products.

Designing things should ideally start with a consideration of the end users' requirements in as much detail as possible and end up by producing a building or product that is a delight to behold and use. This requires a marriage of human needs or desires with the technology available at the time, balanced against various constraints. Therefore, design evolves over time as developments in materials and technology provide new opportunities for better or different ways of doing things. This chapter introduces some of the more important milestones in design evolution since Roman times that have emerged through man's needs, discoveries and inventions and how these have influenced the appearance of things. These include the emergence of the local vernacular, inventions such as the arch, dome and truss, and the effect of technological discoveries in materials and innovative structures employed in buildings, furniture, products and other designs. The three-dimensional form of a particular object is often determined by the forces it has to withstand and therefore this chapter includes examples of some of the ways that principal forces can be better resisted through the manipulation of shape.

Cultural forces and changes in fashion also strongly influence the appearance of things, as noted in chapter one. For example, car design is as much about fashion as it is engineering and we often 'read' meanings into inanimate objects that someone from a different culture may not understand. These more subjective issues have effected changes in design evolution just as much as technological developments and this chapter introduces some human notions about the design of objects shared by many cultures, such as classic versus romantic, masculine versus feminine, zoomorphism and the evolution of visual identity and branding.

introduction

To acquire an appreciation of or good taste in a particular subject requires an ongoing education in that subject in order to gain some understanding of the thinking behind why a certain building (or other design) is a good or bad example of its type. The previous chapter shed some light on the relationship between good taste and good design but there are also other, more objective reasons, as to what makes design successful. Designing things should ideally start with a consideration of the end users' requirements, in as much detail as possible, and end up by producing a building or product that is a delight to behold and use. This requires a marriage of human needs or desires with the

technology available at the time, balanced against various constraints (including the vital one of cost). Therefore, design evolves over time as developments in technology provide new opportunities for better ways of doing things. Human expectations and requirements also change over time.

The relationship between human beings and shelter is fundamental to survival and therefore architecture would seem to be a good starting point with which to consider design evolution. Architecture has form and function analogous to a human being. A building must have a sound structure so that it doesn't fall down and this structure is usually apparent in its outward form (although nowadays visible evidence of structure is no longer considered a prerequisite for good design). Similarly, a human being needs a muscular/skeletal structure, which is expressed in the outward form and articulation of its parts. The doors, rooms and corridors of a building must be of a shape and size to allow the accommodation and passage of people. The windows must be of a particular height if people are to see outside and if they are also to allow sunlight and fresh air to enter. Therefore, a building's function and aesthetics are strongly related to the human form and scale, and this relationship has, of course, been a fundamental principle since human dwellings and artefacts first appeared.

This became a particular focal point for artists and architects during the Italian Renaissance, especially in relation to geometry, and writings by the first century Roman architect and engineer Marcus Pollio Vitruvius were very much admired during this time. Vitruvius was a soldier in Julius Caesar's army and later served as a military engineer and architect under the Emperor Augustus, to whom he dedicated his *Ten Books of Architecture* – a massive work covering almost every aspect of ancient architecture, types of

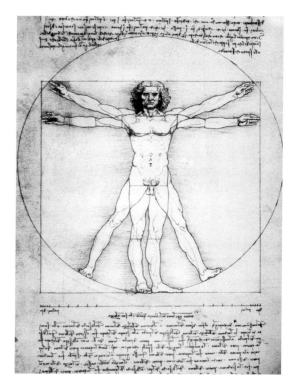

Fig 19 Vitruvian Man – by Leonardo, c.1450 – 'Man is the measure of all things.'

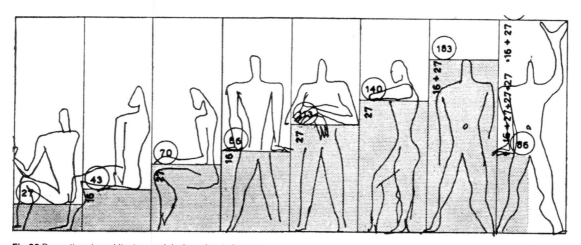

Fig 20 Proportions in architecture and design relate to human proportions. Le Corbusier's *Modulor*. 1948.

buildings, materials and even town planning. Vitruvius said that: 'geometry is the very footprint of man' and that towns and villages should be laid out on a squared grid. Symmetry was essential to beauty and 'no temple can be put together coherently without symmetry and proportion; unless it conforms exactly to the principle relating to the members of a well-shaped man … only a man well-shaped by symmetry can be made to produce the circle and the square.' Vitruvius believed it is because a man's body is symmetrical that architects should follow ancient precepts about symmetrical building. See Leonardo's famous *Vitruvian Man* drawing in Figure 19.

In the first half of the twentieth century one of the founders of the Modern Movement, Le Corbusier, attempted to further quantify human proportions as an aid to designing buildings, furniture and fittings for architects and designers. Figure 20 shows an illustration from his two-volume *Modulor*, first published in 1948, in which, for example, Le Corbusier's recommendation for the ceiling height of a house should be set at the height of an average-sized man with his arm and hand stretched vertically upwards. William Hogarth made similar comparisons regarding the proportions of doors and windows in the eighteenth century. As useful as these and other more recently collated anthropometric data are to designers, such information only takes us so far. A building or a telephone may indeed be designed with the human form in mind – however, we still find ugly buildings and products. If we can pursue this a little further we could say that, like most humans, most buildings and products function reasonably well but truly beautiful man-made objects are rarer.

Proportion in architecture, then, is strongly related to human proportion. If the giraffe had evolved to become the most intelligent creature on the planet, it too would need shelter in northern climes and cars to travel around in. What would giraffe architecture or cars look like? You would probably get buildings that seemed strange to us, even ugly perhaps, but to an intelligent giraffe some of these buildings would look beautiful indeed. So human factors, in combination with the available materials and technology in any given period, have together affected the size and shape of the things that man has designed since the Stone Age and this will continue into the future.

There follow some important examples of milestones in design evolution (in architecture and manufactured products) that have emerged through man's needs, discoveries and inventions since Roman times.

evolutionary design and its influence on aesthetics

The philosopher Santayana had this to say about evolution in building design:

Houses and temples have an evolution like that of animals and plants. Various forms arise by mechanical necessity, like the cave, or the shelter of overhanging boughs. These are perpetuated by a selection in which the needs and pleasures of man are the environment to which the structure must be adapted. Determinate forms thus establish themselves, and the eye becomes accustomed to them. The line of use by habit of apperception becomes the line of beauty. A striking example may be found in the pediment of the Greek temple and the gable of the northern house. The exigencies of climate determine these forms differently (because a steeper roof better promotes the run-off of rain and heavy snow) but the eye in each case accepts what utility imposes. We admire height in one and breadth in the other, and we soon find the steep pediment heavy and the low gable awkward and mean ... In this manner we accept the forms imposed on us by utility, and train ourselves to apperceive their potential beauty.[1]

Historically, the sheer variety of dwelling designs worldwide is largely due to the availability of materials and resources in a particular region. At the extreme end we have igloos made from packed snow, but more usually shelters or houses were built with the local mud (dried, baked or fired), stone and/or timber, to designs capable of withstanding the local climate and sometimes extremes of temperature, as well as coping with other local conditions such as marshy ground, or providing security against wild animals or pests. Thus there are usually very good reasons why a traditional building in a particular region looks the way it does and is not simply the result of a designer's whim. Knowledge of what worked in practice in a particular region was handed down through many generations of local builders, though this knowledge didn't travel very far in the days before mass communications and therefore local designs became stereotyped over the years and acquired the status of accepted good design in a particular region.

Buildings in a particular region have evolved naturally into villages and towns having their own very similar design characteristics – the local vernacular. This includes common elements such as the colour, texture and size of the local stone, the steepness of northern roofs or the conservation of precious rainwater in more southerly climes. The Roman villa often employed inward sloping roofs in order to direct rainwater into a central open area inside the house that collected water in large pools (often very elegantly designed pools). The outer walls of the villa were either solid or generally pierced with just a few window openings, large enough to allow some daylight into the outer rooms but small enough to keep the interior cool at the same time. Probably the best examples of these remaining houses are at Herculaneum near Naples, preserved under volcanic ash since the catastrophic eruption of Mount Vesuvius in AD 79 and rediscovered in the nineteenth century (see Figure 21).

Stone is almost universal as a building material due to its availability, strength in compression and durability. It is not strong in bending or tension however and this places limits on the type of structures that can be made with stone – for example, too large a span between two columns and the straight stone beam bridging them will obviously crack. In some of today's neoclassical buildings the gaps between the columns are far too large for the 'stone' architrave above (for example, the White House portico in Washington, DC) – a sure giveaway that there is a steel girder hidden in there somewhere. The type and size of stone in a particular region often leads to unusual or unique designs. For example, flint, a stone naturally plentiful in certain regions such as Suffolk and Sussex in England, is a very hard material that has been used for purposes other than building. It can be chipped to produce a hard-wearing sharp edge, used by Stone-Age man for axes and the tips of spears, and also knives to skin and butcher animals. It has, of course, also been used to create sparks to ignite gunpowder in the 'flintlocks' of early muskets and guns. However, building with flint stones, or any other similar sized rounded stones that are very small compared to bricks for instance, creates a particular problem at the corners of a building. Therefore, flint-stone houses were usually designed with bricks at the corners and also around the windows and doors. This is because small stones can be embedded quite deeply in the mortar along a straight flat wall, but at the corners much more of each individual stone would be left exposed and therefore prone to coming loose or being accidentally knocked out by passers by. This is also the reason why many early church towers in these regions were cylindrical – a design without corners that saved having to import stone or brick from elsewhere. The traditional Suffolk flint house also exploits the reeds growing in and around local waterways for its roofing materials.

Fig 21 Roman Villa at Herculaneum. c.AD79. The inward sloping roof and opening allows rainwater to pour into the central pool.

We can add to these practical elements other more culturally driven design traits influenced by religion and local customs, such as a preferred taste in decorative elements or paint colours established over time. The local government of Lanzarote in the Spanish Canaries has imposed a strict colour code for the island's houses and buildings – white for a building's walls (but built from the local black volcanic rock) and a particular green for painted woodwork, although blue woodwork is acceptable for buildings near the coast. This was a recommendation by the local artist César Manrique and was put into practice by the Island Council in the 1970s. It is still in force today (although a few residents still try to flout the rules). The number of storeys for buildings on the island is limited to a maximum of three, a far-sighted decision when you consider the number of coastal resorts ruined by the sheer density of high-rise hotels built in recent decades.

The Arch

In addition to using local natural materials, evolution in technology, materials science and construction methods has strongly influenced the design and appearance of buildings over time. The Romans were the original inventors of the simple semi-circular arch constructed from individual blocks of stone or brick over 2,000 years ago (Figure 22) . In France in the Middle Ages the semicircular Roman stone arch was superseded by the Gothic pointed stone arch (Figure 23). Many people think that the Gothic arch was merely a stylistic change applied to cathedrals and churches, symbolically 'pointing' the way to heaven, as do traditional church steeples. Although the pointed arch and steeple do turn our thoughts 'upwards to heaven', the real reason for the introduction of the pointed arch was of a structural nature, allowing designers much more freedom in the design of churches and other buildings. The design of the pointed arch alters the direction of compressive forces in the stonework,

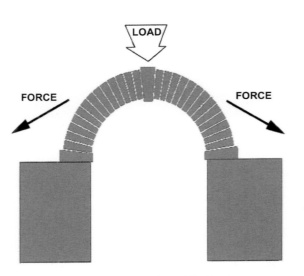

Fig 22 The Roman arch requires substantial buttressing to withstand sideways forces.

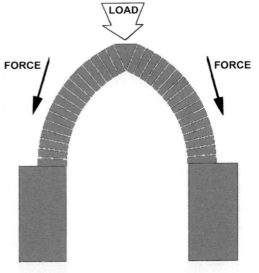

Fig 23 Gothic (pointed) arch forces require much less buttressing.

making them much more vertical compared with the Roman arch and this can reduce sideways forces by as much as 50 per cent.[2] Therefore, the Gothic arch requires much less in the way of buttressing compared to the semicircular arch (although sometimes both types of arch were reinforced by placing a horizontal metal tension rod across the base).

Because of the much-reduced need for massive buttressing against sideways forces, the Gothic arch opened up the structure of churches allowing more space and light to be created within the building, and also paved the way for the inclusion of large areas of stained glass. The 'flying buttress' was a direct consequence of the Gothic arch, its form delicately counteracting the line of forces produced by the pointed arch or vaulting, replacing the previously solid buttressing walls necessary to the Roman design. Sometimes the vertical element supporting or 'anchoring' the base of the flying buttress was extended upwards into a pinnacle (or other design of decorative stonework) in order to increase the weight and downwards thrust on the anchor to further counteract any sideways forces (see Figure 24).

The pointed arch also circumvents another problem of Roman vaulting where two vaults of different widths intersect, resulting in two different heights of arch (Figure 25). Awkward 'stilts' for the smaller arch enabled both arches to be the same height, but this is far from an elegant solution, resulting in a wavy groin where both arches meet, as shown in Figure 26. By employing the pointed arch the heights of the two intersecting vaults can be made the same simply by slightly altering the curve of one of the arches, as shown in Figure 27.

Fig 24 Gothic design – flying buttresses of Notre Dame Cathedral, Paris. c.AD1280. (Note the upward extension of the vertical pinnacles above the stone arches.)

Fig 25 Intersecting Roman vaults of differing widths.

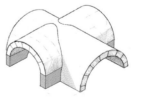

Fig 26 Same as Fig. 25, but using 'stilts' (shown in solid tone). This results in wavy groins where the two arches meet.

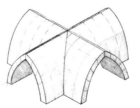

Fig 27 Intersecting Gothic vaults of differing widths but of equal height.

Fig 28 Aerial view of the Pantheon's concrete roof, Rome. AD123.

Fig 29 The pointed Dome of Santa Maria – Florence, by Brunelleschi, completed AD1436.

The Dome

The forerunner of modern concrete was invented by the Romans, using a heavily compacted mixture of lime and a little water, plus aggregates of broken bricks, hollow ceramics and pumice stones (for lightness), and pozzolana – a volcanic ash from Pozzuoli near Naples. The dome of the Pantheon in Rome finished in AD123 (Figure 28) was constructed using this material and, at 42.5 metres (142 feet) in internal diameter, remained the largest unsupported span for well over 1,000 years until overtaken (though only by less than 3 metres (ten feet)) by Brunelleschi's pointed dome for Florence Cathedral in 1436 (Figure 29). Nowadays, concrete reinforced by internal steel rods enables much larger structures to be cast in an endless variety of shapes.

The dome could be described as an arch revolved through 360 degrees and, as such, it produces an outward thrust all the way around its base – a force that would cause it to collapse if not counteracted. This analogy with the simple 'two-dimensional' arch however is slightly misleading, as a pure dome consists of compound curves in three dimensions, like an egg, seashell or an animal's skull, and is therefore an extremely strong shape. Because of this the dome's skin can be much thinner than that required for an arch having the same span (today's Formula One racing cars use this principle in the construction of 'monocoque' composite carbon-fibre shells surrounding the driver). Thick buttressing with walls at the base of the dome could be one solution to counteract the outward thrust, as employed in the Pantheon design and also at the Church of Hagia Sophia in Istanbul finished in AD537 (although this also uses smaller half domes on two opposite sides of the main dome in the east–west axis, in a way anticipating the flying buttress). Hagia Sophia's main dome is about 30 metres (100 feet) in diameter but the two half-domes increase the apparent span in the east–west direction to around 60 metres (200 feet).

Another way of counteracting the outward thrusts of a dome would be to use many tension rods (or a tensile sheet) across the open base, tying together the opposite ends of each arch member. This would not be a very elegant solution, however, and the view up inside the dome would be obscured by these tie rods or the sheet. Sometimes the dome is placed on top of a cylindrical 'drum' (for example, the Capitol building in Washington), which also rules out external buttressing. The simplest and most elegant solution is to place a tension member such as one or more iron chains (hoops) around the base perimeter of the dome – as used by Brunelleschi for the dome of Florence's Santa Maria Cathedral in 1436, Michelangelo's design of 1546 for St Peter's in Rome (redesigned by Della Porta into a more pointed form and built after Michelangelo's death) and Sir Christopher Wren for the dome of St Paul's Cathedral in London, finished in 1710. These iron chains were hidden from view by stonework and the somewhat rusty iron chain of St Paul's was replaced by several stainless-steel ones in 1925. In the case of smaller domes using wooden structures, the same effect could be achieved by joining together all the ends of the arched members around the perimeter base with timber struts in tension (which would require sound carpentry joining methods). Modern pure geodesic domes are by their very structure 'tied together' and usually need no other reinforcement to stop them from spreading. However, on closer inspection, larger geodesic designs are actually triangulated spaceframe structures 'curved up' into domes and spheres that prevent them from flexing too much and collapsing.

'Gothic' was first used as a derogatory term during the Italian Renaissance when referring to buildings of the Middle Ages. Not belonging to the Classical tradition of post and beam, these pointed-arch designs were regarded as ugly unsophisticated products, akin to the 'uncivilized and barbarian' Goths and therefore completely lacking in artistic merit. The Goths were a northern Germanic people who invaded much of central Europe after AD238, which included the sacking of Rome in AD410. However, Filippo Brunelleschi's design for a pointed dome on Florence's cathedral (finished in 1436) was greatly admired (Figure 29) and was itself a brilliant feat of structural design and execution.[3]

The building of the cathedral had begun in 1296 but had stopped after reaching the crossing in 1367 when it was realized that no one knew how to vault such a huge space. At the time many considered the placing of a dome on the top of the cathedral an impossible task, given the very large span required, without the use of massive buttressing placed around the outside of the building. It is also said that the dome was built without the use of wooden centring – support for the dome during construction. This may be due in part to Brunelleschi's 'herringbone' (or zig-zag) brickwork design for the inner shell of the dome. Herringbone pattern brickwork is a much stronger construction method than simply laying horizontal courses of bricks on top of one another. This method interlaces or 'keys' each brick to several other bricks, thus making for a much more secure shell structure that was less likely to collapse inwards as the curved dome was slowly built up.

Nowadays the term 'Gothic' is generally used to describe buildings between the Romanesque and Renaissance periods. Different nations often produced their own peculiar brand of Gothic, for example, 'Venetian Gothic' or 'Belgian Gothic',

Fig 30 Sloping rafters produce an outward thrust and can be considered as an arch comprising just two elements.

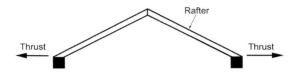

Fig 31 A schematic of a roof truss design for the Banqueting House ceiling. 1622.

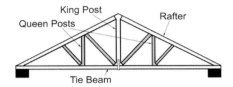

Fig 32 Innovative roof truss design. David Mellor Design Museum, Hathersage. 2006.

which still employed the pointed arch or dome but differed in the detailing and ornamentation. This variation also occurs in other styles of architecture. For example, many later Classical-style buildings (using the Greek post-and-beam method) also incorporated the Roman arch. Later, as a product of the Italian Renaissance, greater expressive design and ornamentation led to what is now termed Baroque and Rococo architecture. The terms 'neo-Gothic' or 'Gothic Revival' refer to a renewed interest in the Gothic style in the nineteenth century, and many new Gothic-style churches and other buildings were built during this period, promoted especially by A. W. N. Pugin in England, as previously noted. A prime example of this revival architecture is the Houses of Parliament in London built between 1840 and 1888, designed by Charles Barry in collaboration with Pugin.

The Truss

In Italy from the sixteenth century onwards, developments in wooden roof truss design led to increases in the span of ceilings. This meant that larger interior spaces could be created without the need for obtrusive supporting pillars. Prior to this, the roof space in most buildings were simply left 'open' and relied on the strength of the walls or buttressing to resist the outward thrust of the inclined roof (Figure 30).

The Banqueting Hall in Whitehall Palace, London, had the largest unsupported ceiling span (at 12.6 metres (42 feet)) in Great Britain when it was created by Inigo Jones in 1622 using a type of wooden truss design he had seen on his travels in Italy. Shortly afterwards Sir Christopher Wren created designs with spans of up to 21 metres (70 feet). Inigo Jones is also credited with introducing the first Classical-style building into the UK, in the form of Queen Anne's House in Greenwich,

Fig 33 Joseph Paxton's prefabricated design for the Crystal Palace. 1851.

completed in 1635 (which still exists and is well preserved).

The roof truss employs a tie beam (in tension), which counteracts the outward thrust of the principal rafters (in compression), reducing the need for thick walls. The addition of a 'king post' (in tension) supported at the top by the two sloping rafters and fixed to the horizontal tie beam at the centre, prevents the tie beam from sagging under its own weight and that of the ceiling, making the whole structure much more rigid (Figure 31). Secondary or 'queen posts' further strengthened the truss, as did additional diagonal struts – helping to prevent the sagging of the rafters under the heavy weight of the lead or slate roof covering.[4] Such were the advantages of these seventeenth-century designs that they would not look out of place on a modern building site today.

Figure 32 shows a contemporary design for a roof truss used for the David Mellor Design Museum in Hathersage, UK, built in 2006. This uses the same principles as the truss design by Inigo Jones – two rafters in compression, with the original king post and tie beam tension members replaced by three steel cables, all joined at a point higher up than is usual compared with the traditionally straight tie beam (or tie cable). This particular design however puts each cable under greater tensile forces, but has the advantage of providing more roof space when a flat ceiling is not required.

Iron and Steel

The introduction of iron-trussed roofs in the nineteenth century, stimulated by the railway and shipbuilding industries, led to much larger spans. Different types of truss design can also be seen in various bridge structures. Cast and wrought (forged) iron structures revolutionized building methods during this period and these buildings were in a sense the forerunners of twentieth-century modernist architecture using steel. One of the most famous of these iron structures was Joseph Paxton's design for the Crystal Palace in London (Figure 33). This was the winning design in a competition (which included a proposal by Isambard Kingdom Brunel) for a building to house over 100,000 exhibits of manufactured goods from around the world. It was intended for inclusion in Prince Albert's Great Exhibition of 1851 in Hyde Park, following an idea by Henry Cole (a member and leading activist of the Society for the Encouragement of Arts, Manufactures and Commerce). The aim of the exhibition was an attempt to raise the quality of British manufactured

Fig 34 ''Undecorated' claret jug design by Christopher Dresser. c.1879.

goods on the world stage and, at the same time, to educate the public in matters of good design and taste. Paxton's design for the building (which was hated by John Ruskin and William Morris) was of prefabricated cast iron and glass construction assembled on site and erected at great speed in about four months.

The son of a farm labourer, Joseph Paxton had joined the Horticultural Society's gardens at Chiswick House in London as a young labourer and gardening trainee in 1823. Chiswick House was the first Palladian Villa to be built in Great Britain (by Lord Burlington in 1727) and was owned by the sixth Duke of Devonshire – who in 1826 employed the twenty-three-year-old Paxton as his head gardener and landscape architect at his Chatsworth Estate in Derbyshire. Paxton was knowledgeable about greenhouse and conservatory design (known as stoves) through his training at Chiswick and went on to design iron and timber glass houses for a variety of plants and fruit trees at Chatsworth. Paxton's design for the Crystal Palace was based on his experiences at Chatsworth but represented a huge leap of faith necessitated by the sheer scale of the proposed new building.

It could be said that the Great Exhibition signalled the start of industrial design proper in the UK – which demonstrated that design does not need to plagiarize historical styles but should embrace modern production methods of the day instead. The American exhibits such as the Colt revolver demonstrated that standardization of parts, simple and honest construction, were a better way forward – the machine aesthetic was a valid outcome in its own right without any need for 'constructed decoration' ornamental applications typical of much Victorian designs of the day.

Christopher Dresser was Great Britain's first professional designer to put these ideas into practice with his designs for metal, glass and ceramics (Figure 34). Dresser admired the simple yet elegant designs of Japan and saw nothing wrong with using contemporary methods of production – his ideas and designs anticipating the Modern Movement of the twentieth century. After the Great Exhibition closed the Crystal Palace was dismantled and re-erected (with additions to the building and also the creation of large gardens with fountains designed by Paxton) at Sydenham in North London in 1854, where it had a variety of public educational and amenity uses over the ensuing years (often narrowly escaping bankruptcy) before being destroyed by fire in 1936.

It has been known for centuries that steel has a much greater tensile strength than iron (it is claimed that steelmaking began as early as 500 BC in India). Up until the latter half of the nineteenth century, however, steel artefacts such as tools, armour and weapons could only be made in relatively small quantities due to steel's complex and costly conversion from iron ore. Steel was therefore not used in buildings in any significant way. However, the advent of cheap mass-produced steel made possible by the new Bessemer process (invented in England by Henry Bessemer in 1855) meant that stone and iron structures could be replaced with the simple straight steel girder, in a way harking back to the Classical post-and-beam stone structures of ancient Greece. The steel post and beam designs enabled much faster construction of buildings and, as such, had a strong influence on modernist architects with the girder's combination of high strength and simplicity. Mass produced steel made possible the building of the first (10–20 storey) skyscrapers in the 1880s and the fact that tall buildings are extremely economical in terms of land use, together with developments in elevator design, plumbing, heating and the

telephone, soon led to the construction of much higher buildings at the beginning of the twentieth century. Now, of course, skyscrapers dominate the skylines of many cities.

There are many different types of structural elements such as panels, shells, beams and tubes used in the construction of buildings, bridge designs and vehicle frames. Structures have to be strong enough to withstand considerable forces – often different forces acting simultaneously. As well as coping with static forces, such as the weight of the walls in a building, structures are often subject to changing forces over time (dynamic forces). For example, the variable wind load on a high building or the different loads a road bridge has to support – a much greater weight of traffic at rush hour compared with other times of the day or night. The family car has to cope with variable numbers of passengers, their individual weights and distribution within the car, as well as resisting bending, twisting and g-forces whilst the vehicle is in motion. Also structures are affected by temperature, for example, steel expands in hot weather and therefore gaps, flexible mountings or other methods must be employed where elements meet to avoid dangerous distortions occurring. The expansion of adjacent steel plates could actually cause shearing of the bolts holding them together as they expand and slide past one another.

Beams, Tubes and Boxes

As outlined above, the particular shape of a structural member, such as an arch, a shell or the introduction of a diagonal element, can have a considerable impact on the effectiveness of a design to resist forces, sometimes deflecting the direction of forces or thrusts acting upon it, like the gothic arch, and designers have exploited the different shapes

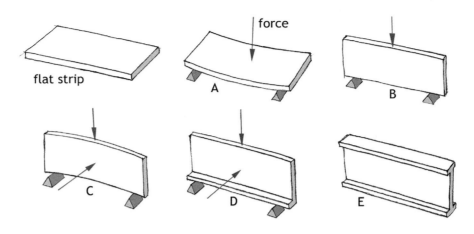

Fig 35 Ways to counteract bending forces.

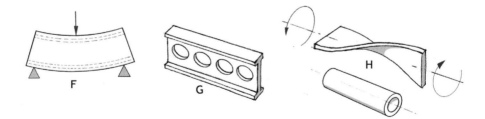

Fig 36 Compression and tensile forces under bending (F) weight reduction (G) and counteracting torsion (H).

of components to more elegantly solve particular problems. Today's cars are much lighter in weight, to aid fuel efficiency among other things, and yet are much stronger structurally than designs of even just a decade ago. Although a detailed study of structures is outside the scope of this book, it is worth looking at some of the principal forces and some of the shapes of some components (not already mentioned) used to counteract these. Obviously the shape of a component, determined by the forces it has to withstand, has a huge impact on the appearance of a particular design and therefore its resulting physical beauty – whether used in a bicycle or a building.

For our purposes here, forces can be classified into five main types:

- compression;
- tension (tensile, stretching);
- bending;
- torsion (rotating, twisting);
- shear (sliding).

The effects of some of these forces are illustrated on the previous page. A simple beam represented by a flat strip of material is subjected to a bending force in Figure 35 (A). The strip obviously better resists bending when turned on its edge as there is more material being used to resist the direction of force (B). This 'edge on' beam is still weak in lateral bending however (C) but the introduction of a flanged edge or edges, for example, 'L' steel angle, 'U' channel or 'I' beam (shown in D and E) strengthens the original strip and to a large extent prevents it from twisting sideways to the direction of the force and then buckling under the load. Another way of strengthening the strip (C) without the use of flanges would be to introduce vertical folds or curves along its length, thereby producing a zig-zag or serpentine shape (corrugations). We see this sometimes in brick walls – a straight wall of about the height of a man made

from a single thickness of brick would be relatively easy to push over but the serpentine (wavy) wall of the same thickness would be highly resistant to the same force. Of course, corrugated sheet iron and steel have been used for roofing for a long time because of a combination of light weight and strength.

When analysed further in Figure 36 (F), we can see that the top layers of the simple beam in bending are under compression, while the bottom layers are being stretched. As we move further towards the central layers of the beam, however, we can assume that, increasingly, the material is doing less and less work in resisting the load – neither being stretched nor compressed. Therefore, to save weight, a lot of the central material could be removed without having an adverse affect on its overall strength, as long as the top and bottom layers were still rigidly attached to each other. One result of this is the perforated 'I' beam (G) – a type of beam used in many buildings and also those large factory or warehouse 'sheds' often seen on industrial estates. The 'I' beam or girder uses four flanges that provide a much greater resistance to buckling than the single-flange design. The flanges also make it easier to bolt two or more beams together, whether in line or at right angles to each other.

However, a weakness of the simple beam (whether flanged or not) is its relatively poor resistance to torsion (twisting), so it is not a good idea to use it under situations prone to twisting forces as indicated in (H). Replacing the simple beam with a tubular design circumvents this problem as a tube is highly resistant to torsion as well as bending. This is one reason why tubes are used for motorcycle and bicycle frames, among other things. On a more mundane level every gardener knows just how strong bamboo stems are for supporting growing plants. Bamboo's tubular structure is extremely strong yet very lightweight and resists bending in any direction (as it would also resist torsion) and, of course, bamboo has been used in furniture design for centuries (and also for bicycle frames in the Far East). The cross-section of a tube can be of just about any shape, and for a tube subject to bending as well as twisting forces, an elliptical or rectangular tube should be chosen with its widest axis in line with the direction of the bending force. This is sometimes used in bicycle frame design, where another benefit of choosing the elliptical section tube is the reduction in the front-facing area, thereby reducing wind resistance.

An aeroplane's fuselage is in effect a large tube and of course needs to resist large bending and twisting forces, especially on take-off and landing. One of the most innovative designs of aircraft frames of the twentieth century was Barnes Wallis' design for the Wellington Bomber in 1936. This used a lightweight 'geodesic' latticework of curving aluminium struts which formed the 'cylindrical tube' of the fuselage. Because of the inherent strength and 'open' structure of the latticework the aeroplane could withstand much damage and yet remain flying (also many of the incoming bullets would pass straight through the holes in the latticework and out the other side). The Wellington's strength and superior performance greatly exceeded the initial contract specification from the Ministry of Defence.

The continuing industrial revolution in the nineteenth century saw the introduction of fabricated and riveted iron girders and rectangular section tubes, components that were used for bridge and large shed construction due to their ease of manufacture – flat sided elements can be easily drilled and riveted together. Flanges were simply bent strips of wrought iron riveted along the length of the main beam. Examples of these can be seen in any large Victorian railway shed or station, as shown in Figure 37, which includes an example of a fabricated version of the perforated 'I' beam mentioned above, having criss-crossing triangulating struts joining the two flanges together. Modern hot-rolling methods, however, can turn a red-hot solid slab of steel into long lengths of 'H' section girders (or other cross section flanged beams or rails) without any joins and are therefore even stronger than riveted girders.

Modern methods of large-diameter pipe manufacture and welding techniques (borrowed from offshore oil-rig construction) have enabled structural designs to be made using continuous hollow steel tubes (instead of riveted sheet/plate fabrications), which can be shaped, cut and welded to each other, thereby providing stronger (as well as watertight) joints that also produces a more elegant and cleaner visual aesthetic. It is also usually easier to curve a rounded section tube than a square one, which might more easily kink. A square section tube is also prone to distortion when subject to heavy bending loads – exactly in the same way as a pin-jointed square frame distorts by parallelogramming sideways. As with the square frame this can be prevented by triangulation, cross bracing or the placement of internal flat panels at intervals along the beam's length. This is analogous to a cardboard box with a close-fitting lid – without the lid the box can be easily parallellogrammed but once the lid is replaced the resulting cube is extremely rigid. Thus our square section steel girder with internal panels has become a series of boxes – hence the name 'box girder'.

A car's body could be considered as a box construction and is therefore basically a very strong shape. That is, of course, until you start cutting holes in the shell for the doors and windows. The more doors a car has the less it can

Fig 37 Fabricated and riveted iron girders forming a vault over
the railway tracks. Tie rods across the base of each arch cancel
out outward thrusts on the supporting outer walls. Darlington
Railway Station, built c.1875.

resist twisting and bending forces – a problem greatly exacerbated with an open-top design, which needs some (visually subtle) reinforcing methods to maintain a stiffness comparable with the closed-top version. This is also true of boat design – a boat with a deck is in effect a box (or a tube) and is therefore highly resistant to twisting and bending forces. However, an open-topped boat, like a simple rowing dingy, does not have a deck and relies to a large extent for stiffness on its shell-like shape of compound curves. Also 'flanges' running round the top edges of the hull, together with a central 'main beam' (the keel or crease) running the length of the bottom of the hull from bow to stern, greatly add to the boat's strength.

Additionally, in the absence of a deck, the positioning of longitudinal thwarts (a seat fastened to the hull at its top and bottom) at intervals along the length of the boat will locally stiffen it as it makes that part of the hull into a tube – as long as the thwarts are firmly fixed to the hull. Sometimes open boats have 'boxes' integrated in the front and/or rear of the hull structure and also continuous seats running from stem to stern on each side, designed as flat topped 'tubes' that you can sit on.

Some of these hulls are made from glass fibre/ epoxy resin composites, such as glass-reinforced plastic (GRP), and some weight-saving experiments have been carried out in recent years with these using a sandwich construction – a double

Fig 38 Norman Foster's spaceframe design for the Sainsbury Arts Centre, Norwich. 1977.

thin-skinned hull with the gap (or core) between the skins filled with various materials – plastic foam, aluminium honeycomb or even balsa wood – and bonded to both skin surfaces. Theoretically these 'cored' hulls should be very strong as they mimic the action of a beam in bending – one skin in compression while the other is in tension – as well as being shell shaped (made up of compound curves). However, in practice this design is controversial as the hull only remains strong for as long as there is a perfect bond between the two skins and the internal core. Once the core material detaches from either skin, or breaks up due to water ingress, the two surfaces no longer act together (analogous to a H beam with the middle part missing), lose their rigidity and there-fore reduce the boat's original performance and, if water has penetrated, the boat becomes very heavy and is easily damaged. Many boat builders using GRP have reverted to designs just using one single thick skin, as before.

Frames

Technological evolution means constantly having to modify our perceptions of man-made beauty – particularly as new materials and processes are invented. The iron arch replaced the stone arch, iron being superseded in its turn by the steel beam-and-post construction, and the introduction of the triangulated tubular steel space frame design (first invented by Alexander Graham Bell). This is a sort of three-dimensional version of the old wooden roof truss, based on the simple triangle which is an extremely rigid shape, and used to great effect in Norman Foster's Sainsbury Arts Centre in Norwich shown in Figure 38. Space frame designs usually employ rigid struts in compression and tension (like the roof truss) and have been used in applications other than buildings for many years, for example,

automobile designs like the Lotus Seven (and more recently Alex Moulton's bicycle frames). Most car designs of today, however, employ a 'monocoque' shell-like frame fabricated from welded-together pressed-steel components and fabrications, onto which everything is attached. Early cars had separate 'rolling' chassis and bodywork which were then bolted together.

Tubular steel frames have been, and still are, commonly used for motorcycle frames, providing the main chassis for supporting the engine and other components (Figure 39). Some of these more recent frames are proper triangulated spaceframe designs but others simply try to look as elegant as possible whilst holding everything together. Attempts at reducing weight and at the same time increasing stiffness have led to some interesting designs where the engine has itself become a stressed part of the frame, up to now probably the German manufacturer BMW has taken this idea the furthest (Figure 40) – you could say that the engine *is* the frame. Note also the modern cast magnesium alloy wheels (instead of assembled spokes and rim), discs in place of drum brakes, and fatter tyres – all technical devel-opments that contribute to the motorcycle's visual and sculptural evolution. With these and other improvements, modern road-going motorcycles for sale in high street shops today would easily outclass the factory tuned racing motorcycles of just twenty years ago.

Tensile Structures

Other structures use rigid members in compres-sion in combination with flexible members such as wire cables, which are only useful in tension. Although providing a strong visual statement, the 'X' cross-bracing tension members on the Pompidou Centre in Paris (Figure 41) are not mere decoration.

Fig 39 BMW R51/3 Motorcycle, 1951–6. 'Traditional' tubular steel frame design, within which the engine is mounted.

Fig 40 BMW R1200 RT Motorcycle, 2004. The engine provides the main frame component.

Cross-bracing prevents the structure from 'parallelogramming' – collapsing sideways (a weakness of four struts arranged in a square or rectangle). Cross-bracing can be effected by simple tension members such as steel cables, where one or the other cable is in tension at any one time, doing away with weighty compression members. Wire cables have been used in suspension bridge design since the nineteenth century (replacing iron chains) and nowadays more unusual expressive designs of suspension bridges can be seen in the work of Santiago Calatrava. Cross-bracing wires were also used on early biplanes as well as many other more mundane structures, such as freestanding bookshelves in the home – sometimes replacing panels that would otherwise do the same job.

Although commonly used in bridge design, developments in tensile (tension) structures are increasingly being applied to new buildings, Some 'supersheds' use steel cable in tension and steel posts and struts in compression (for example, Norman Foster's design for the Renault Distribution Centre in Swindon). Suspending the roof of a building from above maximizes the volume of unhindered space inside. Of course tensile structures have been with us for thousands of years in the form of tents. The earliest tents used the branches of trees to support a covering of animal skins, such as the American Indian's wigwam or the desert Arab's tent. Advances in synthetic materials in the twentieth century have led to the creation of huge tent structures, used in stadium design and outdoor concerts, for example. It is also known that some natural fibres, such as that produced by the silkworm, have greater tensile strengths than steel, and material scientists are currently investigating how the common spider produces the filaments that go into constructing its immensely strong and resilient web, with a view to repeating this process synthetically in man-made

materials. Probably the most well known of synthetic tensile cable and sheet structures to date are the polyester sheet tents of the German architect Otto Frei, who designed the tensile roofs for the 1972 Munich Olympics shown in Figure 42 (and more recently Richard Roger's tensile design for the Millennium Dome in London). Otto Frei also designed pneumatic (air-supported) domes, which used sheet materials in tension. These are supported with the assistance of a slightly higher internal air pressure (being pumped inside) compared to the external atmospheric pressure.

The properties and behaviour of different materials provide significant constraints as well as opportunities for the design and shapes of objects. However, the sensitive handling of these materials and structures by the designer is crucial and can make the difference between an elegant design and an ugly one, even though both designs may function well. Ship and aeroplane designs are significantly constrained by the medium they have to travel through and must resist the stresses and strains to which they are subjected. Streamlined shapes obviously travel through air and water more efficiently and circular 'porthole' and rounded windows prevent stress cracks from starting – a problem with square-shaped windows or holes, which concentrate the forces at the corners.

Plywood, Plastics and Composites

The introduction of new materials and construction methods – and the resulting different shapes for once familiar objects – has always been treated with suspicion by the public. In the first half of the twentieth century plywood structures were first used in furniture design, replacing 'proper' traditional solid timber construction, which provided opportunities for new forms due to plywood's high strength, shock-absorbing properties and springy nature (resilience) – for example, Alvar Aalto's chair No. 41 (Figure 43). The American designers Charles Eames and his wife, Ray, pioneered many experiments with moulded plywood and produced a variety of chairs and other products (for example, a splint for broken legs) made from moulded plywood between the 1940s and 1960s. Notably, several of these designs are still in production today. Plywood's greater strength compared to a solid piece of timber having the same dimensions is due to the bonding together under pressure (using adhesives) of several thin sheets of wood (laminates) having alternating directions of grain – solid timber has of course the grain only going in one direction. As well as plywood's greater strength, the potentially catastrophic splitting along the grain of solid wood is therefore avoided.

Plywood is still used today for a wide variety of applications including furniture and boat construction. Perhaps the most famous demonstration of plywood's strength, however, is its use in the construction of De Havilland's 1941 Mosquito bomber (Figure 44), which was originally designed to save on scarce aluminium and viewed as a stop-gap by Great Britain's Air Ministry – until it proved itself to be the fastest aircraft in Bomber Command for the next ten years. Regarded as a most beautiful aircraft by its crews, the fuselage was a sandwich of balsa between two skins of birch plywood built on spruce stringers and glued together under compression until dry (cured), and is about half to three-quarters of an inch thick. The main wings used birch plywood for the upper and lower surfaces, two skins for the top surface and one for underneath. The top skins were screwed to the internal spruce spars and ribs in addition to being glued because of the enormous aerodynamic upward suction forces on the wing when in flight (in more than one early test flight the top skin was ripped away). The engines and undercarriages are mounted to the wings via welded tubular steel frames.

Aluminium alloys have gradually replaced timber in the construction of aeroplanes since the early 1900s and today carbon-fibre composites are replacing metals in many applications that require lightness and strength. The 1980s US 'Stealth' aircraft (Figure 45) uses composite materials in its construction, its surfaces coated with radar absorbing materials (rather like matt black paint absorbs visible light and infra-red to some extent) and its faceted forms help to reflect radar waves at oblique angles – away from the radar transmitter and receiver.

'Buckminsterfullerene' (named after the American architect and inventor Buckminster Fuller) is a special geodesic construct of carbon molecules – currently found only in stars – that herald future materials having strengths over a hundred times that of steel. Maybe this is the sort of material the science-fiction novelist Arthur C. Clarke had in mind when, decades ago, he predicted an earth-to-geostationary satellite connecting cable having sufficient strength to support itself and provide a means for an earth-to-space 'elevator' – which would make those awe-inspiring terrestrial rocket launches (and the Dan Dare aesthetic) redundant. Applications of such novel materials would mean new and unusual shapes for familiar man-made objects – the bicycle is already morphing into shell-like structures as carbon composite materials are applied to the frame and wheels (but what would a future Buckminsterfullerene bicycle look like?). Furniture design is going in this direction too, requiring our adjustment to new and unusual forms. Our notions of beautiful shapes are therefore constantly evolving. No doubt there will be elegant composite furniture as well as ugly composite furniture – how will we decide which is

Fig 41
'Cross-bracing'
– Pompidou
Centre, Paris.
By Richard
Rogers & Renzo
Piano. 1977.

Fig 42
Tensile roof
structures for the
Munich Olympics
in 1972. Otto
Frei. View of
the roof of the
Olympic Stadium,
designed by
Gunther Behnisch
with Frei Otto as
roof consultant.

which? (More importantly, how will we recycle it?)

Early modernist designers such as Mies van der Rohe, Marcel Breuer and Le Corbusier experienced a similar situation in the 1920s with the introduction of tubular steel furniture (Figure 46). Many people, used to solid timber furniture, severely criticized these new designs at the time. Now however they are regarded as design classics and many of these designs are still in production. Developments in plastics technology in the twentieth century also led to the introduction of 'disturbing' new forms in furniture design. Following on from earlier experiments with plywood furniture, Robin Day's injection moulded polypropylene stacking chair (using tubular steel legs) for Hille International (Figure 47) was the first of its type in 1963 and is still mass-produced today. The chair is cheap, extremely resilient and resistant to abuse, and is therefore widely used in the public sector. The first all-plastic chair was designed by Verner Panton, a stacking design made in polyurethane (the first prototype being made in glass-reinforced plastic) that went into production for Herman Miller in 1967, and since 1999 has been produced in injection-moulded polypropylene (Figure 48). Today, carbon fibre and similar materials are being introduced in furniture designs where a combination of strength, light weight and resilience is required.

Convergence, Change and Beauty

Today's cars, bicycles, tools, houses and the built environment are a part of a continuing technical evolution, started many thousands of years ago with the appearance of bone and stone artefacts.

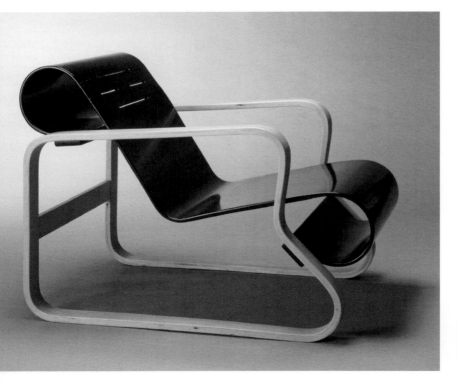

Fig 43 Alvar Aalto plywood 'Paimio' chair (1931). Still in production today as Artek number 41 chair.

Nowadays research and development take place among many different fields of technology simultaneously – for example, materials science, chemistry, thermodynamics, electronics and computer science, electro-mechanical engineering and also space exploration and (increasingly in the future) sustainable energy power sources. These, often very different technologies, continually converge into new and/or better products as engineers and designers learn to combine them in new ways. The family motor car combines all the foregoing technologies into one product – a fast lightweight car (in future powered by hydrogen fuel cells) including GPS (global positioning system) instruments that enable the driver to navigate with the help of geostationary orbital satellites in space.

As cars and other products increase in complexity, the role of the human factors specialist is becoming more crucial to the understanding and safe operation of machines. This includes everything from the satisfactory physical 'fit' of the human body with a product (ergonomics), for example, an office chair, to the design of the computer interface with its often very complex programs. Most of us have experienced frustration with computers in some form or other but this becomes a matter of life and death when the GPS system in the car becomes too distracting. The human factors specialist's job is to make complex things simple to understand from the point of view of the user and simplicity is often a very difficult thing to achieve. Although human factors, ergonomics and interface design can contribute to beauty (both physical and conceptual beauty) through their impact on the design of products, these are subjects largely outside the scope of this book and are covered in depth elsewhere.

Early man-made products have a beauty of their own which we can still appreciate today.

Fig 44 Plywood construction Mosquito aircraft. 1941.

Fig 45 Composite construction B-2A Stealth Bomber. 1988.

Certainly ancient civilizations placed a high value on an object's form, colour and decoration, much of which carried symbolic meanings. Many ancient and modern tools combine form and function that are inseparable from each other – the basic shapes of knives and forks are determined by the shape of our hands and mouths and the task of

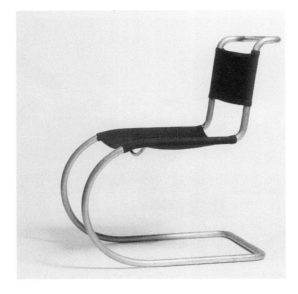

Fig 46 Early tubular steel furniture – Mies
Van der Rohe Chair. c.1927.

Fig 47 Robin Day's polypropylene stacking
chair. 1963.

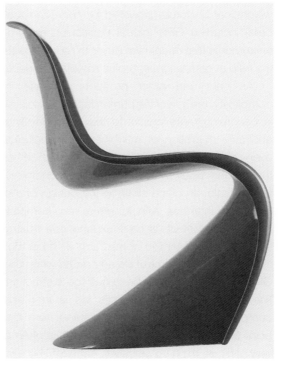

Fig 48 Vernor Panton's all-plastic
stacking chair, first produced in 1967.

cutting food into manageable lumps. But why are some cutlery sets more elegant than others? These are vexing questions. Like cutlery, a chair is designed to fit the human form and also to be strong enough to support the user's weight without breaking. Many such chairs perform this task admirably, yet some will be more visually attractive than others.

It has been said that the most elegant forms are those achieved by the perfect integration of form and function without the need for any decoration. The architect Le Corbusier's maxim 'a house is a machine for living in' became the motto for generations of architects and designers throughout the first half of the twentieth century, although today many would disagree with this philosophy, especially postmodernists. However, modernist designers have produced many wonderful examples of pared-down elegant designs. For instance, Mies van der Rohe's tubular steel chair, pictured in Figure 46, was designed in 1927 and is still in production today. Ideally, new buildings and products should be a seamless integration of function, form and expression of purpose, as well as being a spiritual delight to behold and use – for example, Zaha Hadid's Nuragic and Contemporary Art Museum at Cagliari (Figure 5 in Chapter 1). These iconic buildings can be very expensive to build, however, and although they may never become mainstream design, they are sure to influence the everyday work of future generations of architects and designers in perhaps more subtle ways.

All natural life forms on the Earth have evolved through natural selection into the most efficient designs, materials and structures suitable for survival in a particular set of circumstances. The human form encapsulates the most complex and efficient 'machinery' (both physical and mental) for its survival, inside a very small and extremely

efficient package – form definitely follows function here! By any definition this must be an elegant solution – there's not much room for useless parts in the context of survival. However, as we have seen in Chapter 1, when it comes to judging man-made designs there are no universal guidelines to help us decide which design is elegant and which is ugly.

Culture and taste also evolve over time and notions of beauty and other forms of excellence are subject to changing opinions and fashions with every successive generation. Richard Dawkins describes a form of cultural evolution, which is just as real as physical evolution (only much faster), and this has a considerable effect on our well-being and outlook as social animals. Dawkins refers to 'memes' as the cultural equivalent of 'genes', being slightly modified with each successive generation. Thus different societies have different notions of beauty depending on their own set of circumstances and evolving culture, as we have already seen. In addition to understanding how technology influences design (perhaps we could regard technology as 'genes'), we need to be aware of cultural notions (memes) which also have a profound effect on design evolution, and these can differ depending on which particular culture you are referring to. There follows a brief outline of two of the more obvious cultural notions – classic/romantic and female/male.

Classic Versus Romantic

The terms 'classic' and 'romantic' can be applied to various fields in the fine and applied arts and it is important to understand the difference between the two terms. Deciding which work belongs to which category involves subjective judgements and, like much in the arts, these judgements are open to individual interpretation. Classicism and

Romanticism (with capitals 'C' and 'R') also refer to particular historical periods, specifically Classical Greek architecture and sculpture between (roughly) 500 BC and 300 BC and early nineteenth-century 'Romantic' artists and painters such as William Turner and Eugene Delacroix. These different approaches are particularly striking when comparing the emotionally charged paintings of horses by Delacroix with the classical studies of horses by the eighteenth-century English artist George Stubbs. Works of literature, music, theatre, performing arts, the visual arts, architecture and design, all usually have tendencies to one or the other term. Frequently a piece of work can express both romantic and classic tendencies at the same time – compare the largely classical music of Mozart with the largely romantic music of Wagner. Romanticism usually involves a deeper emotional response in the observer compared with classicism, which usually appeals to our intellect more than our hearts.

Fig 49 'Mannerist' or Baroque Church of St. Carlo, Rome. Borromini. c.1640.

There are many examples of renewed interest in the Classical style of Greek architecture in the years since the Renaissance (and also a return to Classical themes in painting in the late eighteenth century). Even today Neo-Classical architecture is still being built and our fascination with Classical design seems undiminished. In general however it is more difficult to distinguish between classic and romantic (small 'c' and 'r') tendencies in architecture and design. Buildings and furniture produced by the twentieth century Modern Movement are generally regarded as classical (with a small 'c') because of the logical and rational thinking behind them, analogous to the structural logic behind Classical Greek and Roman architecture.

The artists and architects of the Italian Renaissance in the sixteenth and seventeenth centuries combined elements of Classical Greek and Roman styles with a more expressive dynamic. Thus this art and architecture began to express a more romantic, emotional or 'theatrical' appeal – see Francesco Borromini's sculpturally expressive treatment of the Church of San Carlo in Figure 49 – and this shift towards more expressive or emotionally charged works became known as 'Mannerism'. Although there has always been a strong link between architecture and sculpture (as exemplified in Michelangelo's designs for St Peter's and other buildings in Rome), there is a significant difference between meaningful sculpture and mere decoration or 'entertainment'. It could be argued that the columns on the façade of Borromini's church are not really holding anything up – they are decorative rather than structural.

Classical Greek and Roman sculpture was very restrained in its forms; its statues of human figures usually expressed little or no emotion, perhaps only one of understated gesture (though there were exceptions). The artists of the Renaissance, however, were more interested in showing figures engaged in some dramatic or emotional event – for example, a heroic figure involved in some struggle, or a mother's grief for her dead son. This 'Mannerism' led to what has become known as the 'Baroque' in architecture and art. Later on however this interest in the development of the Baroque style got somewhat out of hand, resulting in over-blown garish ornamentation and decoration in architecture, with interiors festooned with carved plants and cherubs - the 'Rococo' style.

Rather confusingly in today's Western society, the term 'classic' is also given to particular designs (whether inherently romantic or classical in nature), which are recognized as significant and have stood the test of time. Probably car design exemplifies this best – the original Fiat Panda and the Porsche 928 are both modern classics but the romantic associations of travelling in speedy comfort to exotic locations are best conjured by the Porsche. Most of today's four-wheel drive vehicles are bought largely for romantic reasons – these are lifestyle purchases and most will probably never be used off-road.

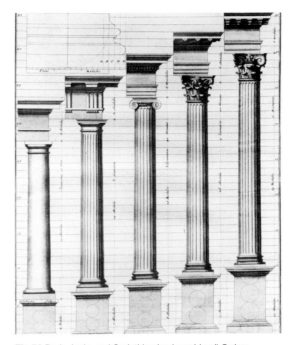

Fig 50 Doric, Ionic, and Corinthian (and combined) Orders. Expressions of gender? The Orders of Architecture from Ordonnances des Cinq Especes de Colonne by Claude Perrault. 1676.

Masculine and Feminine

Many societies refer to inanimate objects as being either masculine or feminine, though this may have nothing to do with their appearance. For example, the French refer to a yacht as male, whereas a car is female. In the United Kingdom ships are regarded as female – 'god bless all who sail in her' – but the British do not seem to have the equivalent for 'male' objects, perhaps British culture doesn't regard males as 'beautiful' – a quality that can probably be more easily ascribed to a ship. It is true however that in Western society certain cars are regarded as more appealing to women than men – masculine tastes tend to prefer more aggressive forms whereas women tend to prefer softer shapes, although a member of a different culture would probably not understand these varying tastes as applied to particular objects. Western thinking also tends to attach objective (function) qualities to masculinity and subjective (form) qualities to femininity – though many artefacts will of course have elements of both.[5]

The attaching of male and female values to designed objects is probably as old as civilization itself. The neo-Classical architect Quinlan Terry has suggested that the different orders of Classical Greek architecture have different personalities – the Doric Order has a manly beauty, Ionic is more feminine and the Corinthian Order expresses a more flamboyant personality and could be either male or female (Figure 50). This follows Vitruvius' original assertion of the male/female nature of

Doric and Ionic capitals, but the Corinthian joins them together to create a symbol of nature's regeneration. Many built or manufactured objects can express a tendency towards either gender – compare Robin Day's and Vernor Panton's chairs above, most people would probably choose the Panton chair as being more 'female'. So different objects can have masculine or feminine, classic or romantic tendencies, many of which will be examples of good design, but our personal preferences for each are issues of taste.

Zoomorphism

In addition to deciding which objects are male or female, most cultures will ascribe other animal characteristics to inanimate objects. A Japanese person will not buy a car with an 'unhappy face' for example (Donald Norman once described direction indicators as a 'facial expression' of the car). This should not be surprising as human beings are programmed to spot living creatures against the background environment – our very lives once depended on it (and of course still do in some cultures). We often describe a house as friendly or welcoming and another house may appear soulless or even hostile by comparison. We can 'read' someone's facial expressions and body language even before we enter into a conversation with them and, from these visual clues, judge their internal emotional states. We can usually tell if they are jolly extroverts or quiet introverted types from a distance, by their body language.

The philosopher Alain de Botton has attempted to describe the different 'personalities' of buildings, furniture and objects, and how these can impinge on our emotional wellbeing.[6] Many designers would not take this topic very seriously but designs and environments can definitely affect our mood and should also be fun from time to time.

Some of the many kitchen products and gadgets made by the Italian company Alessi do have a deliberate element of a 'happy creature' about them and have proved very popular, prompting other companies to follow suit. This is a fashion that may not last, however – to surround yourself completely with whimsical objects might eventually drive you mad.

evolution of visual identity and branding

Evidence of a visual ancestry can be seen in the products of all well-known and long-established companies and organizations. This is usually obvious in a company's two-dimensional graphic identity – you can usually spot the petrol company's identity half a mile away from the motorway filling station. Also the visual identity of a particular company evolves over a period of years, usually determined by fashion preferences prevailing at the time. However, this visual identity of a company is also the case in three dimensions, for example, you only have to glimpse at a Dyson vacuum cleaner or BMW car to know which company produced that particular product – even before you spot the familiar logo or badge. In the two images of BMW cars (Figures 51 and 52) it is easy to spot the ancestry of the twin 'nostrils' radiator air intake. However, there are also much more subtle developments to be discovered in terms of perceived 'muscularity' and 'personality' in the development of a family of cars – analogous to the appearance of our own family members through the generations. No doubt car stylists have a heightened sensitivity to these factors, perhaps even subconsciously drawing curves and details, which automatically fit the family album.

Fig 51 Early 'nostrils' – BMW Roadster 328. 1936.

Fig 52 Later 'nostrils' – BMW Concept M5, 2004. Neo-Baroque meets zoomorphism – headlamps as eyes?

Car design at the start of the twenty-first century has evolved into more expressive use of form and detail as exemplified in the BMW illustration. Commentators have named this 'ugly design' or even 'neo-baroque' (or 'modern baroque') – harking back to the expressive theatrical and romantic forms of the late Renaissance, where designers such as Borromini applied dynamic curving forms to otherwise classical buildings.

The visual identity of a particular company and its products can be protected by law under the registered design and registered trade marks facilities at the Patent Office. These images, symbols, shapes and forms are vital pieces of intellectual property essential to the long-term success of a particular business, preventing unscrupulous competitors from producing products pretending to be something they are not. This has become a real problem for many companies, especially in the field of fashion design where counterfeit clothes and accessories can be made in a very short space of time, appearing in the marketplace not long after the launch of the genuine articles on the catwalk. This is also true of perfumes and packaging. The brand itself has, in one sense, become almost more important than the product in terms of financial clout, allowing the owners of brands to outsource manufacturing wherever it is cheapest in the world.

The owners of many brands nowadays have become mere 'badgers' – sticking their badge or logo onto products made by others. Thus the brand itself becomes even more financially important – it is sometimes a company's only main asset – and firms will go to great lengths to protect it. This has also introduced a political element with the exploitation of local labour forces in regions where the choice of alternative work is severely limited. Branding, or the 'designer jeans' syndrome (a term usually hated by designers themselves) has therefore become a double-edged sword, especially for the high-end fashion houses whose only real defence is to change the designs frequently in an attempt to outrun the counterfeiters.

case studies

Ducati 998 Motorcycle

Fig 53 Ducati 998, 2002.

The first motorcycle to use the inline V twin-engine layout was built by Harley-Davidson in 1909. This engine layout has been used many times since then by a variety of manufacturers due to its slimness (less air resistance compared to across-the-frame twins and other multi-cylinder designs) and relative simplicity, Harley-Davison have stuck with this layout ever since. Following the Second World War many European racing motorcycle designs in the 1950s were of single cylinder design – for example, the Manx Norton – but towards the end of that decade and ever since, factories have employed multi-cylinder designs. As many as six cylinders have been used for comparatively small engines, for example, the six-cylinder Honda 250cc ridden to victory in the 1967 Isle of Man TT races by Mike Hailwood (despite bad handling). Multi-cylinder designs have advantages and disadvantages – for example, gas flow is more efficient compared to a single cylinder engine of the same capacity and therefore revs per minute and acceleration rates are usually higher; however, more cylinders usually mean more weight and complexity.

The Italian manufacturer Ducati built its first roadgoing 750cc V twin-engined bike in 1971, known as the GT750. Originally designed by Fabio Taglioni, a racing version of the bike successfully beat a field of world-class competition at the Imola race track in 1972, taking first and second places, in the hands of the Englishman Paul Smart and the

Italian Bruno Spaggiari (Ducati produced a one-litre limited edition version of Paul Smart's bike in 2006). An 864cc version of the bike was raced to victory by Mike Hailwood in his amazing comeback at the age of thirty-eight in the Isle of Man TT in 1978. Ducati has employed the V twin layout in many bikes since and has developed it to such an extent that Ducati racing motorcycles continued to beat the multi-cylinder competition (to several world championships) even at the start of the twenty-first century. Ducati also pioneered the desmodromic valve – this physically opens and shuts the inlet and exhaust valves using cams, whereas traditional engines rely on cams to open the valves but compression springs to shut them – the desmodromic design thus avoids 'valve bounce' at high revs.

Ducati's 998 production model (Figure 53) was first available to the public in 2002 and had, like all Ducati motorcycles, greatly benefited from race-breeding in all respects including the engine, frame, suspension and brakes. Although production ceased in 2004 with the 998S Final Edition, the design continues to be popular to this day – a sure sign of a design classic in the making.

The original lattice (or space) frame for the GT750 was designed by the Englishman Colin Seeley and used the engine as a stressed member of the 'overall' frame. The 998 with its nose-down 'ready-to-charge' stance, under-the-seat exhausts and single-sided rear swinging arm is a visually stunning machine, a work of art deceptive in its apparent simplicity and beautifully finished in terms of paint quality and other materials. It has been suggested that the fork yokes alone could be displayed in a museum of modern art, such is their beauty, the quality of their castings and machining work. Although the engine is by now liquid cooled (earlier versions being air-cooled), the bike still retains a spare elegant look even with the fairing removed, unlike so many visual nightmares of plumbing seen on some other liquid cooled machines.

Product Design – Mixer-grinder for India
By Sean Hughes, Creative Director, Philips Design, Hong Kong

One of the more memorable design challenges early on in my career was the development of a product for a country, culture and environment that was completely different from my own point of reference. As a recent design graduate from the UK, working at Philips Design in Holland I was challenged to design a new product for the Indian market. The brief was to establish a new design direction for a flagship mixer-grinder for Philips Domestic Appliances, India.

As the international market leader in the food preparation appliances, Philips aimed to cement this position by developing a new and innovative approach to the mixer-grinder category in India. A mixer-grinder is a basically an Indian specific variation on the food processor that has been designed, developed and engineered entirely to meet the needs

Fig 54 Philips Mixer Grinder for India, 1996.

of preparing foodstuffs for the Indian table. A food processor developed for the Western palette, cuisine and kitchen, transplanted to an Indian context would not survive very long in the more challenging environment of the Indian domestic kitchen – grinding Indian ingredients such as hard nuts and spices is a very abrasive process when compared to western foods. This requires much harder wearing materials to be used in appliance design, such as metals rather than plastics, which of course also has a big impact on manufacturing methods and cost.

This project provided an opportunity to put into practice many of the design philosophies I hold dear. Namely you cannot produce meaningful innovations without fully understanding the three pillars of the consumer, the business and the technology. In the case of this project all were completely outside of my existing experience or frames of reference. These three pillars when combined provide the framework that either enables or inhibits innovation. The designer has a duty to understand the challenge from these often divergent perspectives in order to create meaningful and relevant design solutions.

It was clear from the outset that the only to way properly develop a solution that would resonate with our intended consumer was to fully immerse myself in the market, production and consumer contexts. Therefore, I spent many weeks on location in India working with marketing, development and design colleagues in order to create and shape the new product concept. Enormous amounts of information was gathered during this period. This process included visiting people's homes and observing how existing products were used, in what sort of environments and also co-analysing with these users those problems that the existing products did and did not solve, as well as asking how they would like them improved. Research also took into account the retail environments and seeing first-hand how the products were sold and, from questioning sales staff, enabled a thorough understanding of the retailers as well consumers' concerns at the point of purchase. This helped us to gain critical insights into the issues that would ensure our product would 'win the battle' on the retail shelf. Lastly a full understanding of the project from a business and production perspective was gathered through meetings with suppliers, engineers and marketing managers who could relate relevant experiences, define key components and finalize the product's performance requirements.

All of this information was captured, documented and discussed before a single sketch was made. As a result of this process many of the preconceptions I held prior to my visit had to be reviewed – my outsider's view was complemented by my newly acquired insider's view of this particular world. Armed with this information I was able to offer a new design approach that mixed the latest design trends from world markets with local needs so that the new product could be reliably placed into the Indian market. Perhaps the biggest design challenge was to convince the key stakeholders in Europe that a dramatically new design approach was needed in order to maintain our leadership position and to align our products with global trends. It was clear from the research that our consumers were not as conservative as perhaps we first thought, and were ready to accept a more ground-breaking approach to design. By reviewing global trends in the kitchen, as well as the design language of kitchen appliances, it was clear that a new and simpler product characteristic would be a highly appropriate next step. In order to deliver on this a creative workshop was held and a number of proposals developed. Our stakeholders were confronted with these new design directions and an agreement on a winning proposition was reached. This resulted in the product we see today, which set a new direction in the Indian market and has held its own as a staple part of the Philips Domestic Appliance product portfolio over the years. It remains on the market today and is an attractive proposition delivering an enhanced product experience, a timeless design that improves people's lives along the way. Proving that a research-led, people-focused design approach leads to value creation for both our retail customers as well as end users.

Racing Yacht Design
By Tony Castro of Tony Castro Naval Architects and Yacht Designers, Southampton

There is a seemingly endless number of different designs of boats, and the particular shape of a hull depends upon the purpose and function of a particular boat – whether a sailing boat or a powerboat without sails. It can also be a family cruiser where speed is not important but comfortable accommodation and stability is, or it can be a racing yacht where speed is the overriding factor. Generally the wider a boat's hull is the greater the stability it will have, and the more resistant it will be to heeling over sideways. However, a wide hull produces more drag (as there is a bigger surface area in the water) and therefore slows forward motion – not such a good thing when it comes to racing. As well as cutting through the water more efficiently, a narrow hull uses less material than a boat of the same length and is therefore lighter and more responsive. A deep V shape towards the front of the boat's hull reduces 'slamming' head-on to the waves (analogous to diving into the water as opposed to a 'belly-flop') which is a good thing for comfort but, again, this increases the hull's surface area in the water and offers less damping to pitching oscillations.

There are many compromises and trade-offs even within yacht designs of the same class. For example, what makes a boat fast downwind will probably make it slow upwind and the things that make a boat safer will ultimately make it slower. A 'safe' boat usually means that it's unsinkable and self righting – a heavy lead 'bulb' at the bottom end of the keel (the 'wing' that sticks out vertically from beneath the hull) helps to right the boat in the event of a capsize but, of course, this adds to the weight of the boat and therefore reduces speed and acceleration. On the plus side, the use of new materials such as carbon fibre and Kevlar have led to significant weight savings without compromising strength and this

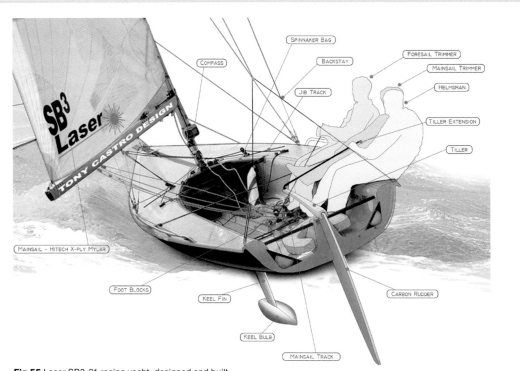

SPINNAKER BAG
COMPASS
BACKSTAY
FORESAIL TRIMMER
MAINSAIL TRIMMER
HELMSMAN
JIB TRACK
TILLER EXTENSION
TILLER
MAINSAIL - HITECH X-PLY MYLAR
FOOT BLOCKS
KEEL FIN
CARBON RUDDER
KEEL BULB
MAINSAIL TRACK

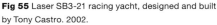

Fig 55 Laser SB3-21 racing yacht, designed and built by Tony Castro. 2002.

has mitigated to some extent the disadvantages of heavy keel bulbs, thereby increasing speed without compromising (relative) safety. Sail design is also a complex science of cloth strength, area, height, shape and the flexibility of the mast. It is no use trying to maximize the area of a sail to catch the most wind if this results in the yacht tipping over into the water. The sails, mast and rigging must be designed in such a way as to catch as much wind as it is safe to do so, while 'exhausting' the excess wind that would cause problems – a function among other things of shape of the sail and the height and flexibility of the mast. Much development has gone into providing yachts with sails that maximize forward speed whilst reducing heeling forces and the designs of asymmetric spinnakers – those 'ballooning' sails commonly seen at the front of today's racing yachts – have played an important role in increasing speeds up to 40 knots without unduly compromising safety. Carbon fibre has also revolutionized mast design allowing the designers to put the most material where the greatest stresses occur. Masts are now up to 50 per cent lighter than aluminium masts and the designer can build in greater control and flexibility nearer the top. Look how 'glass-fibre' poles revolutionized the heights that pole-vaulters now achieve (heights unimaginable in the days of timber or aluminium poles).

The flexible yet strong masts of today can store up large amounts of bending energy without breaking, and 'give this energy back' to the boat automatically when the opportunity arises – analogous to the athlete's bending pole storing up the kinetic energy of his/her run up to the jump and giving it back to increase the vertical height achieved. The sails of course must make the most efficient use of the wind from a multitude of directions, depending on which direction you want to go in. In ordinary circumstance a sailing boat would have to 'tack' in a zig-zag manner to make progress against the prevailing wind. All yachts have to do this to some extent but the larger the sideways zig-zagging results in it taking longer to get where you want – not so good when it comes to racing. The 'closer' to the wind direction the less distance will be travelled but this can result in a slower speed. Therefore, the skill of the racing skipper counts for a great deal in these circumstances.

Swiss Re Office Block by Norman Foster and Partners

Norman Foster's office block for Swiss Re (nicknamed the 'Gherkin') in the City of London won the RIBA Stirling prize for new architecture in 2004. Although geodesic buildings have been with us for many years, for example, Buckminster Fuller's geodesic domes of the 1950s, the Swiss Re building is the first such office tower in the heart of a major city. It rises forty-one storeys and provides more than 76,000 m^2 of office space. The top of the building contains a double-decker private bar and restaurant and gives a 360-degree view of London.

Although often referred to as a 'work of art', there are logical reasons for the Gherkin's shape. The building looks curved but all the glass panels are flat, each secured in the outer apertures of a triangulated steel structure that allows for a fully glazed surface. The only curved piece of glass is the cone at the very top of the building. The building's base tapers to a smaller diameter than its middle, allowing greater pedestrian space and lines of sight at street level than would have been the case if designed on a rectilinear plan with vertical sides (or even a cylinder). Pedestrians will also benefit from reduced extremes of wind around the base compared to conventional buildings with sharp corners. The tapering shape also makes it look more slender than a straight sided block of the same volume and also serves to reduce the glare from reflections while increasing transparency. Because the building curves inwards towards the top, an observer at its base looking up cannot see the top half of the building and therefore it looks a lot less high and imposing compared with its neighbours.

The building also has passive air circulation. The internal atria spaces that spiral up the height of the building exploit the differential in air pressure at opposite sides of the building (no matter which direction the wind is coming from). Fresh air is sucked in naturally from outside and distributed throughout the internal spaces. Only in extremes of hot or cold weather will it be become necessary to use energy to power the climate-control systems.

This, along with other energy-saving measures, reduces the tower's reliance on air conditioning and enables the building to use up to around half the energy consumed by similar volume air-conditioned office towers. Because the tower looks the same from any angle, we can enjoy seeing it from any vantage point – it doesn't have a front and back, unlike many buildings whose rear faces may not be so appealing. The two-tone upward spiralling glass patterns of its skin help to break up what might have been an otherwise monotonous surface; the subtle colours of the panels combined with strips of bright coloured ribs invariably direct our eyes towards the conical focal point at the very top. These elements combine together to produce a visually vibrant yet wonderfully graceful structure.

Fig 56 Swiss Re Building (The 'Gherkin') – By Norman Foster, London. 2004.

theory box

Cultural Relativism (Twentieth Century)

Darwinian and psychological evolutionists say that our physical and mental capacities are the result of millions of years of natural selection since our early hominid ancestors first appeared in Africa. Denis Dutton suggests that our minds at birth are therefore already equipped with a set of tools that enable us to cope quickly with life and provide certain survival skills, such as a propensity for language and built-in preferences that help us to avoid danger. Even animals, birds and insects have some level of danger avoidance and survival strategies, such as nest building or seeking out hiding places, already programmed into their brains at birth. Dutton goes further in proposing that all humans have a common preference (within limits) for particular types of beauty. For example, certain pieces of music or types of calendar art can appeal to individuals across many societies and cultural divides.

Cultural relativism on the other hand proposes that all judgements of beauty and taste are entirely culture specific, that is to say that notions of beauty are learned by an individual according to the culture in which he or she grows up, and these notions become that particular society's shared standards of beauty – we come to admire the things we are expected to. In *Practical Criticism* (1929), the British critic Ivor Armstrong Richards describes experiments he carried out with literature students, which purported to show that even highly educated people are conditioned by their education, the conventional wisdom of the times they live in, and other circumstantial factors of their own society when it comes to judgements of beauty or taste. In these experiments students were asked to criticize anonymous poems – poems from which the names of the authors, the historical period in which they were written and other contextual details were removed (one 'worthless' poem was also included – which many students preferred). This shows the difficulty of judging a work of art (in this case using poetry as the bait) and elucidating meanings without any hint as to the work's provenance. Thus cultural relativism says that it is difficult or even impossible to properly judge works of art that have been divorced from any knowledge of the culture that produced it.

Other writers have pointed to the powerful conditioning effects of tradition and fashion, factors that do indeed have a strong bearing on notions of beauty and elegance in any society. Marxism goes further and argues that art cannot exist on its own (art for art's sake) outside of the society that created it – rather, art reflects the underlying economic forces in a particular culture and only becomes 'great art' when it is 'progressive' – that is, when it supports the cause of the oppressed classes (for example, in the case of communist regimes) and/or other values and principles of the society in which it was created.

chapter three

---

composition

chapter outline

This chapter provides examples of basic visual conventions that need to be borne in mind when composing in two or three dimensions. These conventions are to be used only as a guide and can be deliberately and intelligently ignored depending on the nature of the particular design project in hand. These notions include the balancing of different elements in order to create overall harmony and the balancing of opposing positive and negative components such as walls/spaces in buildings and letterforms/spacing in graphic designs. Also issues of deliberate distortion are introduced and discussed we sometimes need to resort to distortion in order to make something more visually elegant and/or easier to understand.

Although all letters and alphabets perform the same literary function, small visual design variations on the same letter shape, or three-dimensional object, can express a different 'personality' (it is no coincidence that letterforms are called characters). This is true for things other than letterforms; for example, tableware, buildings or cars – we can easily perceive the difference between a 'fun' car and an executive's limousine. The personalities we 'see' in these objects are largely culturally determined however. This chapter also discusses notions of ideal proportions that have emerged over many years, including the 'Golden Section' from Classical Greek times and later notions of how geometry might relate to the human form and be applied to designs.

When we look at a particular design, our eyes are 'taken for a walk' around its elements – a tour of its shapes, forms, details, colour and texture – and a skilled designer can help to make this a more logical and pleasant experience for the observer through the application of visual grammar. This can be achieved in various ways, such as by introducing lines (actual or virtual), the creation of important and hierarchical focal points, the massing or grouping of elements, the elegant resolution of 'collisions' (handshakes), as well as creating underlying but unseen structures of order, including grid systems for the layout of type, the façade of a building or product. Just as grids can help us to understand and navigate design elements in two and three dimensions, so underlying structures can help us to more easily navigate around virtual objects, such as a website, or a physical device with a user interface, such as a ticket machine.

This chapter also looks at the analogies between visual composition and musical composition. There are many similarities between music and architecture. For example, we automatically look for patterns or grouping of elements in a building and the terms 'frozen music' or 'frozen gesture' are often applied to a building's form and detail. The sculptural properties of everyday objects are also discussed. This includes car design as nearly everybody who needs one has to make visual and emotional choices when deciding which model to buy (although cost is also an important factor in any purchase). The sense of touch also plays a vital role in our lives and, like our other senses, can provide us with sensual and pleasurable experiences. It is a small step from noticing the surface texture of objects and materials, to recognizing pattern and our liking for pattern probably stemmed from the human trait for noticing repetition. Therefore, issues of touch, texture and pattern design are included here.

introduction

Composition – the creative bit. How does an artist, designer, musician, writer or any creative person start to compose a piece of work? As well as man's artistic endeavours we are also surrounded by the fruits of centuries of scientific, engineering and technological creativity – putting a man on the moon is pretty creative stuff. You could also say that this was one of man's greatest artistic achievements – the view of Earth from the Moon certainly made us see our home in a new, more profound light. Science and art are often two sides of the same coin in any case and you can be creative in most walks of life. We have our education and training to rely upon when it comes to composing a painting or designing a building. We also have access to an almost limitless history of a variety of artists, designers and composers' work to admire and provide us with inspiration. We cannot avoid being influenced by others, past and present. This is to be celebrated but sometimes we can inadvertently allow ourselves to be trapped by tradition and the usual ways of doing things.

This chapter provides examples of basic conventions that need to be borne in mind when composing in two or three dimensions. Like most rules, however, they are to be used as a guide or intelligently ignored. The list is by no means exhaustive and designers are constantly producing better and/or different ways of doing things. However, if you are not aware of some of the more established concepts and conventions, then you are missing out on a lot, as well as being condemned to making avoidable mistakes in the future.

balance

Human beings prefer balance over imbalance. Designing a machine to stand up on two legs, walk or run without falling over is technically quite difficult to achieve, yet we do these things every day without thinking. We are essentially vertical creatures in a horizontal landscape and we can see at a glance if someone, or something, is in danger of toppling over – which is why the extreme angle of Pisa's Leaning Tower is so startling. Our visual sense alerts us to this fact immediately and a good sense of balance is of course vital in the survival stakes for all animals. Having to maintain a balance is also one reason why we usually prefer symmetry to asymmetry.

We sense, then, a balance in the design of paintings and objects. The more educated we become in the process of looking, the better we become at discerning balance between two (or among several) elements in a particular composition, whether in two or three dimensions. Often artists and designers deliberately use 'off balance' elements in their work to stimulate the attention of the observer and a sloping or leaning element can imply movement and direction. For instance notice how a piece of italic text set amid ordinary text *appears to speed up*. The early twentieth-century Italian Futurists often exploited these ideas in their paintings and sculptures to express speed and turmoil. We are also disturbed by details that are slightly off centre – for example, a door not quite in the middle of a building. In most cases it is best to move the door a little bit further off centre so that its position looks deliberate and not a mistake on the designer's part. Most designers and artists usually aim to achieve a balance, or harmony, in their works. On a simple level this can be analogous to a see-saw or weighing scales where the visual 'weight' of two objects are placed in

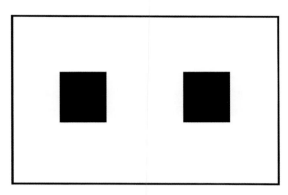

Fig 57 Two squares symmetrically balanced left and right in a rectangle.

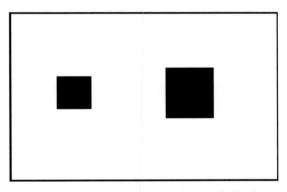

Fig 58 Smaller left hand square requires leftward shift of both squares for overall composition to remain in visual balance.

relation to each other in such a way as to balance each other (see also Chapter 4 on balance in colour compositions). Figure 57 shows two black squares of the same size balanced symmetrically, side by side, inside a rectangle. Figure 58 then shows a smaller left hand square – both squares have had to be shifted to the left to maintain a balance within the space of the same rectangle. They balance each other visually even though the overall design is asymmetrical, analogous to the balancing of a heavy weight on one side of a 'see-saw' scale, by a lighter weight placed further away from the fulcrum on the other side.

The sensitive placing of rectangular, round, or other shapes in a composition can be applied to many areas of art and design, be it the windows, doors and other details on the façade of a building, or perhaps the positioning of dials and knobs on a control panel. Figure 59 shows a schematic drawing of a display panel with an ill-considered arrangement of dials. Placing shapes too close to (or too far from) each other, or too near the edge can be disconcerting – the two large circular dials lack room to breathe and are 'restless'. Figure 60 shows a better solution. As a general rule, the distance between elements should be smaller than the distance between the elements and the outside edge of the panel or shape. This also relates to 'massing' or grouping of elements as well as typographic layout described later.

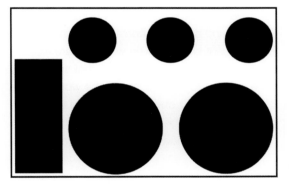

Fig 59 Ill-considered layout of displays.

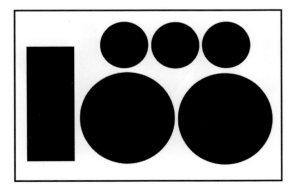

Fig 60 A better solution.

positive and negative

The important relationship or balance between (positive) objects and the (negative) spaces between them is often overlooked. This is most easily grasped in two dimensions – for example, the decorative black and white figurative designs on Greek ceramics and geometric frets, Egyptian wall carvings or the lettering on this page. As much care and attention needs to be spent on getting the negative spaces 'right' as is spent on the positive shapes – the words in this book would not make much sense without the spaces separating them. The artist M. C. Escher has taken this to extremes in his compositions of animals and figures where, for example, the negative shapes between individual birds flying in formation, on closer inspection, turn out to be other birds flying in the opposite direction. Our eyes and brains are constantly on the lookout for significant shapes, even when we are reading we still subconsciously see things that aren't really there in order to make sense of the world. Figure 61 shows a rather obvious example of a 'missing' letter in a word – this doesn't stop us from recognizing that word however. There are many other examples of positive and negative, or opposites, in life, such as: night and day, birth and death, good and evil, beauty and ugliness. It would seem that nature is always balanced between opposing forces in some way – the earth's orbit around the sun, for example. Eastern cultures call this balance Yin Yang. In three-dimensional design, positive and negative forms also have equal importance – for example, the 'positive' walls of a house create the 'negative' spaces of rooms and corridors. The columns of a Greek temple 'create' the spaces around them.

distortion

Ever since the creation of early cave paintings and physical artefacts, artists have employed distortion in their work to emphasize or symbolize particular meanings. In early portrayals of the human figure, for example, the breasts and hips of the female form were often enlarged in sculpted artefacts as expressions of fertility. Later, the artists of the Italian Renaissance sometimes altered the proportions of the human body to exaggerate the muscular power of a figure – a device frequently used by Michelangelo, where the head of a figure is drawn far too small in proportion to the body. An everyday example of distortion in illustration is seen in caricatures of real people drawn by cartoonists. These images of people can appear 'more real' than photographs – by exaggerating certain features, we immediately recognize an individual by a few well-chosen lines in a drawing.

Design is an applied art that also employs distortion for a variety of reasons; sometimes for symbolic purposes, to increase beauty, or to make something more easily understandable. For example, the Parthenon's four corner columns are of a slightly larger diameter than the others.

UNZIP

Fig 61 We still read the 'missing' letter.

The gaps either side of these corner columns are slightly smaller than the gaps between other columns, which has the effect of slowing down the eye at the end of a run of columns, and visually 'strengthens' the overall design. If this were not the case, when corner columns of the Parthenon were seen from an angle against the daylight, the perceived gap against the glare would be greater and the corner column would appear thinner than the others.

These smaller gaps between the corner columns of the temple and their neighbours also resolve to some extent the irreconcilable desire for the spacing of the triglyphs above the architrave to be equal in distance to each other along the four sides and, at the same time, be placed exactly above and between the centre lines of each column and yet meet at the corners. The designers first proposed a gradual increasing of the distances between the last three triglyphs at the corners but eventually settled on moving the corner column inwards instead, keeping the distances between all the trigyphs equal (Figure 62). Thus each of the four corner triglyphs is not in the centre line of the column immediately below it, but this is nevertheless an ingenious and elegant

Fig 63 The Parthenon, Athens. c.450BC. The fluting on the columns modulates the depth of shadow to emphasize roundness. This illustration also shows the Triglyphs spaced at equal intervals above the architrave (main beam).

.

solution. We hardly notice these adjustments and consider the Parthenon to be just about as perfect a building made from stone as is humanly possible (Figure 63).

Columns are often slightly swelled out around the middle (entasis), which gives them an appearance of strength – akin to the muscular arms and legs of the human form. If the columns were exactly straight sided they would appear to be 'waisted' – slimmer towards the centre and therefore visually weak, an optical illusion. Also all of the columns slant inwards slightly – they would meet at a point roughly one mile above the base. If they were exactly vertical they could appear to be leaning outwards. This slight leaning inwards may also help the building to withstand earthquakes. The platform of the Parthenon on which the columns stand (the stylobate) also rises upwards slightly

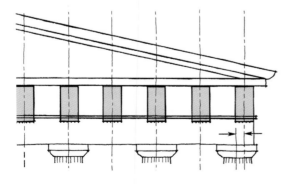

Fig 62 Solving the triglyph problem (adapted from Gelernter).

Fig 64 The Temple of Hera at Paestum. c.550BC. Detail showing 'squashed' capitals that were prone to damage. The Temple of Neptune can be seen beyond.

towards the centre forming a very shallow dome. Seen from the sides, if perfectly flat, the platform would appear to sag in the middle under the row of columns.

The vertical fluting running along the vertical length of each column serves to emphasize its roundness. The glare of bright sunlight bouncing off a smooth white marble is reduced by fluting –

graduating the strips of light and shadow around its curved surface (Figure 63). Therefore, in addition to manipulating materials and structures, architects have to compose their buildings in terms of light and shade – Norman Foster has referred to building design as the 'poetry of light and space'. Another interesting fluting detail on columns is the particular shape of the proud edge where each hollow flute meets the next at a ridge. A sharply pointed stone or marble ridge is easily damaged and therefore flats on the top of each ridge were created to avoid this danger. Sometimes this was only carried out on the bottom six feet or so of a column – the maximum height of passers by – to help prevent accidental damage. The stone columns of classical buildings were originally tree trunks in ancient dwellings. The triglyphs running around the architrave are said to be an abstracted form of roofing supports that used tree branches laid horizontally on top of the vertical trunks (making up the walls), to support roofing materials such as earth and reeds. Each triglyph design is said to originate from the end of a branch or beam – the three vertical lines represent rainwater dripping off the ends. We can still see this sort of 'triglyph' detailing on some house eaves detailing today.

The Parthenon in Athens did not suddenly emerge perfectly formed from out of the blue, nearly two-and-a-half thousand years ago. The Greeks had previously experimented with form and detail in various 'prototype' temples, probably the most famous being the three built in close proximity to each other at Paestum near Salerno in southern Italy, once part of the Greek Empire, with the last temple completed within 100 years of the first. The oldest of these, built around 550BC, was known as the 'Basilica' (Figure 64) as eighteenth-century archaeologists originally thought it was a civil building and not a temple. It is actually the Temple of Hera. This building used an odd number of columns (nine) on the front and rear, and even numbers (eighteen) along each of the two sides. This meant that it would be awkward to introduce a central entrance to the front of the temple, the middle column effectively splitting the building in half. The columns in this temple have a more pronounced swelling (entasis), and the rounded conical parts (echinus) of the capitals appear 'squashed' and are fragile compared to later designs.

The second temple to be built at Paestum around 500BC is now known as the Temple of Ceres, but was in fact dedicated to the goddess Athena. This used an even number of six columns on the front and rear faces thus providing for a central entrance if required. This temple still stuck with the squashed capitals design however. The third and last temple to be built is known as the Temple of Neptune, god of the sea, completed around 450BC. This has six columns along the front and fourteen along the sides. The columns have a slimmer profile and the capitals are more gracefully tapered (the Parthenon's columns are slimmer still). This temple also incorporates a slight curving of the horizontals, imperceptible to the eye, to avoid the optical illusion of the platform sagging in the centre, the same device used in the Parthenon's design.

The swelling of forms, as employed in Greek columns, is still used today in many buildings and products, and is often very subtle. Slightly convex (distorted) surfaces can give more visual 'satisfaction' than flat-sided products and can actually prevent a flat side from appearing concave or 'sinking in'. Even today's many apparently flat-sided vehicles, such as vans, are actually convex upon closer inspection – this actually strengthens the panel (like a shallow shell form) as well as preventing 'drumming' to some extent when driving over rough surfaces. The 'flat' sides of the traditional Rolls Royce radiator surround are slightly curved before being welded together, for the same reasons as above. Deliberate distortion to make things look right, increase visual impact, or to make us see and think about the world in a new way, has been used in art and design ever since the earliest cave paintings and artefacts first appeared.

In the field of typography the layout of type is often distorted – the actual spacing of letters next to each other is an art; there is no set number of fractions of a millimetre (or 'points') from one to the next. Instead, you should aim as far as possible to maintain a similar area between each letter – there shouldn't be any 'holes' in a word nor should there be any crowding together of letters either, though of course you may want to flout these rules for a particular effect. Typographers use 'point sizes' when specifying the measurements of type heights and line lengths; the British and American standard point is about 1/72 of an inch (or approximately 0.35 mm). The first priority of typography is clarity – ease of readability – especially relevant when speeding down the motorway looking for a particular sign to your destination, for example. 'Artiness' takes a back seat here. The design of a motorway typeface for the UK was the scene of much controversy in the late 1950s.[1] However, a typeface that needs to be easily read can also be beautiful.

The legibility of a particular typeface, its size, contrast with the background, overall 'grey' tone of body text, spacing of letters and words is very important. There are many examples of designs using small sizes of typeface – especially on business cards – often produced by young designers (with perfect vision) for reasons of aesthetics or fashion but these are usually unreadable by the majority of any population. The

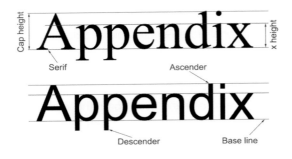

Cap height

Serif   Ascender

x height

Descender   Base line

Fig 65 Some typeface terminology. Also note the slightly different 'x-to-Cap' height ratios between Times New Roman (top) and the Trebuchet MS font underneath.

ascenders in a line of type play a more important role than the descenders in aiding legibility (see Figure 65. Cover up the descenders on a line of type on this page (with the edge of a sheet of paper) and you can still read the line fairly easily. Cover up the ascenders, however, and the line becomes much more difficult to read. Graphic designers hate underlining words that contain descenders, as the underline can crash into the descenders – for example, in the word <u>appendix</u> – very inelegant. It is better to use emboldening or italics or, if you must underline something, make sure that the line is placed lower down or alternatively include gaps to avoid such collisions. Increasing the size of letters on the page can obviously make the text easier to read, but if you compare different fonts having the same *overall* height size you will see that some have larger lower case letters even though the capital (upper-case) heights are the same (Figure 65). You would think that this must lead to better legibility but, of course, larger lower case letters means shorter ascenders (leading to less legibility) and therefore a balance needs to be struck in the ratio between the two.

Many people think that a 'serif' typeface is easier to read than 'sans serif'. The serifs are those little twiddly bits on the ends of a charac-

ter's strokes. Sans serif means *without* serif (from the French) and modernist designers prefer these 'non-ornamented' typefaces. The Times New Roman font in the top line of Figure 65 is a serif font (and regarded as old-fashioned by modernists), whereas Trebuchet MS (shown on the line below) is sans serif. Conventional wisdom says that the serifs help to link letters together to form words and most people recognize whole words without the need to read individual letters.[2]

However, serif fonts can be confusing to people with dyslexia and many sufferers find a simple and clear sans-serif font like Helvetica (as used for this book) or Arial easier to read, particularly if presented in a slightly larger point size than usual.

Some fonts tend more towards calligraphy than others. Writing script by hand with a broad nib or brush produces lines and arcs having varying widths of strokes, depending on the direction of hand movement dictated by a particular letter shape. For example, the two slanting lines making up the capital letter 'A' in Times New Roman (top line in Figure 65) are of different widths, exactly the effect you would achieve wielding a broad nibbed pen in the right hand. Compare this with Trebuchet's capital 'A' shown beneath. These effects can also be seen in Arabic and Chinese fonts.

There is much subtlety involved in typographic design that has a strong relevance to other areas of design, whether this is the façade of a building, the layout of a car's dashboard or the design of a control panel on a domestic appliance. When considering which typeface to go with a particular product, it is sometimes a good idea to choose one that has an empathy to the product or business itself – for example, you may want to choose a softly rounded shaped typeface to promote a bread and pastry shop – though

MILAN

Fig 66 Automatic spacing of letters using Microsoft Word software.

MILAN

Fig 67 Letters equally spaced – unbalanced result.

MILAN

Fig 68 Shortened horizontal leg of 'L' – optimum result.

unless handled carefully this sort of literal translation can easily end up as kitsch.[3] It takes years to become a competent typographer or graphic designer and to get a feel for the subtleties of letter design. To a layman two similar fonts might look almost identical, but experienced designers can infer such abstract notions such as colder, friendlier, aggressive, aloof and endless other terms to describe the 'emotional' qualities of a particular typeface when compared with others.[4]

Spacing of letters is called 'kerning' and computer software does this automatically to some extent; look at the different spacing between the letters spelling MILAN in Figure 66. This was typed using Microsoft's Word program and you can see how the potentially large 'hole' between the letters L and A has been somewhat mitigated by placing these two letters closer together compared to the rest. You can also see that the space between the letters A and N is also slightly less than the spacing of M, I and L – in order to

cope with the 'hole' produced by the slanting A. Compare this with Figure 67, where the spacing between all letters is equal. For an important sign, graphic designers might take this variable spacing further by trimming a little off the end of the horizontal element of the letter L and moving the A slightly to the left, as in Figure 68, thus reducing the 'hole' still further. Barclays Bank logo takes this one step further by actually joining the letters L and A together (Figure 69). Incidentally, using all CAPITALS in a word or sentence is the graphic equivalent of shouting.

The overall impression of a paragraph should be one of uniform density, ideally without any 'holes' or 'rivers' running through it. Rivers are the appearance of more-or-less vertical white rivers of word spacings accidentally created by several near-alignments of word spaces above and below one another in lines of text. This is exacerbated when the spaces between words are wider than the spaces between the lines. In addition to rivers, typographers have terms for other visual faults; for example, a 'widow' is a word left on a line of its own at the end of a paragraph and an 'orphan' is the same thing carried over to the top of the next page. The use of hyphenated words at the ends of lines in the body text can usually result in getting around these problems.

Letters based on a circular form are often slightly larger than straight-sided letters in a particular typeface; otherwise they would appear to be smaller to our eyes than the others. For

Fig 69 Barclays Bank logo showing L and A actually joined together.

Gill Sans MT

Fig 70 Curved letters slightly larger than rectilinear letters.

ABCDEF
BCDEFG
CDEFGH
DEFGHK

Fig 71 Visual adjustment of letter starting positions.

or indent at the start of the line (Figure 71). Again, this is something to watch out for in any composition of varying shapes.

The above guidelines have become conventions in design over the years, however you may wish to intelligently ignore this advice for artistic or other reasons. Perhaps you want to spread out the spacing between letters and words as a stylistic device, or maybe get rid of spacing altogether using colour or tone as an alternative to word recognition, see Figure 72.

When placing shapes within other shapes you need to consider the apparent halfway height of the inside shape. This is best seen when looking at pictures set into mounts inside a frame. If the picture is at the exact centre of the mount it will appear as if it is below halfway. Look at any properly mounted picture and you will see a slightly wider mount margin at the bottom compared to the margin at the top. This is because the picture

example, 'O' and 'C' are larger than 'N', and 'H' and, as such, the bottom of the curves on Os and Cs must be placed slightly below the line on which N and H sit. The tops of Os and Cs slightly protrude above the height line of the other letters, as illustrated by the classic example of Eric Gill's 1928 typeface shown in Figure 70. These adjustments are something to watch out for in any composition of square and circular forms, not just typography. Sloping letters like the CAPITAL 'V' and 'open' letters like the capital 'L' are particularly difficult customers to deal with when placed next to other letters as they also have a tendency to produce 'holes' in the text. If you are starting a line of text with a capital V (or any other sloping letter) you will need to position it ever-so-slightly to the left of any square letters immediately above and below it, otherwise you will end up with a hole

THIS SPACING MAY SUIT A PARTICULAR SUBJECT

howeasyisittoreadthis?

Fig 72 Readability without spaces between words.

Fig 73 Centre rectangle at the visual centre of outer rectangle.

has visual 'weight' and, mounted properly, will appear to be at the correct height even though its actual centre is slightly above the halfway line of the frame (Figure 73). One of the most familiar examples of distortion in graphic design is the London Underground map – geographically incorrect but deliberately skewed in order to make it more easily understandable. The original map of 1908 (Figure 74) was replaced with the classic version we now use, said to be based on electrical circuit diagrams (Figure 75), the first version of which was created in 1931 by Harry Beck, a draughtsman working for London Transport.

personality

Although all letters and alphabets each perform the same written function, small shape variations on the same 2D letter (or 3D object) can express a different 'personality' (it is no coincidence that letter forms are called characters). This is true for things other than letterforms, for example, tableware, cars or buildings – we easily perceive the difference between a 'fun' car and an executive's limousine. The personalities we perceive in these objects are largely culturally determined – a person from a different culture (or time traveller) would not have the same understanding as ourselves. Different design personalities are most easily detectable in typeface design, where centuries of designs by individuals has left a rich and varied legacy of letterform families. Typefaces are sometimes named after the person who invented them, and the tradition continues today. Each character is carefully constructed to fit a particular family type and very subtle differences in dimensions and proportions can make big differences in the personality of a particular alphabet (whose complete set of characters, numbers, punctuation

marks and symbols are known collectively as a font). You can usually detect the underlying structure of a particular typeface (a sort of engineering drawing) that the designer employed – see the font design in Figure 76, adapted from a 1525 alphabet design by Albrecht Dürer. Because different fonts have different personalities the designer must be sensitive to the context in which a particular font is to be used – for example, compare the 'serious' Dürer typeface design with the more 'fun' shapes of Quentin in Figure 77, used in this case to advertise a circus. So graphic designers exploit the different personalities of fonts to better express the message. In their book on type design.[5] Erik Spiekermann and E. M. Ginger state that: '… choosing a typeface to set a word in is part of manipulating the meaning of that word.'

Although graphic designers and typographers tend to work in two dimensions and architects and industrial designers in three dimensions, there exists a strong relationship between two- and three-dimensional design. The façade (or front elevation) of a building can almost be treated as a work of two-dimensional graphic design, however architects can also play with the changes in the effects of light and shadow on the details as the sun moves across the sky during the day – an element denied to the designer in two dimensions. Prior to a building being constructed, plan and elevation drawings are drawn up to work out the shapes, sizes and relationships between the various elements (such as windows and doors) and these drawn elevations are often beautiful in themselves. On a smaller scale direct comparisons can be made between two-dimensional letter forms, or fonts, and the construction of three-dimensional products such as cutlery. Also an engineering drawing for a cutlery design would look somewhat similar to the Dürer 'engineering drawings' for the letters of the alphabet in Figure 76.

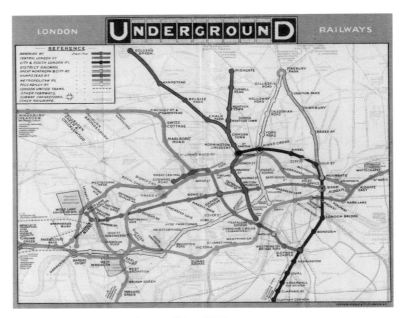

Fig 74 The original London Underground Map of 1908.

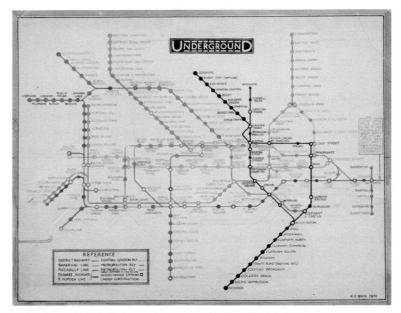

Fig 75 The model for today's map, first conceived by Harry Beck in 1931.

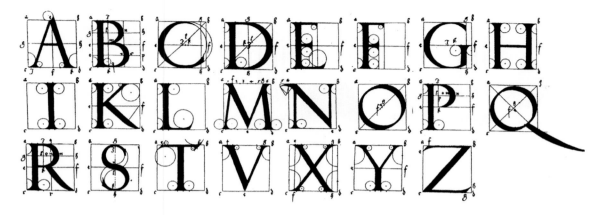

Fig 76 Constructed Roman Capitals. Adapted from a sixteenth-century design by Albrecht Dürer.

Cutlery design is an especially good illustration of the relationship between letter forms and physical objects – compare the 'personalities' of David Mellor's Classic and Odeon cutlery sets shown in Figures 78 and 79. All the pieces in a particular cutlery set need to work together as a family and, although different in function (and therefore different in basic shape), each piece needs to relate to all the others visually, just as different letters and numbers in a particular font need to visually relate to each other even though their individual functions are very different. In addition to cutlery design, David Mellor's work can also be seen on just about every UK high street, in the form of lamp posts, traffic lights, bus shelters and modern letter boxes.

be places of importance – for example, the main person in a group picture, the main entrance to a building or the controls on a food mixer. The eye is attracted to strong logical shapes in order to recognize which is top, bottom, front and back and which parts are the handles and which are likely to be hot! The eye is also attracted to symmetry and balance – the external human form is symmetrical (for all intents and purposes) and so we are naturally impressed with this aspect of nature. In early hunter-gatherer times, symmetrical objects lurking in the bush usually meant it was something to eat, or something was coming to eat you![6] Vilayanur S. Ramachandran points to experiments that show that: 'when choosing a mate, animals and humans prefer symmetrical over asymmetrical

taking the eye for a walk

When we look at a painting, building or artefact, our eye does not like to be confused. It prefers order to chaos, to be led or 'walked' is preferable to getting lost. Whilst on this walk it will need resting places, or focal points, these might

Fig 77 Quentin 'fun' font – used to advertise a circus for example.

Fig 78 David Mellor's 'Classic' cutlery set.

Fig 79 David Mellor's 'Odeon' cutlery set.

ones and evolutionary biologists have argued that this is because parasitic infections – detrimental to fertility – often produces lopsided, asymmetrical growth and development.'[7]

So our admiration for symmetry was originally a means of survival – we are programmed to watch out for it! However, symmetry can also be boring – do not be afraid to experiment by deliberately skewing a design. This can often lend a visual dynamic to a particular composition. It should look deliberate though; it should not appear as if a mistake has been made. There are many examples of asymmetry in product design and architecture nowadays.

focal points

Painters sometimes use visual tricks to lead the viewer's eye to important focal points. For example, these could be perspective lines leading to vanishing points, perhaps obvious, perhaps only hinted at. The use of colour attracts our attention and, conversely, camouflage is *meant* to be confusing. On product designs it should be obvious where the handle is and sometimes it's useful to give clues through choice of materials, colour and soft shapes to aid the eye and brain in making decisions where it would be most comfortable, and least dangerous, to grab hold of and pick up an object. This is particularly important for those users with impaired vision, where strongly contrasting tones and colours can be extremely helpful, for example, helping to locate a handrail when boarding an underground train, or finding the release button on a hot pressure cooker. Similarly, we need to know where the entrance to a building is and, once inside, we need to find our way around. However, much of today's painting and architecture relies less on focal points, being more open to other notions of composition, meanings and expression. In 1999 the artist Bridget Riley had this to say about focal points in paintings:[8]

There is seldom a single focal point in my paintings; in general, my paintings are multi-focal. You can't call it un-focused space, but not being fixed to a single focus is very much of our time. It's something that seems to have come about in the last hundred years or so. Focussing isn't just an optical activity; it is also a mental one. I think this lack of centre has something to do with the loss of the certainties that Christianity had to offer. There was a time when meanings were focused and reality could be fixed; when that sort of belief disappeared, things became uncertain and open to interpretation. We can no longer hope as the Renaissance did that 'man is the measure of all things'.

proportion

As previously noted, the proportions of architecture and the everyday products we use are strongly related to human proportions – the heights and widths of doors allow our passage through, and

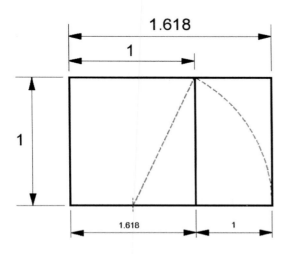

Fig 80 Golden rectangle.

the dimensions and layout of a mobile telephone fit our mouths, ears and fingers. Other notions of elegant proportions in nature have been proposed in the past, perhaps the most famous ideal proportion is the 'golden section' – a mathematical ratio of the length of one line compared to another, or the height of a rectangle compared to its width. Examples of the golden section can be seen in Greek temples as well as paintings from the Italian Renaissance and also in some modern buildings. It goes like this – take a line of any length and cut (section) it at a point somewhere along its length so that the ratio of the shorter length to the longer length is the same ratio as the longer length is to the overall length. It turns out that this ratio is 1 to 1.618. Therefore, the golden rectangle would have a width of 1.0 and a height of 1.618, or vice versa.

You can construct a near-enough golden rectangle starting with a square and, finding the centre of one of its sides, draw an arc from the corner as shown in Figure 80. Geometry has always fascinated us, probably since man noticed that the sun and moon were circles, and has been of huge significance in mathematics and physics as well as art ever since.[9] It has been suggested that the golden section is also apparent in many life forms, from the way branches of a tree are spaced out up and around the trunk, to the spiral of a snail's shell (Figure 81). This may have something to do with the Earth's gravity affecting the way things grow, placing a limit on the proportions and maximum size to which earthbound creatures and plants can attain. The size and proportion of each species is a balance between a creature's various functions (for example, walking or flying) and the restraining force of gravity. Every time you double the scale of an animal or object, the mass or weight increases eightfold and therefore the largest land creatures on Earth, the dinosaurs, were about as big as animals could get without

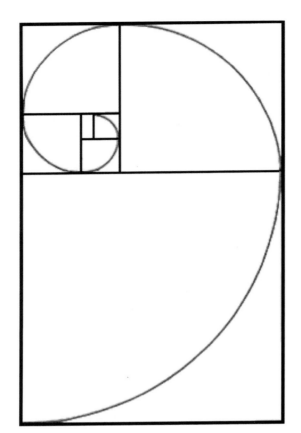

Fig 81 Golden spiral.

as being an elegant proportion (or mathematical notion) it probably has no more significance than any other shape in the universe. Interestingly, however, something like the golden ratio occurs in mathematics in the 'Fibonacci series' – named after the thirteenth-century Italian mathematician, Leonardo Fibonacci de Pisa, who came up with the series where each number is the sum of the previous two – 1, 1, 2, 3, 5, 8, 13, 21, 34, 55 and so forth. By comparing any two adjacent numbers in this sequence, for example 3 and 5, the ratio of these numbers is similar to the golden ratio.

Although the anthropomorphic principle will always be a strong factor in design, it is not always relevant to man-made artefacts. A suspension bridge may be a huge structure, necessary to span a wide river. Its height and length do not bear much relation to human scale but this does not detract from its elegant proportions and beauty. The function of the bridge's materials and the laws of physics largely determine the form – although the width of the roadway relates to human scale in that cars containing humans need to pass. Perhaps there has been too much emphasis on the human form determining proportions in design – we are in danger of falling into the same trap as William Hogarth with his example of chair legs following the serpentine form of human long bones. To quote Bridget Riley again:

Our bearings still suffer from the concept or suppositions of Renaissance theory, which is 'man is the measure of all things'. But man is part only of a bigger whole and this whole is neither centripetal nor centrifugal. It is much more open and egalitarian; and the structure of this whole, as opposed to a circle (Renaissance), is an infinitely subtle grid.

becoming so heavy that it became impossible to stand up or walk. The height of trees is limited in similar ways – too tall and the tree is unable to support its own weight. Perhaps on a smaller inhabited planet orbiting another star in another part of the universe, the plants and animals will have very different sizes and proportions compared to life on Earth.

The golden ratio is also supposedly to be found in the proportions of the human body (the Vitruvian man mentioned earlier) although you could probably find any geometric shape in the figure of a human being if you looked long enough. So while the golden section may be trumpeted

massing

Massing is the term given to the arrangement of the main components or forms of a product or building. This helps us to 'read' a product or a building in three dimensions when we see it for the first time – we should know almost immediately where the door (or the handle) is and the object's other main parts. An example of massing in product design can be seen in the telephone keypad in Figure 82 – the handset and the receiver make up the two main masses, but this also extends to the controls themselves, the massing of elements and 'grouping' of the push buttons help us to make conceptual links about the various functions of the machine and make it easier to understand and control. In two-dimensional design the graphic massing of text literally does help us to make sense of a page of type, for example – imagine how difficult it would be to navigate around your daily newspaper if all text, headings and spacing were the same size.

visual grammar

Just as we use spacing and punctuation marks between words in order to make sense of a piece of text, we can also carry this analogy further to suggest that written punctuation has a direct comparison with visual punctuation. This is some-times referred to as a 'handshake' where two or more elements in a design meet together. It is good manners to shake hands or verbally greet one other when we meet another person – each acknowledges the presence of the other. In text this is achieved through full stops, commas, sen-tences, paragraphs and so forth and helps us to make sense of the written article. Also, just as large entrances and smaller internal doorways help you

find your way into and around a building – in written work the text headings and smaller subheadings, make for a more efficient navigation around the page in a newspaper. The philosopher Sinclair Gauldie calls these handshakes 'collisions':

One of the key problems of architectural detailing, namely the 'problem of 'collisions'; for it is at the meetings of one plane or shape or material with another that the question of fit, both in the practical and in the aesthetic sense, becomes acute and it is here that all sorts of ill-considered design deci-sions come home to roost.[10]

Where two or more elements in a design meet, maybe a window in a wall, or where a column meets the architrave (main beam), we usually need some elegant way of introducing them to each other. This also has the happy effect of letting the window express its 'windowness' and the wall express its 'wallness' without each interfering with the other's individual qualities.

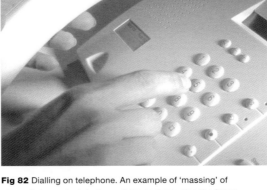

Fig 82 Dialling on telephone. An example of 'massing' of elements in product design – sizing and grouping the finger buttons according to functions.

Fig 83 Constantine College today – the 'stripped classical' style.

Figure 83 is an illustration of the University of Teesside's Constantine building, opened in 1930. Look at how much care the architect has put into the handshakes where the wall accepts the windows, the roof meets the walls and the walls meet the ground. The strongly expressed vertical and horizontal structural elements of this particular façade (without an arch in sight) is analogous to Classical Greek column-and-beam structure and therefore buildings of this type are sometimes referred to as the 'stripped classical' style. These handshaking details of a building can also be applied to product designs where two components meet – for example, the soft form of a handle where it meets the sharp blade of a knife, or the handle of a kettle where it meets the lid or main body.

The philosopher Roger Scruton examines this handshaking problem using examples of the post-and-beam in building construction.[11] In Figure 84, the left-hand sketch shows a simple post and beam. This could be understood by an observer as the post penetrating the beam, that is, the beam is free to slide down the post. The right-hand sketch introduces a 'cushion' or capital between the post and beam, this now reads as though the post is supporting the beam. Scruton refers to an earlier account of the post and beam from Sinclair Gauldie (Figure 85) in which Gauldie states that:

The business of a column, which is to hold up the lintels above it, could be done by a fat enough pillar without any capital at all … but a pad between the lintel and the column-head makes it look more comfortable, and it needs no calculation of bearing-pressure to show why: you can sit more comfortably on a shooting-stick … (of the fold-out leather seat type) … than on the knob of a walking cane. A simple square block … is enough to remove the sensation that the column is boring into the lintel ends; but it seems, if anything, to

accentuate a certain abruptness about the junction: the horizontal movement of the eye along the lintel-line trips over the block and is pulled almost peremptorily down the vertical line of the column. At this point one becomes aware of the block as an intruder. The lintel is rectangular and horizontal (which is obviously the natural thing for a lintel to be), the column is cylindrical and vertical (which is equally proper), and there is no quarrel between them as functionally distinct entities: if anything, one would say, 'Vive la difference.' But here now is this block which confuses the whole visual issue. It is rectangular like the lintel but does not belong to the lintel: it does seem to belong to the column but it is the wrong shape.

Once a shape-conscious designer is aware of this problem, he becomes interested in correcting both the feeling of abruptness and the feeling of intrusion, and there is a certain satisfaction in finding that the double correction can be made in one move by putting a more or less conical cushion between column and block. This is a solution, moreover, which feels right in a structural sense: one can visualize the column as a pipe conducting the downward flow of force, and the capital as a funnel directing the force into it.

A particular type of handshake should obviously take account of the materials and manufacturing processes involved. The Greek columns and capitals would still 'work' on a new building in stone today. Norman Foster's Stansted Airport building uses steel tubes and struts for its structure and the handshakes between the various elements are careful, elegantly engineered solutions in themselves and need no further elaboration (Figure 86).

Much detailing or handshaking can also be seen in nature. If we again take the human animal

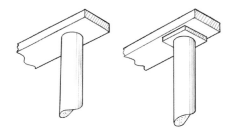

Fig 84 Is the post penetrating or supporting the beam? (Adapted from Scruton.)

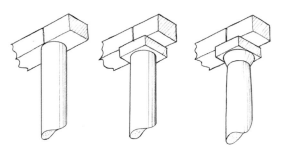

Fig 85 Classical solution – also introduces subtle curvature in cone and column (adapted from Gauldie).

as our yardstick, we can see that our heads aren't just stuck on top of the shoulders – a neck intervenes. The fingernails nicely finish off our fingers. Each eye sits happily in a discernible socket, rather like the windows nestle in the wall of a nicely detailed building – like those in Figure 83 – or a button that sits in a dished depression in the surface of a product (Figure 87). Our eyebrows protrude and protect the eye; the overhanging eaves of a building provide shelter, either from the rain or the sun. A house with small eaves looks somehow 'mean spirited' compared to its neighbour with larger eaves. We are all programmed through evolution to look for shelter; therefore any indication of shelter is far more satisfying to behold than none. Perhaps this is one reason why

Fig 86 Stansted Airport (detail). 1991. Sir Norman Foster.

Fig 87 Control buttons nestling in dishes.

we find traditional Italian architecture, with its large sheltering eave designs, so appealing.

Much scarring to the faces of houses has occurred in recent years in Europe and elsewhere with the fitting of replacement windows using plastic-framed double glazing. On the face of it there is nothing inherently wrong with PVC (polyvinylchloride). It is a good enough material for the task. However, the production process requires a lot of energy and PVC is not as easy to dispose of or recycle as wood. Very often the replacement design bears no relation whatsoever to a particular house's original window design – a design with which we have become comfortable and perhaps have admired over many years. You often see large 'gaping holes' where once nicely detailed windows used to be – the architect and designer Eileen Gray said that windows without shutters were: 'like eyes without eyelids'. The old saying 'God is in the details' certainly applies to windows.

music analogy

According to research by Dr Geraint Wiggins music is a uniquely human trait.[12] Our brains 'automatically' search for patterns in sounds and different people pick out different patterns, or rhythms, from the same constant beat – for example, some might hear 1,2,3 – 1,2,3 – 1,2,3 and others might hear 1,2 – 1,2 – 1,2 etc. Music directly affects our emotions and is also strongly related to movement – it is difficult not to tap your feet or move to the music when listening to something you like. In a visual sense this is analogous to moving through a building or 'reading' a painting. Probably our tendency to notice patterns, repetition and the relationships between things triggered the birth of mathematics – for example, Pythagoras (c.500BC) discovered the mathematical relationship between the subdivisions of the length of a piece of string and the harmonious tones they made when plucked.

There are many analogies between music and architecture (and design); again we automatically look for patterns or grouping of elements in a building. The term 'frozen music' (usually attributed to the German philosopher Goethe (1749–1832)) or 'frozen gesture' (Gauldie) is often applied to a building's form and detail. A Greek temple probably provides the simplest explanation, although by extension the analogy can be applied to almost any building or product. The temple columns express the main rhythm, the 'beat of a drum', or repetition as the observer walks through the building. The fluting of the columns, details of the architrave and triglyphs provide supporting notes – smaller elements in harmony with the main rhythm. The overall expression of a building can be sombre or light hearted, classical or romantic, noisy or quiet, and can affect our emotional state. A veritable symphony orchestra can be contained in a Victorian building's façade. This analogy with music is more difficult to discern in smaller product designs, nevertheless a product can also be said to demonstrate rhythm, expressed through its main elements with 'harmonics' in the detailing and a product can also be sombre or light hearted.

Musicians often refer to 'colour' in music, and different conductors can give a different colour to the same piece of music. The art historian Kenneth Clark has compared the music of Bach and Handel with Baroque architecture and the paintings of Jean-Antoine Watteau (1684–1721) to the Rococo style. Perhaps jazz finds its architectural equivalent in Art Nouveau?

grids and grid systems

A grid system could be described as a visual form of rhythm or repetition. The term 'grid system' is usually associated with the subject discipline of graphic design and describes the layout for a page of print, or print and pictures, and gives a logical and visually strong structure to the appearance of the page. Typically a magazine or newspaper page will consist of columns of type, the dimensions of which will usually be consistent throughout each page of the entire publication. Images or insertions could take up more than just one column width across the page. Figure 88 shows a typical page layout for a magazine with the lines of the grid

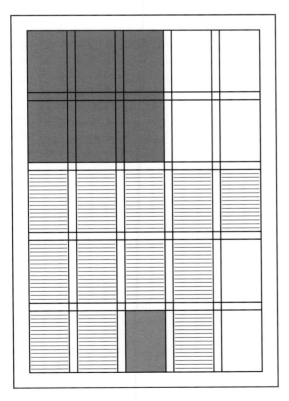

Fig 88 Typical grid for a magazine page layout. Lines in the boxes represent type, the grey areas represent images

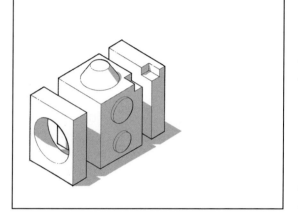

Technical Illustration:
an introduction

Module ref DES 102PD
Year One - Semester 2

Fig 89 Deliberate use of white space and asymmetry for a more interesting layout.

superimposed. There are specific margin widths around the edges and gaps between the columns, the central margin or gap where the paper folds is normally wider so that text isn't lost in the crease. One should not be trapped by the grid, however. It is often a good idea to deliberately skew a design and use lots of white space for a more sophisticated layout, as shown in Figure 89, for example.

Grid systems are not confined to graphic design, however. They are also used in architecture and product design as a useful method for the visual ordering of various elements and thus help to ensure the harmony of the whole. The arrangement of doors and windows on the façade of a building usually does conform to some under-

lying grid system. Theoretically there is no limit to the number of columns on a page or elements in a design, however an over-complex grid would probably lead to visual chaos.

systems design

Just as grids help us to understand and navigate design elements in two- and three-dimensional designs, so underlying structures can help us to navigate around virtual objects, such as a website, or a physical device with a user interface such as a ticket machine. Beautiful design is not restricted to the way things look. Objects can also be beautiful in an abstract sense by the way in which they are designed to interact with the user – the pleasurable ease with which objects can be used versus the horrendously complicated. Good systems design, sometimes called interaction design, is the term given to the method by which a device is designed so that its operation is friendly to the user – its purpose made obvious and its user interface easy to understand and navigate, even by a new user – although there is always a learning curve, even with simple devices. The task of designing something simple to operate can be a very complicated one however, especially when the user has a wide variety of options to choose from. How do you hide complexity yet retain access to a simple versatility? Donald Norman's three principles of good product design can also be applied to systems design – simplicity, versatility and pleasurability.

Good systems or interaction designers always construct experiments to establish the worth of their design ideas. There really is no substitute for making and testing prototypes, as things you take for granted are often not understood by others and people sometimes find unforeseen or even bizarre ways of using things as well as inadvertently or deliberately abusing objects. These discoveries are useful for the designer provided they happen during the early stages of the design process. It is therefore essential to enlist the help of outsiders – potential users – in evaluating new designs: people who have no prior knowledge of the project and are therefore impartial. However, such people can be eager to please and say good things about the design – not wishing to say negative things even though they may be thinking them. Human nature is such that it is difficult not to have an affect on the thing you are trying to measure – being watched while you try to make sense of something is not a pleasant experience for most people. Nowadays interaction designers try to construct experiments in which potential users do not even know they are taking part in an experiment, perhaps by placing the device in a 'real' environment using hidden cameras to capture user interactions. This raises obvious ethical issues but it is probably the only way of objectively assessing a particular design proto-type (unsuspecting users can always be asked for their permission afterwards).

The nature of a particular design project can vary hugely, but there follows a list of general guidelines as an introduction to good systems design:

• **Anticipation** – the design should anticipate the user's needs. For example, is the purpose of the design obvious? Is that machine at the railway station something you can get train tickets from, or a cup of coffee? What visual clues does it display?

• **Metaphors and symbols** – these need to be chosen carefully; for example, a symbol of a spy-glass used in computer tool bars can mean either zoom or search. Words are often a better choice than a symbol, though sometimes both are used – for example, placing the computer's screen cursor over a symbol sometimes produces a short explanation.

• **Actions feedback, visual and/aural** – we need to know that the device has definitely entered/accepted each instruction, leave no room for ambiguity.

• **Status information** – users need to know where they are in the system at any one time. This is especially important if the user is interrupted while using the design. It is also sometimes useful to have a tracking status facility, so the user can avoid useless repetition. For example, some Web search engine headings change colour once visited – you know the next time the heading appears that you've already been there.

• **Consistency and logic** – stick to simple pathways and obvious navigation/doorways. A bad example of this is clicking on the start button when you want to end Microsoft's Windows applications. Sometimes it is necessary to be deliberately inconsistent, for example, when things need to act differently from the norm. Many cash machine displays now offer simple choices with touch-screen 'buttons', which most first time users find reasonably friendly. Touch screens with aural feedback are an improvement on old screen displays that had physical push buttons lined up alongside icons on the screen – which invariably didn't line up!

• **Undo/step back facility** – essential in any system. Also always allow a clear way out from the system completely.

• **Defaults** – need to be intelligently set whilst at the same time making it easy to change to another setting and back again. Some designers prefer to use the words 'standard setting' and 'restore standard settings' rather than 'default'.

• **Protect user's privacy and security** – this is particularly relevant when using high-street cash machines, for example, probably everyone feels vulnerable to some extent when using these machines. We don't like to display our mistakes to the rest of the queue when using a ticket machine for the first time, so privacy is important for mundane tasks as well as dealing with sensitive or private information.

• **Inclusivity** – the design should be easy to use for as large a proportion of the population as possible. Most young designers take for granted excellent eyesight, colour vision, hearing and hand/eye coordination – but it is pointless creating a visually elegant design or system if a large proportion of users have difficulty in operating it.

Fig 90 Philips Food Mixer. Example of blend lines in product design.

form and detail – sculptural properties of everyday objects

The design and appearance of an object is constrained by the very materials and manufacturing processes used in its production. The quantity in which a particular product is to be produced is also a crucial factor. The injection moulding of plastic parts, especially those of complicated form and detail, such as a mobile telephone with a moulded plastic body, requires expensive tooling and machinery – a cost that can only be recouped by selling the resulting plastic product in large numbers. In contrast, a plastic product that will only be sold in relatively small quantities will be made by much cheaper tooling methods, such as by vacuum forming and/or fabrication methods, though the advantages of injection moulding techniques (for example, fine detail, moulded-in webs and pillars, little or no hand finishing requirements) will not be available to the designer. Similarly the design of products in other materials, such as steel, aluminium, wood and composites, needs to take into account the shapes required and again the numbers involved. Metals can be cast, rolled, forged, die-cast and extruded (all of which influence the metal's behavioural properties in service) and are also available in standard off-the-shelf forms, for example, as tubes and sheets, as well as a vast number of standard components, such as fasteners (nuts, bolts and screws etc.) and subassemblies of components – suspension units, batteries, switches, etc. But rather than limiting the industrial designer's scope for form and detail, a good knowledge of materials, components, manufacturing and assembly methods is vital to the design process. For example, a simple injection moulded part made in two halves provides some scope for nice detailing where the two shells come together and trap other components such as surface switches and a mains lead input (see the food mixer example in Figure 90).

The fabrication of forecourt petrol pump housings in sheet steel is another example, this time requiring a good knowledge of folding, joining, fabrication and coating methods in order to create an elegant interesting design rather than a crude box with exposed sharp edges – which would be both dangerous and prone to rust. There follows below a variety of examples of products and buildings that illustrate the ways in which form and detail can be manipulated to make a more pleasing result. The list is by no means exhaustive and new 'tricks' are being invented all the time. These examples include cars, as these are probably the nearest thing to mass sculpture that nearly everyone has to make choices about – choices of shape, form and detail, colour and tactile properties – even when people say they are 'not interested in art'.

The particular shape of a car or product doesn't usually appear out of the blue – this is part of an evolutionary technical, visual and frequently fashion-led process. Every so often in this process one particular version or model becomes an outstanding example of its type – a so-called 'classic'. This is probably best exemplified in car design, where one year's model is superior to those versions in the years both preceding and following it. Sometimes, however, the very first version of a new model remains the best. For example, the first Fiat Punto introduced in 1994 remains, in the opinion of many critics, far superior in visual terms to all subsequent 'facelifts' where the designers introduced various cosmetic nips and tucks, frivolous changes that merely served to destroy the vehicle's original purity of form and detail. Car manufacturers are always under pressure to do something new each year but often changes are made just for the sake of

change and these are not always for the better. So fashion plays a large part in design and the examples illustrated in this book will no doubt date very quickly. Who knows what cars and other objects will look like in ten or twenty years' time? The following basic conventions and visual concepts will probably still be useful however they might be interpreted in the future.

Silhouette

One of the first things we notice about an object is its silhouette – the shape or form enclosed by the object's outer edges – from whichever direction it is viewed. The silhouette is usually the first clue as to what the object is, its size and function, for example, a spoon, car or a building. This silhouette establishes an impression upon which we can judge whether or not its shape or style is likely to please us. If worthy of further investigation we then begin to notice details such as the object's colour, surface textures and the shapes of the component parts that go into its construction, and comparing how these details relate back to the overall silhouette – do these make up a harmonious whole? Probably a good place to start a discussion about the sculptural properties of objects is *lines* – for example, the outline of a car's silhouette helps establish the overall shape, form or style of the car, which usually sets the scene for other 'rhyming' lines making up the shape of the doors, windows and bodywork and other smaller components such as the front grille, lights, badge, etc. (these often small bright metallic parts are referred to as 'jewellery' by car designers). The direction of lines – straight, slightly curving, sharply curving, or increasing curvature with length – affects our response to the object. Is it a fast shape or a slow one (a shark or a turtle)? Is it over- or under-stated? Is the object soft or hard?

Fig 91
Ford's StreetKa
– an example
of 'leaping'
vectors and
'form slicing'.

Smooth or textured? Designers use a variety of line types to describe shapes that promote a particular desirable aesthetic, first using lines to sketch the object and then developing its form and detailing. See Chapter 5 for more on drawing with lines.

Blend Lines

Sometimes used to define where one curved surface meets another curved or flat surface. Rather than blend the two surfaces smoothly to produce an invisible join, it is often a good idea to 'butt up' the adjoining surfaces in such a way that creates a line indicating a change of direction and making it obvious where the two surfaces meet. This is often used as a subtle visual handshake – for example, the blend line in the hand-held food mixer in Figure 90 helps to define where the handle starts and where the motor body ends. This also gives a visual clue about where it is safe to grasp the appliance with the hand. Blend lines help to emphasize form and provide a detail to delight and lead the

eye, especially in car designs, thereby relieving an otherwise bland form. When the product is lit from certain positions the blend line can be clearly seen, enhancing the product's sculptural qualities. Figure 91 shows an illustration of Ford's 'Streetka' design where you can pick out a blend line along the side of the car, passing through the door handle.

Shut Lines, Bead Lines and Vectors

Probably the best example of shut lines is the 'lines' created between a car's body and its doors when shut (actually a linear shadow and highlight where two panels meet leaving a small gap). However, shut lines can be seen on any product that has a lid or where two separate components come together. As well as providing a visual handshake where components meet (thus helping the user to understand which part is likely to open), shut lines are also a practical way of getting around the problem of trying to match two components together so that they meet *exactly* along the entire lengths of their edges. Shut lines also help to take the 'eye for a walk' around the form of an object, directing our gaze along a surface. Shut lines, either real or artificial, can also help to guide the user's eye to an important detail such as an on/off button. You often see a real shut line continuing onto an artificial shut line, or groove, on an adjacent surface. This technique can also be applied to small products and on a larger scale, buildings too. 'Drawing' lines on cars and buildings with thin strips of shadow cast by raised ridges is nothing new, as many Egyptian and Greek carved stone figures show lines 'drawn' using thin shadows, often to show detailed features such as the lips on a sculpted face in stone – where only a change of colour would in reality indicate where the edge of the lip meets the face.

Although describing the effect of lines in drawings, Philip Rawson has the following to say about lines, which also applies equally to designing in both two and three dimensions:

A principal method for uniting elements in the composition of a drawing is by continuities. These are picked up across intervals or breaks, from one line to another. They are based on kinetic reading of the implied vectors of lines across the intervals. Usually the picking up will be direct; one line may pick up, and gather into itself, the projected vectors of more than one other line, and the projection of one line may be ramified into a number of other lines like a growing plant. Quite often, too, the eye may be expected to pick up a continuity that has a step in the interval. All such continuities are most effective when they establish relations between what are, in the world of things, separate objects.[13]

This device is often used to lead the eye and, at the same time, adds dynamism to a design. For example Figure 91 shows separate elements in

a car's bodywork that are 'connected' by virtual or imaginary vector lines, gestures that maintain direction and add visual excitement. This is analogous to the child's pointed finger in Andrea's painting of the Sacred Family, shown in Figure 92, which helps the eye to leap the void onto the other child's arm and continue on its travels around the arms, elbow and heads (focal points) of the other figures in the painting. In architecture linear elements can also connect visually, for example horizontal elements are read as continuous despite the interruptions caused by vertical elements.

In addition to the lines on a car's bodywork, whether silhouette, shut, groove or vector lines, sometimes the eye can be guided by other pathways, such as the curved bead profile running

Fig 92 The eye jumps the gap – Andrea Del Sarto. Madonna and Child with St Elizabeth and St John the Baptist c.1528.

along on the sides of the Ford Transit van shown in Figure 93. This bead travels around the front and sides of the van and is deftly brought to a halt and 'absorbed' by each rear light cluster. Of course such beads and other corrugations serve to strengthen the panel's structure as well as providing a nice visual detail.

A visual handshake, similar to a shut-line, is the deliberate gap left between a product and the surface it is sitting on, usually created by three or four feet stuck to the product's underside. This gap creates a visible shadow under the object's bottom edges (a 'shadow gap') that emphasizes its sculptural qualities, as well as making the object appear to weigh less – it 'hovers' above the surface (like car bodies 'hover' above the ground). Taken together, the shut lines, highlights and shadows created by light help to delight the eye and make the object more attractive. This type of visual device can often be seen in architecture where a vertical surface, such as the façade of a

building, meets the ground. On a small product, leaving a gap underneath also helps in a practical way by using feet to make the object stable on an uneven surface, this also aids cooling if the object is an electrical/electronic device.

Echoes and Visual Rhymes

We are attracted to repetition and soon notice evidence of pattern. Even in apparently non-visual things such as writing or music, a repetition or a hint of repetition seems to please us – for example, words that rhyme in a poem, or a repeating chorus or element in music. These rhymes, repetitions or 'echoes' serve to grab our attention and reinforce a particular design message. In design and the visual arts generally, the shapes, forms, details and colours that repeat themselves in obvious or subtle ways suggest an intelligent order or harmony, a certain level of organization that we perceive as being the opposite of chaos – and is therefore to be valued. Details, such as door handles on a particular car, need to rhyme with the car's overall shape. In some cases, however, case the handle shape may be tweaked to avoid the obvious thereby adding a level of subtlety or vibrancy to the composition. This rhyming is also used when colouring objects – for example, in a two-coloured product using green and grey, a drop of the green can be mixed with the grey to make a more harmonious colour composition overall.

Fig 93 The bead profile running along the side of the van is absorbed by the light detail at the rear corner, and thereby 'introduces' it to a flat area of the rear door surface – a handshake or a reconciled 'Gauldie collision' where two elements meet.

Radii

Product designers are especially keen on the dimensions of the radii along the edges of the product they are designing, probably because small products are handled by the user and the tactile properties become more important than in large objects and buildings, though radii is important here too. A three-dimensional object with almost no radii whatsoever along the edges could be perceived as having sharp edges and therefore might be uncomfortable to hold. Replacing the sharp edges with a small radii can make the object a little more tactile friendly and perceived as more comfortable to hold and use, while retaining a dynamic hard-edged appearance. Soften the radii further and the object becomes much more comfortable to hold and its sculptural quality is much softer and less aggressive. This is why we are attracted to handling pebbles on the beach – ground into soft shapes over years of rubbing down by sand and sea. The colour and reflective qualities of wet pebbles make them even more attractive, and are often far more elegant as body decorations than some contrived fancy jewellery seen in many shop windows.

Depending on the end purpose of the product being designed, you may wish to use very small or large radii, or a mix of both small and large – soft where the held in the hand but 'tight' along the other edges. This adds variety and visual interest: the object is friendly yet retains an air of 'hi-tech' purposefulness and these small differences of radii can have a large visual impact. Adding shut lines and other details into the mix also makes large differences to the appearance of a product. Often the control buttons themselves are slightly convex and sit in a concave dish as shown above – a handshake between the surface and the button, this aids visual delight (an eye in its socket again) and improves the tactile properties of the product. Similar effects of varying radii and curves can also be seen on larger objects such as cars and caravans.

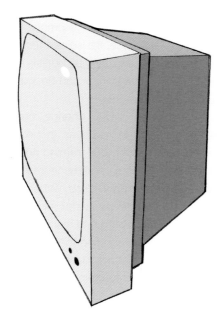

Fig 94 'Slim' television – a useful visual trick.

Pruning (Reducing Visual Bulk)

It is often desirable to alter the perceived visual bulk of an object or building, for instance, when trying to reduce the apparent size of a domestic appliance such as a television, or the mass of a building. For example, the main components of the old cathode-ray television designs are quite bulky and the simplest way to create an enclosure around this assembly would be a straightforward box. However, this would result in an unnecessarily large and bulky appliance. Figure 94 shows a casing designed to make the television appear smaller and lighter, while still enclosing the cathode ray tube and other components. As we walk past the front of the television, the 'thin' box surrounding the screen's edges fools us into thinking just how slim and elegant this product is – we don't really notice the tapered box housing the remaining components sticking out from the rear. Sometimes the rear is coloured differently from the front part to further de-emphasize the unwanted bulk. Of course, flat screen technology has replaced the cathode ray tube but it is a useful visual trick nevertheless, which can be applied to other products or buildings.

This camouflage colour change can also be seen in car design, such as in helping to disguise the amount of metal framing necessary for strength and at the same time increasing the apparent area of window glass. When looked at closely, the outside perimeter of many car windows have a broad border of black (printed on the inside surface) surrounding the window. This is often seen on hatchback designs, where the window glass appears to cover the full width of the rear tailgate door. However, when seen from the inside, the pressed metal frame extends the full extent of the door, passing down behind the black border on both sides of the glass and, as the interior is usually darker than the outside, we don't notice it. This hides the pressed steel frame, gives the illusion of a greater area of transparent

glass and lends the car a more 'airy' structure.

A similar effect is achieved by painting the centre pillar between the front and rear side windows a dark colour (especially effective in conjunction with tinted window glass seen against a light tone of body colour) which makes the two windows (or three in Figure 95) appear as one large aperture by 'removing' a vertical element. A vertical element in a car is at right angles to the direction of travel and therefore 'slows' the car. Conversely a horizontal line can give the illusion of a greater length and also speed (in the direction of the line) of whatever it is applied to, for example, the black bumper strip along the side of the car in Figure 95. In a similar way the bottom skirts of cars are often coloured differently to reduce perceived bulk and emphasize the horizontal 'go faster' aspect. This also helps to camouflage any scratches from loose stones kicked up from the road surface. The 'arrow-like' window and rear light cluster shapes of the car in Figure 95 also serve to emphasize forward motion and direction.

Fig 95 Peugeot 407 SW, showing the dark coloured side window pillars and horizontal door bumper strip.

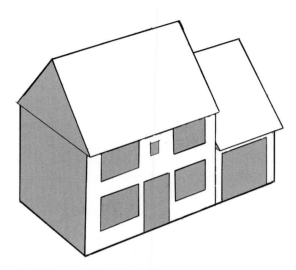

Fig 96 House with 'in-line' extension.

Fig 97 House with stepped-back extension.

The bulky form of products or buildings can also be broken up by clever use of detailing or by 'slicing' into the form, like taking a knife to a slab of cheese, as in the rear of Ford's coupe version of the StreetKa in Figure 91. This reduces the apparent mass of the design as well as providing something to delight the eye, similar to massing, pruning or visual punctuation methods noted previously.

Architects use similar techniques to reduce the apparent visual bulk of buildings. Figure 96 shows an illustration of an existing house and its side extension. Figure 97 then shows the same house with the extension stepped back a little, making the house look smaller while retaining the same interior volume and being less visually 'brutal' – a better mannered solution compared with its former self. This also relates to massing techniques noted earlier and, in this case, also preserves the hierarchy of the two volumes – the stepped back extension acknowledges the 'higher status' of the main house and preserves its dignity.

Friendly Versus Aggressive Forms

Just as different radii can make a big impact on the perceived friendliness of product designs, this argument can be extended to other shapes and forms also (shape usually refers to two dimensions, form usually to three dimensions). Examples of crude and aggressive architectural forms can be seen where 'Gauldie collisions' have not been carefully handled – for example, the absence of eaves where the wall of a house meets the roof, or an extension has been added without proper regard for the original building's design – including its form, detail, colour and textures. We regard sharp pointed things as potentially dangerous – we soon notice a rather sharp-topped pitch roof among more friendly angled roofs. This also applies to furniture designs such as the aggressive and non-too-comfortable looking Gerrit Reitveld's 1934 Zig-Zag chair shown in Figure 98. The lack of detailing or handshakes also emphasizes its barbarity. Friendly or aggressive 'personalities' can also be found in two-dimensional design – as indicated in the earlier examples of different typeface designs.

Texture and Surface Pattern

We delight in the visual and tactile properties of surface texture, for example, natural materials such as skin, wood, stone, rubber or grass, as well as man-made substances such as plastics, metals, carpet and fabrics. The list is endless. Touch is a vital part of survival and, like our other senses, can provide us with sensual and pleasurable experiences. Even the sound of something rolling or scraping across a surface can give us clues as to its likely texture – the momentary screech of chalk on blackboard can even cause physical anguish, 'setting our teeth on edge'. The perception and feel of different surfaces also affects our emotions, comfort and sense of well-being; compare the feel of natural materials such as cotton and linen with 'artificial' polymer-based fabrics such as nylon

Fig 98 The harsh forms of Gerrit Reitveld's Zig-Zag Chair. 1934.

when worn next to the skin. Donald Norman cites a visit to IDEO's American Design Consultancy where the designers had constructed a 'tech box': '…a multi-drawered cabinet containing silky cloth, textiles, sticky rubber, squeezable balls, knobs to turn, etc – (because) good designers worry a lot about the physical feel of their products.'[14] Norman calls this textural quality 'tangibility'.

In his book *The Aesthetics of Architecture*, the philosopher Roger Scruton writes about the anticipation of texture:

… our visual experience is qualified by reference to the other senses. As many critics have pointed out, materials and forms are often endowed with a visual appearance that translates, as it were, their functional and tactile qualities. Rough cast concrete has an unfriendly look, because we anticipate the scouring and bruising that result from touching it, while the wood and paper of a Japanese house are 'friendly' materials, from which we anticipate no harm.[15]

In the context of drawings, Philip Rawson writes about the emotive properties of texture:

Texture is always grasped by being understood as a segment of surface imbued with an emotive quality, very much as colour is. In general smooth textures have a 'cold' quality, implying remoteness and, perhaps unexpectedly, repelling the sense of touch. Rougher textures feel 'warmer', inviting the hand; but much broken texture may be disconcerting.[16]

So even before we've touched an object we can perceive something of the 'feel' of a surface by its appearance. Different surface textures can also make the same colour appear slightly different. Like Scruton's concrete example above, we know through experience that the shiny smooth surface of a ceramic washbasin will be hard and cold to the touch – fine for washing in and also a hygienic material, easy to keep clean. However, smooth ceramic handlebar grips on a motorcycle, although easy to keep clean, would be almost useless and positively dangerous. Apart from ceramic's unsuitability to withstand physical shock and vibration, ceramic handgrips would be difficult to keep a grip on (particularly on a cold, wet day) and fail to absorb sufficiently engine and other vibrations when out on the road – very tiring for the hand and arm muscles and sapping the rider's concentration. On the other hand, rubber, or one of its synthetic equivalents, is ideally suited as a material for handlebar grips – easy to grip over long periods of time and simultaneously providing essential feedback on the bike's performance and road surfaces without transmitting those harsh vibrations potentially injurious to the hands. Rubber also provides good thermal insulation. Rubber washbasins however would be unhygienic, difficult to keep clean and would wear out considerably quicker than ceramic – though such a design would provide a less painful landing if you slipped in the bath! The philosopher George Santayana has this to say about materials:

… we may note that however subordinate the beauty may be which a garment, a building, or a poem derives from its sensuous material, yet the presence of this sensuous material is indispensable. Form cannot be the form of nothing. If, then, in finding or creating beauty, we ignore the materials of things, and attend only to their form, we miss an ever-present opportunity to heighten our effects. For whatever delight the form may bring, the material might have given delight already, and so much would have been gained towards the value of the total result.

Sensuous beauty is not the greatest or most important element of effect but it is the most primitive and fundamental and the most universal. There is no effect of form which an effect of material could not enhance and this effect of material, underlying that of form, raises the latter to a higher power and gives the beauty of the object a certain poignancy, thoroughness, and infinity which it otherwise would have lacked. The Parthenon not in marble, the king's crown not of gold, and the stars not of fire, would be feeble and prosaic things.[17]

Plastic materials can easily be produced with a variety of surface textures. For example, domestic electrical appliances usually have a smooth glossy finish, which, like ceramics, is attractive and relatively easy to keep clean – particularly important in a kitchen environment. It is sometimes useful, however, to vary the surface texture – perhaps in areas where a better grip is required, for example, when using an electric razor in the presence of soap and water. Varying textures on the same product also makes for more tactile and visually attractive product. Textured surfaces are to be preferred to glossy finishes in situations where scratches and soiling need to be disguised – a car dashboard with a glossy surface would soon start to look grubby. A textured finish also helps to absorb light and prevent reflections and glare – particularly important when driving at night. Simulated leather effect finishes on plastic are sometimes used in car interiors, and although not very honest, these help us to feel more comfortable – we are happy to let ourselves be fooled into thinking that this hard surface is somehow soft and warm to the touch.

Different materials and surface textures have obviously been part of architecture and artefacts since civilization began. When composing the façade of a building or product, different textures can be used for a variety of reasons, for example, the introduction of a textural detail in an otherwise blank brick wall helps to relieve the visual monotony and steers us away from brutalism. Varying the brickwork, the application of pebble dashing, or using different coloured stone or pattern in a design must be handled sensitively – just enough is needed to relieve the monotony. It is a human trait to be fascinated by repetition and pattern but on the other hand we soon tire of too much of it. Santayana again, on monotony:

Defects of pure multiplicity ... the power of multiplicity in uniformity; we may now proceed to point out the limitations inherent in this form. The most obvious one is that of monotony; a file of soldiers or an iron railing is impressive in its way, but cannot long entertain us, nor hold us with that depth of developing interest, with which we might study a crowd or a forest of trees. The tendency of monotony is double, and in two directions deadens our pleasure. When the repeated impressions are acute, and cannot be forgotten in their endless repetition, their monotony becomes painful. The constant appeal to the same sense, the constant requirement of the same reaction, tires the system, and we long for a change as a relief.

Surface texture plays a vital role in product design – obvious in furniture design – giving the designer scope to use and mix a variety of materials, colour and texture, such as wood, steel, aluminium, plastics and textiles, although the use of too much variety in a single product can confuse the eye – the elements start to fight each other for our attention, just as too many different colours and patterns in a room would drive us crazy. Here's where the old motto 'less is more' comes in handy – use additions and variety with care! On most plastic products it is easy to see

how the designer has achieved interesting and visually pleasing designs with the careful use of texture. Some of these textures however are invisible - like the rubbery feel of the buttons, which does not become apparent until touched. The element of surprise and delight is, however, a useful tool in the designer's repertoire, whether involving texture or any other element (the element of surprise is also useful at client presentations, helping to regain everyone's attention). It is a small step from noticing the surface texture of objects and materials, to recognizing pattern. In his book *Pattern Design*, Lewis F. Day proposed that our liking for pattern stemmed from the human trait for noticing repetition, and that:

... pattern is, in fact, the natural outgrowth of repetition ... take any form you please and repeat it at regular intervals, and, as surely as recurrent sounds give rhythm or cadence, whether you want it or not, you have pattern. It is so in nature, even in the case of forms neither identical nor yet recurring at set intervals. The daisies make a pattern on the lawn, the pebbles on the path ... the grain of wood, the veining of marble, the speckling of granite, fall so obviously into pattern that they have been accepted in place of intelligent design ... Geometric pattern grew, of course, out of primitive methods of workmanship. No mechanism so simple but it gives rise to it. To plait, to net, to weave, or in any way mechanically to make, is to produce pattern.[18]

Our early preoccupations with pattern design must have included noticing the different patterns and markings on the skins and furs of living creatures. These designs are products of evolution, usually to help camouflage the animal against the background, whether predator or prey, although sometimes markings are used to actually be noticed – for example, the fanned-out tail feathers of the peacock help in impressing potential mates. Humans have always been attracted to texture and pattern and its elements of symmetry, repetition and colour and this has led to their application in artefacts and buildings – sometimes to remind us of the beauty of nature, especially when indoors. Certain cultures regard pattern as more important than form, whereas others tend to give priority to form. All cultures are fascinated by pattern design, however, and there is often a strong inter-relationship between a building's structure and its surface decoration. This is easily seen in Gothic architecture with patterns applied to flat planes and linear elements, but it is especially notable in Islamic buildings where the domes are often decorated with mosaic designs that are easily carried across and around curved (and compound curved) surfaces.

Islamic patterns have meanings deeper than mere decoration, for instance symbolizing the underlying structure of the cosmos. This has led to a rich variety of vernacular and religious designs, such as the geometric Islamic design shown in Figure 99. Note how the *positive* linear elements create the *negative* star shapes of different sizes. Pugin thought that all pattern design should conform to his honesty principle, for example, the 'dishonest' use of illusionist shadows on plant or floral designs, or other attempts to create illusions of depth such as perspective, should be avoided – a flat surface should not pretend to be three dimensional. In any case why would anyone want to step onto a carpet of flowers?

Organic Forms

Architecture and product designs are usually manufactured using components made by machines or industrial processes. For example, steel beams, bricks and glass in buildings, and product design assemblies consist of such things as metal castings, plastic mouldings, extrusions and parts requiring machining at some stage in their production. It is not surprising therefore that buildings and products have largely been geometric in their appearance – straight-edged affairs with the occasional arch, dome or curve here and there. At the end of the twentieth century this geometric state of affairs was developing into a much more organic, free-flowing visual language, expressed most noticeably in the styling of cars. Almost since the beginning of mass car production however, designers have incorporated curves into their designs, usually in an attempt to express speed and also to streamline the airflow around the body, as well as lending a more graceful appearance – somewhat akin to the swelled columns of classical Greek temples or the human form.

The form and detail of cars, products and buildings are becoming increasingly more expressive and developments in manufacturing technology,

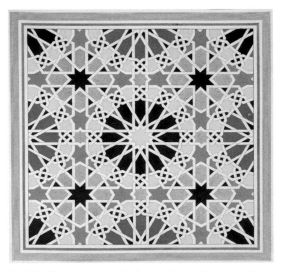

Fig 99 Water colour reproduction of a fourteenth-century Islamic pattern design from Alhambra Mosaic ornament in the south side of the Court of the Lions, Alhambra, from 'The Arabian Antiquities of Spain', published 1815 (w/c on paper) by Murphy, James Cavanagh (1760–1814).

particularly in the area of CAD/CAM (computer-aided design and manufacture) are allowing designers to create more complex shapes easily and very accurately. Who knows where this will lead? Maybe at the start of the twenty-first century we are returning to William Hogarth's eighteenth-century ideal of beauty expressed through serpentine line?

It is hard enough for the beginner to learn how to handle form and detail in terms of 'boxes and cylinders', let alone deal successfully with more organic and free-flowing forms. Life becomes more difficult for the designer when handling more expressive forms, such as the shape of a car or the fashion for soft sculptural forms seen in contemporary product design – to be successful at this subtle art requires great skill. Learning to 'sculpt' organic forms is a highly specialized design skill and takes years of practice to become expert. However, the lessons of visual grammar, for example, visual handshakes where two different elements meet, can still be applied to organic form.

Form and Detail Exercise

A good starting exercise for students new to form and detail is the 'bar of soap project'. This is a traditional favourite used by three-dimensional design tutors as many of the lessons of form and detail, outlined above, can be reasonably and cheaply carried out on such a small form – sculpting plastic foam rather than soap itself however.

case studies

Architectural Façade Design – Pasadena Museum of California Art by MDA Johnson Favaro Architects

Fig 100 Pasadena Museum of California Art. Façade elevation.

This privately funded museum was completed in 2002 and is home to permanent and travelling collections of Californian art, created since the founding of the state in 1850. The museum provides 30,000 square feet of exhibition space and includes parking and a street level lobby at the ground floor. In addition to the main gallery, there is a smaller gallery on the third floor, along with a garden and terrace, providing views of the dome of Pasadena's City Hall to the west and the San Gabriel Mountains to the north.

There is obviously a lot more to consider when designing a building than just composing the façade, for example, the internal layout and design features determine to a large extent the positioning of external windows and doors. Parts of things can rarely be designed in isolation, but this is where the skill of the designer is needed to reconcile such conflicting elements in order to come up with an elegant and well integrated solution. This is why

Fig 101 Photograph of actual museum.

designers prefer to talk about reconciling rather than compromising – and why integration is a key theme of this book. For our purposes here, however, it is nevertheless interesting to consider just this frontal aspect of the museum as an exercise in composition. We could compare it to a Mondrian painting or a Ben Nicholson low-relief sculpture, in that the front elevation is an arrangement of lines, steps, ledges, rectangles and colours – white, black, grey, yellow and blue. These colours, as well as the shape and sizes of the shadows cast by its elements, will change during twenty-four hours – the sky blue rectangle at the top in the drawing will not always be blue, even in daytime California.

The architect could have gone for a completely flat façade, leaving out the low relief steps and hollows. This would have deprived us of the enjoyment of its sculptural qualities however, tripping up our gaze as it travels across the white surface and pausing at the focal points of doors and windows. No doubt disturbing to purists is the introduction of the sloping and curved elements. Whatever you think of them, they certainly add an idiosyncratic and memorable touch. These parted 'drapery folds' of the façade serve as a visual theatrical semantic that reveals the entry points for the visitor and vehicles, and starts a formal vocabulary that repeats and develops on the journey into the interior of the building: 'in the manner of a fugue across the sequence of entry from street level up the main stair'.

Looking at the drawing in Figure 100 – if we take the main entrance as the main focal area, or 'fulcrum' of the façade (or painting), the elements clustered closely to its left are balanced by those elements spread out further to the right (the top aperture and the small grey rectangle at the bottom right hand corner). This leaves an area of white space that also helps to balance the details – resulting in a façade that is not too 'busy', nor, on the other hand, too empty. However, the architect might not have bargained for the street light (shown in Figure 101) placed perhaps randomly on the street directly in front of the building. This might have prompted another return to the drawing board in order to integrate a more elegant street lighting solution into the fabric of the building, and reconciling the building to the street.

Car Design – Aston Martin Rapide
By Marek Reichman, Director of Design, Aston Martin Lagonda Limited

What does it take to make a beautiful object? Understanding beauty is key to my job as a car designer and it forms the basis for my personal design philosophy. I believe beauty is timeless and when you're creating something like an Aston Martin you need to bear in mind that an Aston Martin is a timeless product that transcends fashion.

In my mind an Aston Martin needs to have elegance, power and soul, these are key qualities of the brand. So when it came to creating the Rapide my brief was to make the world's most beautiful four-door sports car. Cars that are typically judged to be beautiful are often two-door sports cars and I didn't want the visual appeal of Rapide to be compromised because of its four doors. I knew it had to have fluidity and an element of movement even while static, through the way the surfaces of the Rapide's body interacted. Above all it had to evoke a powerful message, because at the end of the day an Aston Martin is a sports car.

Fig 102 Aston Martin four-door Rapide. 2008.

When I sat down to work on my initial sketches, I had an image in my mind of a racehorse, I wanted to create the same kind of elegant relationship of muscularity and flowing line that a racehorse in full flight has. I also thought about a beautiful silk scarf; if you let it blow in the wind it flows and looks graceful, but if you scrumple it up in a ball it does not have the same appeal. I imagined Rapide's roof line as that beautiful silk scarf, flowing in the wind. Of course, the challenge for any designer, and the skill one needs to possess, is being able to see the potential of a simple line drawing and visualize how it would translate into a moving three-dimensional object. Here the Golden Section is a key to my work – this relationship of length to height to width is one of the general principles of art and nature. What do I mean? Well a nautilus shell is one of nature's examples of the golden section; its proportions are exact and balanced. In art, if you look at the Mona Lisa the relationship of her eyes to her nose to her lips to her chin and the angle of her face fits precisely into what we know as the golden section. This same principle can be applied to designing a beautiful car in my opinion.

When designing the Rapide it was important constantly to have a great working relationship with the engineering team. You can make a beautiful piece of music but if the conductor has it wrong and the orchestra isn't playing together it sounds awful. Creating a fabulous looking car from a sketch is impossible without the support of a talented team. My team of modellers constantly viewed the early clay models outside in the open air to check the way light fell on different areas of the car from sunrise to sunset. And don't under estimate the importance of things like wheel to body relationships and the amount of lines on a car, good design and creative engineering is the key to this. For example, look at The Kiss, by Rodin, its clear that its hewn from a solid block of marble, but imagine a joint line between the two heads, it's just would not be as beautiful. I wanted Rapide to have as few lines as possible, to make it as pure and beautiful as possible and to give Rapide the appearance that it is hewn from a solid piece of material. An Aston Martin is an experiential car, everything you come into contact with on the car matters, from the door handles to the key to the seats. Although we worked with traditional Aston Martin materials, wood and leather, we paid incredible attention to detail when it came to our choices of grain and cut. I believe this kind of attention goes to make it more beautiful.

To create something beautiful you need to care about what it is you are creating, give it time to evolve and have a passion for it. I believe you need to put some love in the object you are building to make sure you never stop short. It's 'good enough' is a phrase you'll never hear at Aston Martin; we always want to be better than that.

Goudy Typeface Design

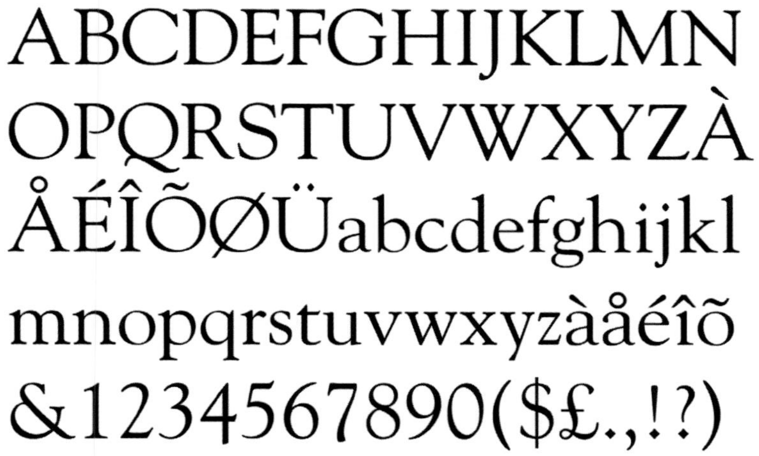

ABCDEFGHIJKLMN
OPQRSTUVWXYZÀ
ÅÉÎÕØÜabcdefghijkl
mnopqrstuvwxyzàåéîõ
&1234567890($£.,!?)

Fig 103 Goudy Old Style typeface. c.1916.

Born in Bloomington, Illinois in 1865, Frederic W. Goudy was one of the best known and prolific American type designers. His first type face 'Camelot' was designed for his own company of the same name in 1896. In 1903 Goudy, together with Will Ransom, created the Village Press in Park Ridge, subsequently moving to several different locations and ending up in Marlboro in 1923. In 1939 the Village Press had a devastating fire and most of Goudy's work was lost, including seventy-five of his hundred type styles. Afterwards, Goudy devoted his life mainly to teaching.

Frederic Goudy is best known for several distinctive typestyles: Old Style, Kennerly, Garamond and Forum, but Goudy Old Style remains his most popular typeface (Figure 103). This is due to its elegance and readability, helped by the use of comparatively tall ascenders on lower case letters and the flow of serifs from one letter to the next. Designing all his typefaces by freehand helped create their unique and friendly characters, forms that were similar to the old type styles but expressing a particular aesthetic that no others could rival. According to Simon Loxley, the Goudy Old Style typeface was often used for the lettering of names of public houses in the UK, chosen for its: 'rare combination of qualities of tradition and warmth'.[19] Frederic Goudy authored *The Alphabet* (1918), *Elements of Lettering* (1922), as well as *Typologia* (1940). He died in Marlboro, NY, on 11 May 1947.

Typographers traditionally construct a grid on which to sketch their designs. This helps to maintain reasonably consistent limits for the heights and proportions of letter forms; capitals, lower case middles, ascenders and descenders, ('middles' are those letters without ascenders or descenders), the designer often overlaying and tracing a particular letter form to help create other characters, thus maintaining a family aesthetic throughout (Figure 104). This relies on the experience, skill and judgement of the designer and is not remotely a scientific process (though early motorway typeface prototypes underwent readability trials). These raw sketches are often beautiful works of art in their own right and, by trying this method for ourselves, we can be introduced to the many different qualities of line – curves, expressiveness, balance and spacing.

These qualities are fundamental to gaining visual skills that can be applied to both two- and three-dimensional design, skills often overlooked today because of too much reliance on the computer and design software. We need to 'fall in love' with creating lines and shapes first as well as exploiting the visceral tactile qualities of paper and pencil and other media and exercising the delightfully creative relationship between hand and eye. Extremely small changes in font design can make a big difference to the look and feel of a page of text. Goudy maintained that the design of beautiful letterforms could be achieved without any sacrifice of legibility and that inherently beautiful designs combined simplicity, dignity, harmony and strength in equal measure.

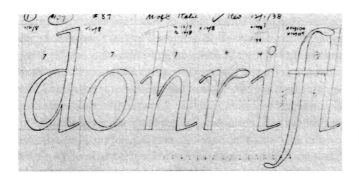

Fig 104 Frederic Goudy's 'University of California Old Style' italic – one of the few sketches that survived the fire of 1939. Note the overlaid letters n and h, also i and l.

Website Design for Ralph Ball (studioball.co.uk)

By Jamie Billing and Tracy Cordingley, Technical/Creative Design Directors, Alte Design Ltd, UK

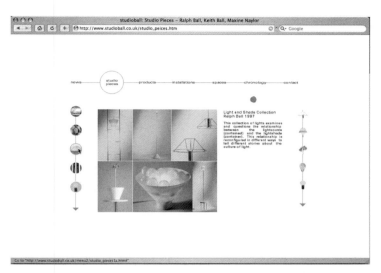

Fig 105 Screen image from www.studioball.co.uk website showing visual design.

Generally speaking the task of designing websites can be split into two main areas of consideration, loosely described as the visual design (what you can see) and the technical design (what you cannot see). There is always a conflict between what is 'creatively' desired and what is 'technically' possible. Some websites such as Google are very technical, employing complex, cutting-edge technology and software to run databases and search facilities. Other smaller websites do not require such technological power and in such cases it is often a simple choice between whether to construct the website using Adobe Flash technology (software program) or using html (Hypertext Markup Language). Since the purpose of Ralph Ball's 'studioball' website (Figure 105) is to publish an online library of creative design work, it only requires the basic (html) technology to enable it to function. This also has the added benefit of requiring very little maintenance work, since it is compatible with most operating systems and Internet browsers.

It is often the case, however, when developing websites using only html technology, that many creative ideas for how the website might operate – such as designed interaction, navigation and user interface – are much more difficult to achieve. This often requires excellent planning and of course, clever design when implementing the visual aesthetics. For Studioball, this took the form of custom-developed iconography and graphics but, most importantly, a well planned design process that included a detailed appraisal of the potential 'Navigational Structure and Flow' of the Website interaction (see below). The working process of designing a website can be summarized into seven important stages:

1 Detailed Planning   Prior to commencement of any work, it is important to establish the appropriate working methods and to confirm all deadlines and delivery dates with all involved. A Gantt chart is very useful here.

2 Strategic Analysis   This is the investigation into target users or markets, project functionality, user requirements and system capabilities (operating systems/platforms and browser compatibility).

3 Creative Marketing Concepts   Development of online brand identity or logo (if required); conception of multiple marketing solutions for use both online and offline.

4 Content Analysis   Analysis into the nature and quantity of the website material both available and required.

5 Design Concepts   The design, development and implementation of the website's underlying strategic concept and design concept. This will consist of two key integral processes:

   1. Navigational structure and flow. Flow diagrams illustrating all aspects of content, required functionality and multi-level user navigation, which can be storyboarded and presented (at the next client meeting, if the project is for an external client).

   2. Graphic identity and interface design. Development of the most appropriate and effective visual method of communicating and delivering the information to be developed. The user interface/graphics will need to be simple, intuitive and attractive with an effective control and navigational system.

6 Design Development   Once the underlying structure and design concept for the project has been agreed, the creation and integration of the website content (this will include all necessary photography, graphics, animation, sound and video) and development of the design concept to prototype stage will be achieved. After the prototype has been tested and approved, the development stage is concluded.

7 Creation of Website Material   On conclusion of the development stage the final website material will be created ensuring that all previous agreed design/functionality guidelines have been implemented successfully.

theory box

Evolutionary Psychology and Perceptions of Beauty

Just as natural selection is responsible for the development of Homo sapien's physical attributes, our current mental capacities have come about through an evolutionary process of psychological as well as genetic development, beginning with our hominid ancestors millions of years ago. Our intelligence, inclinations, fears and desires have thus evolved as advantageous adaptations to life and circumstances over time. These advantages include especially those of spoken language and its usefulness to early Stone Age hunter-gatherers collaborating in small groups, increasingly sophisticated tool making and, more recently, the invention of writing and agriculture and a settled way of communal life in villages and towns from about 10,000 years ago.

The contemporary philosopher Denis Dutton suggests that we should not regard the mind at birth: 'as a content-free blank slate' – instead evolutionary psychology 'posits the existence of innate interests, capacities, and tastes, laid down through processes of natural and sexual selection. Evolutionary psychology replaces the blank slate as a metaphor for mind with the Swiss army knife: the mind is a set of tools and capacities specifically adapted to important tasks and interest.' For example, Dutton cites the smell of bacteria-laden rotting meat as being the most repulsive smell to humans. Thus even as babies we automatically avoid the danger of eating something extremely poisonous. The essentially similar psyche of the human brain across all cultures has resulted in largely similar views on what is important in the arts. Works of art may take many different forms but the 'mind-forces' that produce them are the same. This is analogous to developments in technology since the Stone Age, where similar tools and artefacts can be found wherever human beings flourished. Certain works of art produced by a particular culture therefore can have a resonance across many cultural boundaries. Dutton agrees with Hume's hypothesis that the value of some works of art might be essentially eternal. Those works of art that endure over time 'do so precisely because they appeal to deep, unchanging features of human nature' – for example, the works of Shakespeare have been translated into many different languages and are performed and admired in many countries around the world because they (beautifully) express themes of emotional life such as humour, anger and tragedy that are common to all human beings. Similarly, certain well-known pieces of music continue to be performed by many cultures other than those that produced them.

In the visual arts all cultures show a propensity for a certain type of figurative landscape imagery. Dutton cites worldwide calendar art (and also the design of public parks) as demonstrating significant universal themes across all cultures. Common features include the presence of trees, water and shelter, these preferences being the result of millions of years of psychological evolution in the pursuit of survival.

Psychological evolution may have shaped our brains and minds into what they have become – producing internal forces that influence our everyday behaviour - but psychological techniques can also be applied 'from the outside' on existing mind/brains in order to improve a particular person's poor mental health, for example. Sigmund Freud believed that art can be used as a therapeutic tool – something that can be applied to a person's psychological state of mind in order to improve mental well-being by helping to get to the root of a particular problem, in order to face up to it. Freud said that art can reveal hidden conflicts and emotions and can thus provide a safety valve for releasing tensions (in the observer as well as the artist). As daydreams and fantasies are channelled into art they become a means of confronting previously hidden emotions or interior struggles and this allows the individual to visualize and grapple with his or her problems. Even on a more mundane level, art is well recognized as a therapeutic aid for the improvement of patients' mood in hospital wards.

chapter four

———

colour

chapter outline

Colour is highly subjective and can mean different things to different people. The same colour can have a diversity of symbolic meanings across different cultures. For example in the West, white symbolizes the purity of the bride and black is the colour of death, whereas in some Eastern cultures the colour of mourning is white – on this occasion representing the purity of heaven and the destination of the departed.

For centuries artists have been fascinated by the rainbow that, to many observers including Leonardo, suggested a 'natural order' of colours and colour harmonies analogous to the scales of music. Even after the scientific discoveries of Sir Isaac Newton on the properties of light published in his *Opticks* of 1704, arguments about primary, secondary and tertiary colours continued among artists for many years. The German writer, philosopher and scientist Johann Wolfgang Goethe published his treatise on colour in 1810, in which he stated that the perception of colour was subjective and depended to a large degree on an individual's faculties and local lighting conditions and was not simply a physical phenomenon as proposed by Newton. Goethe also proposed a colour wheel, experimented with the intensifying effects of complementary colours, provided an analysis of the after-image and also attempted to describe how colours might affect human emotions.

The proper scientific basis of colour interaction as perceived by humans was first proposed by the French chemist Michel Chevreul (1786–1889) and the first successful attempts to classify colours in any rational system were achieved almost simultaneously by Albert Munsell and Wilhelm Ostwald in the early years of the twentieth century. Munsell's method became the accepted model for the basis of today's colour systems and is described in this chapter.

Many artists since the Renaissance have attempted to link colour with music. The painter Wassily Kandinsky, who taught at the Weimar Bauhaus in the early 1920s, likened certain colours to particular musical instruments. The colour scarlet was the 'sound' of a trumpet and light blue was that of a flute. Many of his paintings were an attempt among other things to visually express music. Various attempts have been made to construct a 'psychology of colour' and relate colour to the observer's mood. For example reds are usually associated with arousal and aggression, whereas cool blues and greens are said to have a calming effect.

Choice of colour in design is often at the mercy of fashion, whether in clothes, cars, interiors or product design and colour is often vital to the success or failure of a product or scheme. The main aim of this chapter therefore is to provide a conceptual framework for understanding colour and describe the attributes and effects of colour which will hopefully be useful when composing a painting or a graphic design, choosing a colour scheme for an interior, or deciding on a suitable colour for a particular product. Colour attributes include notions of harmony, discordance, complementary and contrasting colours, warm versus cool colours, spatial properties of colours and optical effects such as after-images and others.

introduction

Ideally, colour should be considered right at the start of any design project. This is especially true when helping the user to recognize important controls, read a sign, or assist those users with impaired vision (usually a large percentage of any population). Architectural materials often come with their own intrinsic colour, particularly natural materials like stone or wood, and we are often dismayed by the choice of brick colour (and texture) in houses and other buildings. This is particularly annoying when someone hasn't bothered to find the same brick for a later extension to a house. The architect or city planner also has to deal with three dimensions, place, times of day, weather and seasonal affects on the colours and/or tones of buildings, townscape and spaces – factors that the studio painter does not usually have to contend with. The effects of atmosphere and sunlight can make a huge difference to our perception of a place. According to Tom Porter, architects' use of colour seems to break down into four main functions, as follows:[1]

• *Symbolic use.* For example, matching the colours of a sea ferry with its owner's terminal.

• *Environmental clarity.* For example, colour coding as a 'supergraphic' to discriminate between the forms or main working parts of a building.

• *Blending of architectural form into its setting.* This is a kind of colourful camouflage.

• *Opposite of blending.* This colour approach seeks to detach the building from its setting and uses colour to decorate or refer to concepts and ideas that exist beyond its setting.

Colour is highly subjective and can mean different things to different people – the same colour can have a diversity of symbolic meanings across different cultures. In the West, white symbolizes the purity of the bride and black is the colour of death, whereas in China the colour of mourning is white – on this occasion representing the purity of heaven and the destination of the departed. In his book on drawing, Philip Rawson says about the colour black: 'Only in some tropical countries, such India, does black have positive emotional overtones suggesting the grateful sweetness of shade and the erotic warmth of black hair.'[2] For centuries, in Europe, the colour purple was regarded as the supreme colour by the Church and the nobility and, as such, was reserved for use only by them. Severe punishments would be handed out to transgressors. The colour's high standing was not simply due to the expensive dyes required for its manufacture; purple contains red, the colour of the sun (and also blood), therefore bringer of life. Purple also contains blue, the colour of the sky and heavenly light, and can also contain black, the colour of death. The reflective highlights and dark shadows produced simultaneously by the sheen of high quality purple clothes in natural light reinforced these ideas, expressing both life and death in the one garment.

Black and white were once regarded as primary colours – externally the eye appears black and white but all the colours can be seen within it. Alchemists and artists were fascinated by the rainbow, which, to many observers including Leonardo, suggested a 'natural order' of colours and colour harmonies analogous to the scales of music. Even after the scientific discoveries of Sir Isaac Newton on the properties of light published in his *Opticks* of 1704, arguments about primary, secondary and tertiary colours continued among artists up until the end of the nineteenth century. However, the German writer, philosopher and scientist Goethe published his treatise on colour in 1810, in which he proposed that the perception of colour is subjective and depends to a large degree on the individual's faculties and local lighting conditions, and is not simply a physical phenomenon as proposed by Newton. Goethe also proposed a colour wheel, experimented with the intensifying effects of complementary colours, provided an analysis of the after-image, and also attempted to describe how colours might affect human emotions.

The proper scientific basis of colour interaction as perceived by humans was first proposed by the French chemist Michel Chevreul (1786–1889). The Gobelin Tapestry Company hired Chevreul to investigate the fading of their tapestry threads. In his book on the simultaneous contrast of colours published in 1839, Chevreul shows that the colours did not really fade but instead the *apparent* fading was due to the simultaneous contrast effects between adjacent coloured threads, caused by retinal fatigue in the observer: 'Any given colour would influence its neighbour in the direction of that colour's complementary.'

Isaac Newton had identified seven distinct colours of the rainbow, including indigo (a deep purple/blue) in order to chime with the seven notes of the musical octave. Since the Renaissance, many attempts have been made to link colour to sound and music.[3] For example the painter Wassily Kandinsky, who taught at the Weimar Bauhaus in the early 1920s, likened certain colours to particular musical instruments. The colour scarlet was the 'sound' of a trumpet and light blue was that of a flute. Deeper (darker) blues were the sounds of the cello and, deeper still, the organ. Kandinsky's painting *Composition V1* (Figure 106) is an attempt, among other things, to visually express music.

Artists have always sought to manipulate colour and influence our response to it by creating colour juxtapositions that do not occur in the real world – sometimes these take the form of abstract paintings that, having no other purpose outside of themselves, we nevertheless regard as beautiful, and/or meaningful. The artist therefore 'distorts' colour to create new worlds, analogous to the way in which we have distorted natural sounds via the invention of special instruments to create music. Even the singing human voice can be trained or 'distorted' to increase its emotional range. The opera singer is probably the best example of this.

The nineteenth-century writer and critic Walter Pater said that: 'all art aspired to the condition of music'[4] and Kandinsky believed that colour was capable of having a 'direct influence on the soul', producing an emotional response in the viewer similar to that of music. Johannes Itten, another Bauhaus teacher, said that: 'the deepest and truest secrets of colour effect are … invisible even to the eye, and are beheld by the heart alone.'[5]

It is probable that Kandinsky had a form of synaesthesia, a condition experienced by a small percentage of the population whose senses overlap in the brain to some extent. Some of these people see colours when hearing different sounds (even in blind individuals) and sometimes particular letters, numbers and words are perceived as particular colours, occasionally 'displayed' in three dimensions. Words and sounds are also experienced as taste in certain individuals. Research by Dr Jamie Ward, a neuro-psychologist at University College London's Synaesthesia Research Group, showed a remarkable consistency across many of these individuals, in that deeper sounds produced darker colours while higher notes produced lighter, brighter colours.[6] Professor Vilayanur S. Ramachandran goes further by postulating that the emergence of language is a direct result of synaesthesia, where shapes and tactile properties of objects are related to spoken sounds. In an experiment, normal volunteers (people unaffected by synaesthesia) were shown two different shapes cut out of board; a soft rounded shape and a straight-edged spiky shape and were asked to assign one of two spoken names to each of the two shapes – one sounding like 'Boobah' and the other 'Keekee'. People overwhelmingly chose 'Keekee' for the spiky shape and 'Boobah' for the soft shape. Ramachandran also proposes that this is one reason why we make hand gestures during speaking – to further emphasize the meaning of speech and its relationship with the physical world.

Kandinsky's colleague at the Bauhaus, Paul Klee recognized that 'value' (the lightness or darkness of a colour) could be ordered in a scale between black and white, analogous to the scales of music, but that 'hue' (a particular colour, red or blue for example) was too subjective to classify in any rational sense. However, Klee did attempt to analyse hue in terms of 'weight', 'giving greater psychological prominence to the primaries than to the secondaries or tertiaries.' For example, the colour red has a particularly powerful impression on our senses. Philip Rawson says of the colour red: 'Red, especially the vivid orange-red of many iron oxides, is far from being a material of negative colour value. Its significance is overwhelmingly positive. It lies at the very centre of the "hot" side of the colour circle and is the colour which symbolizes the highest pitch of feeling.'

We often use red as a symbol for something important, either as a warning sign of something dangerous or to attract our attention to something of special significance. Steven Mithen says that: 'Red has been shown to have special significance for humans because of the range of physiological effects it induces, including changes in heart rate and brain activity, and because of the privileged position it bears in the colour systems of all societies.'[7] Red also tells us that some berries and fruits are ripe enough to eat and is also an indicator of the freshness of meat. Red is the colour of fire (dangerous!) and also the colour of spilt blood, which signals injury.

Various attempts have been made to construct a 'psychology of colour' and relate colour to the observer's mood. For example, reds are usually associated with arousal and aggression whereas cool blues and greens are said to have a calming effect (green and its association with nature is a colour often used in hospital wards). This is fraught with difficulty, however, as experiencing colour is highly subjective. On a more mundane level, certain properties of colour are very useful – we certainly notice highly saturated colours against a neutral background. For example, the red traffic light, or the highly visible contrasting yellow and black chevrons painted on the front of a locomotive (Figure 113) as a warning of approaching danger.

Whatever theories exist about colour and mood, the choice of colour in a design is often at the mercy of fashion, whether in clothes, cars, interiors or product design – last year's fashionable colours are definitely 'old hat' this year – and colour is vital to the success or failure of a product. Although colour is one of the least physically complicated components of a car, it is often a crucial deciding factor on whether or not someone buys it.

One of the aims of this chapter on colour is to provide the aspiring designer or artist with basic tools of the trade and what follows is a 'manual' of attributes and effects of colour. An important point to remember is the question of balance in design. This is particularly important in the context of colour composition – a larger area of less saturated colour balances a small area of highly saturated colour, whether it is the same hue or a different one. However, as in design generally there are no rules that say you should compose colours in a certain way – just as knowledge of the alphabet and words in no way confines what you can write. It can be fun anyway going against conventional wisdom. So the colour attributes starting on page 143 are an 'alphabet' of colour for you to use at your own discretion, whether composing that painting, choosing a colour scheme for an interior, or deciding on a suitable colour for a product that you might want to blend in with a particular environment. A lot of office products are grey or neutral so that they stand a better chance of blending in, although, taken to extremes, this can lead to bland and even bleak environments. On the other hand you may want to shout 'look at me I'm different' – the colourful and translucent Apple iMac computer introduced in 1997 certainly did that! Our response to colour is also affected by the material or texture of the product it is applied to. For example a blue leather sofa may seem unnatural or even awful, but a sofa covered with a blue textile material might be more acceptable.

As noted above, to the human observer a particular colour is affected by the placing of other colours next to it and is not a constant entity in its own right (see simultaneous contrast below). Colours and tones are always relative to each other. A simple example of this can probably be found in your wardrobe. Put all your black clothes next to each other and you will immediately see that some are blacker than others. If you want those faded black trousers to look 'blacker' put on a white shirt or blouse – the contrast will emphasize the trousers' blackness and also make the shirt look whiter. Similarly, introducing a new colour into a painting will have an effect on your perception of the colours that existed beforehand – introducing a white or light toned colour will make the other colours appear darker, introducing a green will

make the reds appear 'redder' – for 'contrast' also applies to colours other than black and white. The illustrations within these pages attempt to demonstrate these and other principles.

colour systems, dimensions and classification

There are two methods of colour mixing – subtractive and additive. Mixing paints or inks together is subtractive mixing – for example, if the primary colours of red, blue and yellow paint were mixed together you would end up in theory with black but, in practice, the result is a muddy grey colour. You have *subtracted colour* (Figure 107). However, if you mix the primary colours of light – red, green and blue – (with a projector onto a screen) you would end up with white light; you have *added* colours together (Figure 108). But for practical purposes the remainder of this chapter will refer only to paint, or any other physical pigmented media.

Colours can be arranged in a colour circle as shown in Figure 109. The central triangle shows the three primary colours yellow, red and blue. Primary colours are those that cannot be mixed from other colours. The secondary colours are theoretically produced by mixing the primaries together in various ratios and the tertiary colours by mixing secondaries. In practice however much colour is lost due to the subtractive nature of mixing pigments. When sunlight hits a yellow painted surface, most of the colours in the visible spectrum are absorbed except (mainly) yellow, which we see reflected. Similarly a blue surface reflects mainly blue. However, when mixing blue and yellow paint in an attempt to produce green, for example, the yellow paint absorbs the blue part of the light and the blue paint absorbs the yellow light so all that we see is the small residue of reflected green contained in the original two pigments, as no colour is 'pure'. Green is not 'created' from mixing blue and yellow pigments but is merely a leftover.[8] The same principle is true when mixing red and yellow to produce the secondary colour of orange, or red and blue to produce purple, and so on with the tertiaries. It is therefore impossible to obtain a good range of paint colours from mixing only the three primaries. You will need to buy a wide variety of highly saturated colours to avoid ending up mixing mud.

Every colour has three basic properties (or dimensions): hue, tone and chroma. Altering just one of these properties usually affects the other two in some way. For example reducing the saturation of the bottom red in the right-hand chroma diagram in Figure 110 also lightens its value. In colour terminology, lightening a colour by adding white is called a tint, darkening a colour by adding black is called a shade – 'a tint lighter or a shade darker'.

Many attempts have been made over the centuries to classify colours in a systematic way; however the first real practical systems were invented independently by Albert Munsell in 1905 (Figure 111) and Wilhelm Ostwald in 1916. The Ostwald model is a 'closed' system however and the 'open' Munsell method eventually became the accepted standard on which more recent systems are based. The Munsell system allows the addition of more highly saturated colours to be added as manufacturers develop them, whereas the Ostwald system does not.

The Munsell and more recent Pantone systems give specific reference numbers to particular colours; this enables users to specify colours remotely over the telephone for example. The Pantone reference system is the one most used by designers, but the simplest conceptual model of colour is the Munsell System. This system of colour categorization distinguishes uniform steps of difference in the appearance of colours when compared with each other. The system takes the form of a three-dimensional 'solid' or tree and has five principal hues and five intermediate hues arranged in a circle surrounding a central vertical axis:

• principal hues – yellow, green, blue, purple, red;

• intermediate hues – green/yellow, blue/green, purple blue, red/purple, yellow/red.

A Munsell specification consists of a hue reference, followed by a value and then a chroma reference, so that we get GY 6/4 (green/yellow), for example, with the oblique stroke dividing the value and chroma reference numbers. These reference numbers are internationally recognized colour standards.

Wilhelm Ostwald's system uses the same vertical central axis as the Munsell system, with black at the base through to white at the top. On a particular hue's 'page', however, the colours increase in saturation with each step towards the outside of the solid, converging on the single most saturated colour for a particular hue, thus completing a 'hue triangle' with its three corners of black, white and the most saturated hue. This fixed triangle therefore makes it impossible to add more colours.

In theory the three primary colours of red, yellow and blue could be used for printing coloured illustrations on paper using inks. From these three primaries, the secondaries and other intermediate colours can be produced but, as we have seen above, mixing the three primaries together does not in practice produce black. Therefore, the standard method of printing coloured images uses these three primaries as well as black, in printing terms these are referred to as CMYK – Cyan (process blue), Magenta (process red), Yellow and Key (black). Rather than mixing these coloured inks together, the coloured image is built up on paper using a grid of separate tiny dots of each colour, in varying quantities, placed adjacent to (or overlapping) each other, to produce a reasonably wide range of colours. This is analogous to the 'Pointilist' painting methods of the post-Impressionists at the end of the nineteenth century, in particular Georges Seurat, who discovered that more colourful and vibrant images could be created by placing small spots of paint next to each other – spots that appeared to blend together when seen from a distance. This avoids subtractive mixing where a lot of saturated colour is lost in the process of mixing the pigments together beforehand. Although CMYK is adequate for most printing requirements, better quality colour images can be produced by using six base colours, the four of CMYK plus orange and green, and this is the basis for Pantone's 'Hexachrome' colour system.

So much for classifying colours into systems. As designers and artists we now need to know what happens when *composing* with colour – what are those special attributes and effects of colour that are created when we place different colours next to each other? There follows a list, by no means exhaustive, of things to watch out for and use (or intelligently ignore) according to your intentions.

attributes and effects of colour

1. Complementary Colours These intensify (contrast) each other – and are those colours lying opposite one another on the colour circle. This is used a lot in the visual arts, interior design and advertising to catch the eye. In the example shown in Figure 112, the reds in the two smaller squares are identical, but one can be made to appear redder (more highly saturated) by surrounding it with a different colour, in this case green – red's

complementary. A combination of contrasting coloured designs is often used to express fun or excitement, for example the colour schemes used in toys or the packaging designs for fireworks.

2. Contrasting Colour As well as the complementary colour contrast above, other juxtapositions of colours can also provide contrast, for example warm colours next to cool colours or a light tone next to a dark toned colour. Colours are often placed against a black background in order to make them stand out, for example by placing flowers in front of a dark fence in the garden. This is also why flowers appear more colourful after the rain, as well as the surrounding soil becoming darker, the wet petals reflect more light. The use of the contrasting (hue *and* value) striped chevron design in Figure 113 helps to attract our attention to possible danger, said to originate from the appearance of a wasp or other stinging insect, and we also automatically look for 'edges' of things – there are a lot of eye-catching edges in the chevron design. The message is 'notice me and keep away!' – a striking design even in black and white.

3. Harmony Colours lying close together on the colour circle/solid are said to be harmonious (Figure 114), that is, non-contrasting colours. Some commentators have argued however that the *complete* colour circle is harmonious because, going around the perimeter, no two opposites are placed next to each other and each hue can blend smoothly into the next one without sudden change. Johannes Itten said that different colours having a similar tone (lightness or darkness) can also be harmonious when placed together. Like much in art and design however, this is open to interpretation, and many individuals regard certain colour combinations as harmonious even though they may be made up of completely different hues. Many well-known paintings in fact confirm this principle, although this also may be to do with 'balance' (see below).

Too much harmony, however, can lead to visual boredom and it is often a good idea to introduce a small splash of colour and/or pattern to relieve the monotony. The harmonious warm colours of the room surfaces and furnishings illustrated in Figure 115 are spiced up a little by the inclusion of the reddish painting on the wall (and could be spiced up further by the placing of a green plant adjacent to the red painting). Cover up this painting and see the difference. This is another example of a small element or detail having a very large impact on the overall design.

4. Discordant Colours The opposite of harmony. The reversal of natural tones of colour when placed together, for example pale violet against dark orange, is generally regarded as giving unpleasant combinations (Figure 116).

5. Simultaneous Contrast Identical areas of tone or colour can be made to appear different by placing other, differing tones or colours around or next to them. The example shown in Figure 117 shows an illusion by Edward H. Adelson – the two squares A and B are in fact the same tone of grey, as demonstrated in the second image.

6. Colour Modification Similar to simultaneous contrast – any colour is likely to be modified by the colour placed next to it. Figures 118 and 119 show that the identical colours of the small central squares can appear to be modified slightly by surrounding them with different colours. The same orange looks more 'yellowy' when surrounded by red, and more 'orangey' when surrounded by yellow. Surrounding a neutral grey tone with a strong colour has the effect of 'pushing' that grey slightly towards the surrounding colour's complementary. Thus a neutral grey can appear greenish when surrounded by red.

7. Warm Versus Cool Colours The colour circle is often referred to as having a 'warm' side and a contrasting 'cool' side. Reds, oranges and some yellows are generally regarded as warm colours, whilst blue, green and some purples are perceived as cool. However, even a particular hue (colour) can be made warmer or cooler – Figure 120 shows warmer and cooler versions of blue and yellow. Even the colour red can be 'cooled' somewhat by reducing the level of saturation, as shown in the chroma illustration in Figure 110, although generally any red will always remain warm compared to blues and greens. There can also be warm and cool versions of whites and greys, depending on the presence of a small amount of warm or cool hue in the mix. More interesting greys can be produced by mixing complementary colours together, for example red and green pigment, rather than mixing just black and white.

8. Spatial Properties of Warm and Cool Colours Generally, warm colours appear to advance, whereas cool colours recede. This is probably to do with our perception that far away landscapes and mountains become a more blue/purple colour with increasing distance. This is caused by the lower frequency (less energetic) wavelengths of warm colours being filtered out by the atmosphere over long distances.

Light colours or tones tend to enlarge an area or volume, conversely dark colours or tones tend to reduce an area or volume. These effects are used a lot in interior design, for example a dark coloured ceiling appears to be lower than a light coloured ceiling and a white painted room looks bigger than a dark toned room. In the early twentieth century the artists and designers of the Dutch DeStijl movement deliberately used colours to control the perceived spatial qualities of a building, both internally and externally.[9]

Coloured and white surface areas were used to modify the volumes created by a building's physical mass – making walls, floors and ceilings appear to 'float' in space, causing some areas to advance while others receded. Black lines created 'edges' where none previously existed and black border-lines also served to emphasize *real* edges. Colour experiments in DeStijl paintings also explored these themes and colour was used by DeStijl designers in their furniture designs to emphasize solid and surface elements and the spatial relationships between them.

As well as altering our perceptions of space, different patches of colour or tones placed next to each other on a flat surface can also give the illusion of a bumpy surface, so colour can also suggest textured surfaces. For example the strips of adjacent but different greys in Figure 110 may give rise to an expectation of feeling 'ridges' if you were to run a hand across them.

9. Modifying Shape and Proportion Applying *patterns* of colour or tone can affect our perception of an area, or emphasize one of its dimensions. For example if you wanted to accentuate the length of an oblong or similar shape, place stripes in that direction. Similarly if you wanted to minimize or break up the lengthwise dimension, place the stripes at 90°. This is often used in fashion design where an individual may want to appear taller and slimmer, or alternatively reduce his or her apparent height (Figures 121 and 122).

10. Weight of Colour and Perception of Form and Detail A dark-coloured three-dimensional object can appear heavier than the same object painted in a light colour. This is also true in two dimensions – a dark shape has more visual weight than a light shape, for example in a painting or a work of graphic design. A dark colour usually doesn't show a three-dimensional product's highlights and shadows particularly well, some of the form and detail may be lost to the eye. This is sometimes used to advantage in a person's choice of clothes however – a black garment doesn't show highlights and shadows very well as the (often matt) material absorbs light, therefore helping to hide those unwanted bodily bulges!

Colour and surface texture can affect our subjective perception of otherwise identical shapes and forms. For example a particular car seems to work best in a particular colour. A more objective approach however is favoured by car designers when developing and fine tuning a car's form and detail. At some stage in the development of a car's form, designers will use full-scale sculpted clay models that are eventually covered in patches of thin thermoplastic sheet, first warmed in hot water and then stretched over the clay's surface to provide a smooth skin (even over compound curves) that can then be spray painted to better reveal the sculptural surface. Light grey or silver paints are usually chosen having a silk surface finish (somewhere between gloss and matt) as this better shows off the forms under most lighting conditions – without the confusing glare and bright reflections caused by a high gloss surface on the one hand and insufficient visual information given off by a dull light-absorbing matt surface on the other. This is something to bear in mind with the design develop-ment of any three-dimensional object where form and detail are important.

11. Flicker Effect The illusion of independent movement, where two colours very similar in tone, but otherwise extremely different in hue, are put against each other (Figure 123). The black-and-white receptors in our retina have difficulty in finding an edge where the two colours meet – therefore the elements can appear to move or float about independently. This is most apparent with blues and greens seen against oranges and reds (contrasting warm and cool hues). This effect is often seen on the covers of children's books – for example red text on a blue background and on advertising hoardings and magazine adverts. This juxtaposition of colours is often also used to enliven certain products, for example toys and bicycles.

12. Zing   A small patch of highly saturated colour amidst less saturated colours or greys (Figure 124). Often used in advertising and graphics generally to attract attention – it also could be used to highlight an important control knob on a product.

13. After-images The apparent reversal of colours and tones when the colours being observed are suddenly replaced by a plain white area. This is caused by the green receptors (for example) in the retina 'tiring out' (a reduction in the frequency of cell firing) after a period of viewing a green surface. Thus, when the image is suddenly replaced by a white sheet, green signals are reduced, leaving red and blue receptors to dominate and 'show' magenta (purple/red) until the eyes recover. To try this reversal for yourself – first of all cover everything on the page except the illustration in Figure 123 with plain white sheets of paper. Stare at the image for a few seconds and then cover the image with an opaque white sheet and stare again. After a few seconds the pattern of colours will be appear in their opposites of green and orange as an after-image. These techniques have been used a lot in Op Art and advertising. The most commonly experienced after-image is the one we 'see' after staring at an illuminated light bulb – the black after-image seems to follow us around for a few seconds after diverting our gaze from the light. This also proves that colours are generated within the brain and do not exist 'out there' – the eye/brain simply converts different wavelengths of light in the visible spectrum into the colours that we perceive.

14. Balance   For example, a small area of red is 'equivalent' to a large area of blue. A highly saturated colour, such as a red area in a painting, immediately demands more of our attention than a dark blue area, for example. If you are going for a balanced composition you will need to 'balance' the red area with a much larger area of another, less attention-seeking colour, as applied to the design of GNER's railway carriage shown in Figure 125. However, there are no rules that say you can't have an all-red train; a line of red carriages seen passing through green foliage would certainly be more noticeable (and safer?) and even could be regarded as kinetic art.

15. Monotone   Rather than make features stand out using different colours, another approach is to colour everything the same. For example the controls on the food mixer shown in Figure 126 are coloured the same as the main casing. Handled properly this 'less-is-more' modernist approach can lend an understated elegance to products and the all-white Kenwood Chef food mixer is regarded as a modern classic of product design.

16. Constancy   The brain intervenes to tell us that different surface areas of an object are the same colour, even though the areas in shadow appear darker.

case studies

Interior Design – Michael Graves' Design for Team Disney

We associate traditional productions by the Walt Disney Company with a certain cheerfulness. The wonderful colour and tonal compositions of Disney's animations, particularly those of his early hand-drawn animated films, serve to manipulate our emotions. For example the shifting colours and tones of a film could make us fearful of the dark interior of a forest at night, or alternatively the lyrical image of a spring morning in the countryside next to a stream can lift our spirits. Colour, light and space continue to affect our mood even when we're not in the cinema or following a story. Michael Graves' mural and colour scheme for Disney's dining room shown in Figure 127 successfully captures that playful, optimistic quality of Disney and happily marries these with the more serious business side of the company. Executives will hopefully return to their work refreshed and uplifted by the interior design.

There is a preponderance of light tones and colours in the interior that contribute to the feeling of spaciousness, as does the use of pillars rather than partitions or walls – providing a balance between openness and intimacy, perhaps appropriate to a 'works canteen'. The colours are mostly on the warm side of the palette and the use of juxtaposed complementary colours adds vibrancy, magnified by the contrasting tone of the dark ring of the ceiling aperture. We physically have to lift our heads to view the mural, the opposite of a cast-down posture – lift our heads and we lift our hearts. The use of contrasting patterns adds to its playful qualities and our eyes can delight in hopping around the details, analogous in music perhaps to a playfully joyous jazz session.

Mark Rothko Painting

In contrast to the cheerfulness of Michael Graves' mural for Walt Disney, many would find Russian-born Mark Rothko's print *Light Red Over Black* a much more sombre composition. It does appear, however, as though there's a red glow behind the dark rectangles, which warms or nurtures us to some extent – we usually regard red as a positive colour but we are prevented from fully benefiting from the 'heat' by the two obstacles of dark depressing shapes hovering in front in Figure 128. This impression might seem to go against the title that Rothko gave to the print but the title probably refers to the patch of lighter red at the top hovering above the dark rectangles. However, Rothko said he did not want his (often huge) paintings to be regarded as mere colour exercises. Rather, he hoped that the onlooker would undergo something akin to a religious experience similar to the one he had while painting them. He regarded his paintings as intimate and intense but he cannot control the response of the viewer and, on one level, we cannot help but be interested in them as colour compositions.

Although regarded as one of the American Abstract Expressionists, Rothko maintained that he was not interested in abstract relationships between form and colour, and that his real goal was the expressions of man's often powerful emotions, for example ecstasy or tragedy, using colour compositions to evoke feelings in the observer. The dark purples and browns of some of Rothko's other paintings appear to many observers as much more depressing than the red and black example shown here. Indeed Rothko did suffer from severe mental health problems and after a long depressive illness ended up taking his own life in New York in 1970.

theory box

Formal Versus Contextual Aesthetics – The Personal and Universal

The eighteenth-century German philosopher Immanuel Kant believed that beauty was not a property of an object and existed only in the mind of the observer. Thus the sensation or experience of beauty is generated in response to an object – a view that is widely accepted today. Kant therefore believed that the experience of beauty was personal and individuals made their own judgements about what was and was not beautiful or tasteful. However, Kant also proposed that in addition to this personal experience there was also the possibility of universal beauty; a formal beauty that has nothing to do with a particular individual's subjective tastes. He proposed that universal beauty could be established if an individual considered an object, or work of art (for example a portrait painting), from a disinterested point of view – that is, view the work as an end in itself and ignore any extraneous notions of who painted it, the identity of the person in the picture, or its monetary value. Critics and philosophers used this argument to defend the emergence of abstract art in the early twentieth century.

These concepts of personal *and* universal good taste were also supported by Kant's contemporary, the Scottish philosopher David Hume (1711–76). Hume also maintained that although we have an inbuilt facility to be impressed by beauty as an initial response, an individual's personal tastes can be improved through learning about 'standards' of good taste that have evolved over time and are held up as good examples by the many. Kant admired the Irish philosopher Edmund Burke's treatise on empirical aesthetics 'A Philosophical Enquiry into the Origin of our Ideas of the Sublime and Beautiful' (published in 1757), which maintained that standards of beauty and good taste are universal, having been judged so by many observers over a long period of time. For example there exists a large consensus of opinion that certain works by Leonardo or Bach are indeed standards of beauty and good taste.

Kant also divided the types of aesthetic response into the beautiful and the sublime. Beauty represents our pleasurable response to an object in terms of its order and harmony for example, whereas the sublime fills us with awe (which may be terrifying) in the face of something overwhelmingly powerful, which can often be formless and not necessarily artistic – for example the mind-blowing properties of the universe and night sky. Kant also said that in order for the object under consideration to be regarded as beautiful, the object should have been created for a purpose, even though we may not know what that purpose is or was. This 'purposiveness' is not the same as function, however, which for Kant was part of utility and maintained that utility has no role to play in our experience of beauty. Interestingly Kant was also reluctant to include colour as a property of beauty. He considered that the design of forms was what really mattered and that colour was mere decoration or afterthought.

Unlike Kant's formalist approach to universal beauty, Georg Wilhelm Hegel (1770–1831) believed that to appreciate a beautiful object properly the observer must take into account the context in which the object was created or observed. Hegel also maintained that in addition to expressing the spirit of the artist who created a work of art, objects of art also had the power to express the spirit of the particular culture to which the artist belonged. Hegel divided up the historical development of art into three main stages:

• *Symbolic* – for example, African masks and distorted figures or Egyptian images of gods – half-man half-animal creations - representing meanings beyond their formal appearances.

• *Classical* – as exemplified by Classical Greek sculpture, which aimed at recreating the appearance of physical perfection, to the exclusion of just about everything else.

• *Romantic* – the expression of the internal emotions of the artist or subject, for example Munch's portraits of mental anguish, such as *The Scream*.

Fig 106 Visual music? – Wassily Kandinsky, Composition VI. Oil
on canvas. 195 × 300 cm. c.1913.

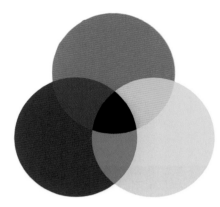

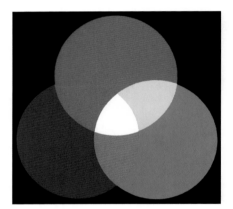

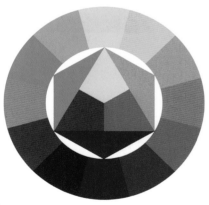

Fig 107 (top) Subtractive mixing with paints.
Fig 108 (middle) Additive mixing with light.
Fig 109 (bottom) The colour circle. Adapted
from Johannes Itten – Bauhaus. c.1920.

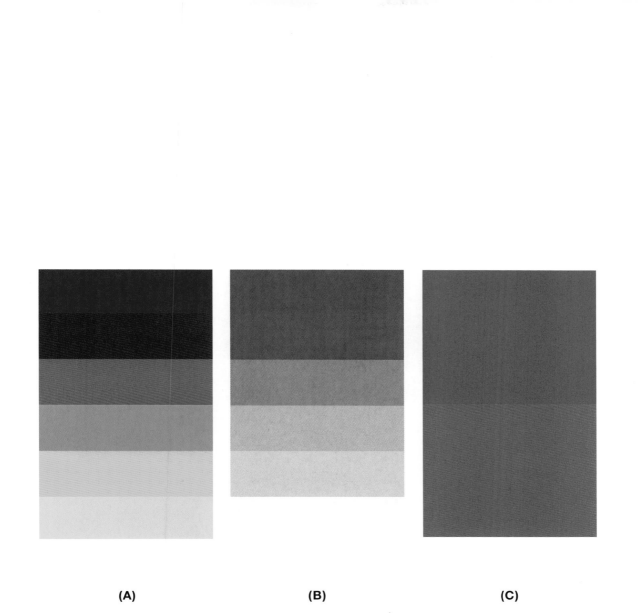

(A)   **(B)**   **(C)**

Fig 110 The three properties (or 'dimensions') of colour: **(A)** HUE – Red as distinct from blue, for example. **(B)** VALUE – The lightness or darkness of a colour, also referred to as TONE. The above shows the grey equivalents of the HUES on the left. **(C)** CHROMA – The strength or intensity of a colour – the top red is 'redder'. Also called SATURATION or LUMINOSITY.

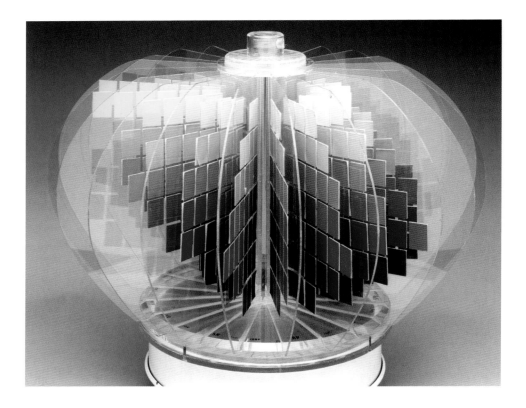

Fig 111 The Munsell colour tree. The colour 'pages' are arranged in a circle around a vertical axis. This axis starts with black at the base, increasing in lighter tones in stages up to white at the top, with each crresponding horizontal line of colour also becoming lighter in tone. The colours increase in saturation (or chroma) with each step towards the outside of each page.

Fig 112 Complementary colours. The two reds are identical.

Fig 113 Chevrons – An arrangement of warning colours (and striking design) –
contrasting colours and tones.

Fig 114 (top) Harmonic oranges and reds.

Fig 115 (bottom) Casa Araras: Bedroom. An example of using colour harmonies in warm muted colours where tranquil environments are required.

Figs 118 and 119 Colour modification. The same colour is
perceived as changing when surrounded by different colours.

Fig 120 Warm and cool versions of blue and yellow.

 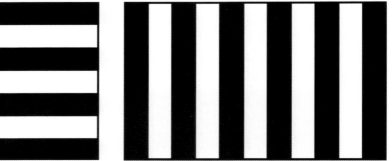

Figs 121 (top left) and **122** (top right) Two rectangles of identical proportions can be made to appear different sizes.
Fig 123 (bottom) Flicker effect – the illusion of independent movement.

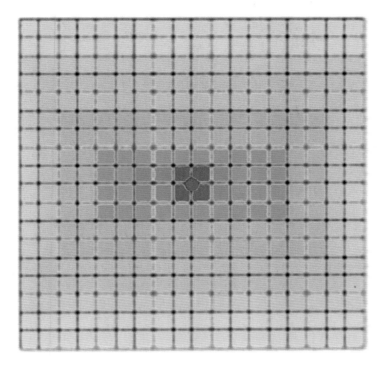

Fig 124 (top) 'Zing' – an attention-seeking colour highlight.
Fig 125 (bottom) Colour balance as applied to Great North Eastern Railways livery.

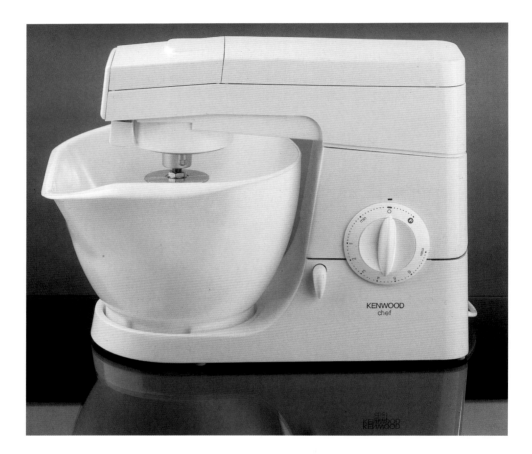

Fig 126 1980s Kenwood Chef KM300 food mixer – the application
of an overall single colour in product design.

Fig 127 A positively cheerful and optimistic interior design and colour scheme for the executive dining room, Team Disney – Michael D. Eisner Building, Burbank, CA. By Michael Graves. 1986.

Fig 128 Light Red Over Black. Mark Rothko. c.1960.

chapter five

—

drawing, communication and expression

chapter outline

Designers need to be able to communicate their abstract ideas and thoughts to other people – their colleagues, the client or simply the spectator in an exhibition. Often these ideas need to be made visible very quickly, perhaps making design changes during an ongoing conversation. Being able to sketch quickly and reasonably accurately can also help significantly in the creative process – by making problems visible and helping to solve them.

Computers are currently far too slow and cumbersome in these early stages of a design process, although some designers like to use digitizing tablets on which they can draw by hand with a stylus – but this still requires good drawing skills. Computers are superb at producing photo-realistic visuals at subsequent stages of the design process, even providing animated 'walk-throughs' and exploded views of buildings and objects, although this realism comes at a cost – the time required for inputting the data can be considerable (although better and faster interfaces will become available in the future).

This chapter begins, however, with the birth of cave and rock drawings and goes on to discuss important developments and milestones in the history of drawing – the different reasons for depicting three dimensions on a 2D surface and different ways of achieving this. These include the 'technical' drawings of the Ancient Egyptians, the probable discovery of perspective by the Greeks, its (clumsy) rediscovery by the Romans and the perfecting of it by Brunelleschi and Alberti at the beginning of the Italian Renaissance. This chapter discusses and demonstrates modern perspective methods and the importance of lines and line quality, light and shadow to better render the illusion of three dimensions, to suggest fast and slow shapes and to indicate different surfaces. Examples of simple construction methods are provided to enable the student to quickly produce reasonably accurate drawings of his or her ideas – whether these are geometrical or more organic flowing forms.

Some simple and quick methods are included for the construction of circles in perspective, the use of ellipse templates and other methods that can provide graphically powerful images with which to impress the client.

introduction

Why do designers and artists need to be able to draw competently? For a start we need to be able to communicate the ideas in our heads to other people – our colleagues, the client, or simply the spectator in an art gallery. How else can we quickly make abstract thoughts about 2D or 3D objects and spaces visible? The drawing needs to be reasonably good so that it's easy to 'read' and therefore easy to understand the designer's intentions. For many non-visually oriented people drawings are definitely not easy to understand and this becomes crucial when we present proposals for a new design to a client. A poor or difficult-to-understand visual will probably result in our not getting the job (for this reason it is a good idea

wherever possible to show the client a physical 3D model as well). Often visuals are posted or emailed to the client, so we sometimes don't even get the chance to present the work ourselves and help explain what the drawings mean. This chapter looks at some concepts and practical drawing methods used by designers today. It is interesting, however, to look first at man's early attempts to represent 3D reality on a 2D surface.

The birth of cave and rock representational drawings emerged about 40,000 years ago, and continued to appear independently at various locations around the world from this date onward (though recently found 'geometric' engravings have been dated to about 77,000 years ago). It has been suggested[1] that some of these drawings were simply ancient versions of graffiti which were

Fig 129 Dotted horse and hand prints, Pech Merle Caves, southern France. c.23000BC.

produced mainly by male 'daredevil adolescents' making images of their own obsessions, as well as trying to impress the girls. However, the anthropologist David Lewis-Williams proposed that drawing first emerged as a kind of tool – that by touching the images of figures and animal spirits drawn on the walls of caves people could actually enlist the help of these spirits in their daily lives, assisting them to catch more prey or cure the sick for example.[2] Only later did 'art' emerge as people noticed that drawings and tools adorned with 'useful' symbols could appear beautiful in addition to their utility.

Lewis-Williams argues that although Neanderthal man and other mammals experienced dreaming sleep, only Homo sapiens possessed a level of intelligence, sufficient memory and a language rich enough to enable them to discuss their dreams with each other and ascribe common meanings to these dreams (within a particular societal group). He proposes that the combination of dreaming and a rich language was the basis for all religious and supernatural beliefs – for example we often 'meet again' the deceased in our dreams. Put simply, nocturnal dreams were glimpses into another world – the dark underworld of human and animal spirits – that could also be entered via rock drawings on the walls of dark caves by shaman (spiritual healers). However, no one can know for certain what ancient rock art and other symbols meant to the people who created them many thousands of years ago. These speculations are nevertheless fascinating in themselves.

But how did Homo sapiens first make the intellectual leap that enabled 3D objects such as bison to be represented in two dimensions on the wall of a cave? Some have argued that this is simply due to the human trait of pattern recognition and that we are constantly and subconsciously looking for connections between things. For example, we often see faces and the shapes of animals in the patterns on a curtain, a cloud formation, or the stain marks on a wall. Others have suggested that drawing originated in face masks, or handprints made on the walls of caves (Figure 129), or even from footprints in the mud.

It is perhaps easy to see that a 2D hand print *looks* like a hand (just like a child today recognizes the shape of his hand after drawing a line around it) and this could have led to the drawing of the complete figure. Lewis-Williams proposes that the images produced by hallucinations and afterimages in the minds of shaman – during altered states of consciousness in dark caves lit by flickering lamps – were actually 'seen' as floating in front of them on the walls and ceilings of caves. Thus the drawings and paintings that followed (on these same walls) were simply attempts to fix such images so that others could see and extract power from them. The floating dark dots in the Pech Merle cave painting in Figure 129 might be the result of after-images produced by flaming torches that were used to illuminate the cave, though of course no one knows for sure.

The ancient Egyptian civilization also believed that drawings and paintings provided points of contact with the underworld of spirits. Egyptian art and hieroglyphs can be found painted or carved into the walls of their tombs. What makes these images so powerful, over and above 'ordinary' drawings elsewhere, is the particular culture and beliefs of ancient Egyptian society, which resulted in a unique way of 'seeing' and portraying people and objects. The images of humans and gods are particularly striking, with an individual's head, eyes, shoulders, hands and feet each drawn from the most recognizable viewpoint. For example, Figure 130 shows a man's head in profile, although his eye and shoulders are seen from the front. These drawings were created as 'technical drawings' of individuals rather than works of art, as the figures and objects they represent had a serious job to do in the afterlife. An arm hidden from view by the body might have implied that the person actually only had one arm, and a one-armed slave might not be so useful to the deceased in the afterlife. The Egyptians believed that a good likeness or 'specification' of an individual was essential in order to ensure their safe passage to heaven and future life thereafter. Thus the production of an accurate mask or bust of an important individual, together with drawings of his slaves, cattle, house, gardens and so forth, were buried with that person's embalmed and preserved body. Any later tampering with or destruction of these images and artefacts would have a dire effect in the afterlife of the person depicted (hence elaborate methods of concealment). As a consequence of these strict rules of portrayal, Egyptian art changed very little over 3,000 years.

Modern perspective drawing methods, or producing images using photography, are *illusionistic*. We have come to accept the invention and conventions of perspective through education – the trick of creating the illusion of the third dimension on a 2D surface. However, as the art historian Ernst Gombrich has pointed out, perspective drawings or photographs require some sacrifice of reality.[3] For example we know a person has two arms, but seen from the side the far arm may well be obscured by the body and would not appear in the picture. Tarzan, brought out of the jungle again, would not comprehend a drawing or a photograph. Lewis-Williams writes: '… one cannot "notice" a representational image in a mass of lines unless one already has a notion of images.' He refers to the work by the anthropologist Anthony Forge who, when he was working amongst the remote Abelam people of New Guinea, found they:

… had difficulty in 'seeing' photographs. If they were shown a photograph of a person standing rigidly face-on, they could appreciate what was shown. But if the photograph showed the person in action or in any other pose than looking directly at the camera, they were at a loss. Sometimes Forge had to draw a thick line around the person in a photograph so that people could retain their 'seeing' of him or her … Forge managed to teach some Abelam boys to understand the conventions of photographs in a few hours, but up until his tuition, 'seeing' photographs was not one of their skills.

drawing

Apart from its magical or symbolic role in history, drawing was, and continues to be, a superbly quick and easy way of thinking around ideas and solving problems. The usefulness of drawing is also true also for disciplines other than art and design – the Oxford mathematician Sir Roger Penrose is well known for using drawing as a tool to visualize concepts and problems in theoretical physics.

The speed of your drawing technique needs to keep up with the speed of your thoughts, otherwise ideas might fly out of the window and be forgotten. Often you can make connections between two drawings of different ideas on a piece of paper in front of you that you wouldn't otherwise have made – thus drawing aids creativity. For these 'quick-and-dirty' purposes it doesn't really matter about the finish quality of the sketches. All that is needed is a good tool to aid the thinking process and record ideas so that you don't forget them. Up until the end of the twentieth century, computers were generally useless at this early stage of the thinking process. They were simply too slow and cumbersome to input drawings at

Fig 130 Egyptian Eighteenth Dynasty Bas-Relief Painting of Horemheb. c.1348–1320BC.

a speed necessary to keep up with the speed of your thoughts. As the designer Richard Seymour said in an article on drawing in 2005: 'You can depict with a few strokes what something is going to be, before it exists, and it is this that sets it apart from 3D computer modelling, where all the data has to be put in before you can see what it is.'[4]

However, in recent years the appearance of flat digital drawing tablets – where your sketch appears directly under the stylus you are wielding (like a pen but with access to virtual colours and other tools) – may yet develop into something that actually betters pencil and paper, analogous to the word processor's impact on writing compared with an ordinary typewriter. However, many people think that pencil and paper will always be with us for both drawing and writing, for sheer ease of recording thoughts.

Developments in software now enable the computer to recognize your drawing style and convert 2D rough perspective sketches into accurate 3D renderings (should you require them) and are extremely useful in certain applications such as automotive styling. However, computers can also hinder the design process. Anything slightly complicated takes time to create – time that could have been better spent thinking and sketching out a lot more ideas on a piece of paper. Weaker students often end up becoming slaves to the computer rather than the other way round. Computers have been good at producing simple shapes with high quality rendered surfaces and colour/lighting options, so design proposals have often been unimaginative, boring and shallow. That is not to say that computers have not helped in the creative process – the opposite is the case and ways of manipulating more complex 3D forms are gradually becoming easier.

An example of computer-aided-creativity is being able to visualize reasonably realistic versions

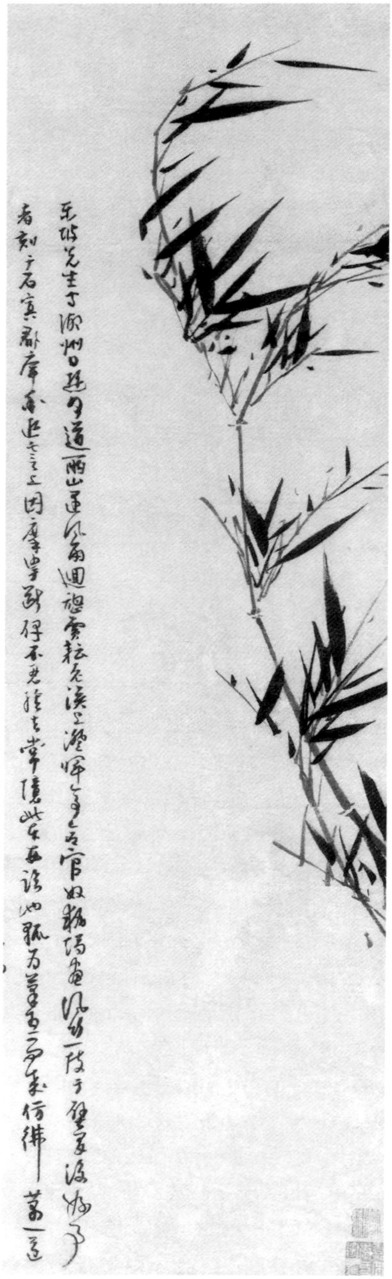

Fig 131 Fast lines – Bamboo in the Wind. Chinese thirteenth century Yuan Dynasty. Ink on paper. Artist Wu Zhen.

of your ideas at several stages throughout a project. This enables you to take a look around a product or walk through a building and maybe improve certain aspects you didn't realize were a problem, or change the colour scheme, lighting and/or texture at the touch of a button. Software can also help test out the physical properties and structural forces of a design proposal before building a real prototype, perhaps for safety reasons, saving time and money in the process.

lines and edges

Human beings and animals have specialized visual mechanisms for edge detection. Recognizing the edges of objects is crucially important in making sense of the world. Even if we see just a small part or silhouette of something we can usually recognize what it is. Our brains can make up edges and deduce meaningful shapes from the flimsiest of information. Although there are no lines around objects in nature, we have learned to use lines in the simplest type of drawing to describe an object's shape or form. Lines, and different types of lines, are hugely significant for artists and designers and can be manipulated in a variety of ways to better express their intentions. For example you may use lines to direct the observer's eye to some important part of the drawing, or better express the 'speed' of an object, or perhaps indicate a change of direction in the surface of something.

The American philosopher George Santayana had this to say about lines:

… the straight line is the simplest and not least beautiful of forms. To say that it owes its interest to the thought of the economy of travelling over the shortest road, or of other practical advantages, would betray a feeble hold on psychological reality.

The impression of a straight line differs in a certain almost emotional way from that of a curve, as those of various curves do from one another. The quality of the sensation is different, like that of various colours or sounds…There is a distinct quality and value, often a singular beauty, in these simple lines that is intrinsic in the perception of their form.[5]

Different types of lines are also used to good effect by cartoonists. Vilayanur Ramachandran proposes reasons why cartoon caricatures of real people are more effective than photographs – that by isolating a single visual modality, for example the outlines of someone's features, and then enhancing or exaggerating that modality (maybe the outline shapes of someone's protruding ears), enables the brain to focus more of its limited visual resources on the outlines, rather than sharing these resources for processing other informa-tion, for example skin colour, surface texture or shadows.[6] This leaves the brain free to concen-trate on the essentials of a person's appearance without distraction. Ramachandran calls this the 'peak shift effect' and says that this is: 'why an outline drawing or sketch is more effective as "art" than a full colour photograph' and 'why more is less in art'.

line quality

The variety of drawn lines is endless – fast lines, slow lines, expressive lines, passive lines, and many other differing line qualities on drawings – lines are among the most powerful tools of expression in the designer's vocabulary. Lots of lines drawn close together can even be used to shade an area to suggest form. Children draw with lines from an early age and, as noted above, our vision is 'tuned' to see the edges of things –

a person, tree, or whatever, that we interpret as lines when we draw. Changing the quality of lines in a drawing can make a big difference to its visual impact – compare the drawing of a bamboo plant in the wind (Figure 131) with the cave drawing of the horse in Figure 129. The 'fast' lines of the bamboo's stems and leaves suggest movement caused by the wind, even though it's only a still image.

Fast lines are also used to suggest movement and potential speed of man-made objects. Straight and slightly curving lines are used to draw sports cars or speedboats (we also 'read' them faster), whereas the meandering line, changes in direction, bumpy or smudgy lines, can convey slowness, or something that is still. As well as suggesting speed and direction, a fast line can indicate a hard smooth surface, and conversely a scruffy line can suggest a rough surface and/ or a soft material. Line quality is also important in engineering drawings where clarity is vital. In fact international standards exist that govern the different types of lines used for particular purposes in a drawing. Figure 132 shows an engineering drawing of a steel bracket where the object and dimension lines are all the same thickness. This leads to visual confusion; it is difficult to pick out the object among all the dimension lines. Figure 133 shows the correct weightings of object and dimension lines – the outline of the components is drawn quite thick, whereas the dimension lines are drawn much thinner – this makes the drawing much easier to understand. These types of 'flat' drawings are called orthographic projections and are probably best imagined as a cardboard box (containing a toy car for example) with the top, bottom, sides and end views of the car drawn onto the relevant box sides. Open the box out flat and the result is an orthographic representation of a 3D object (also sometimes called a develop-

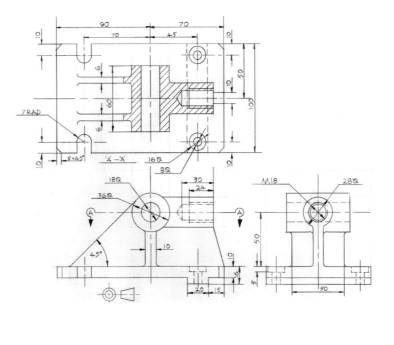

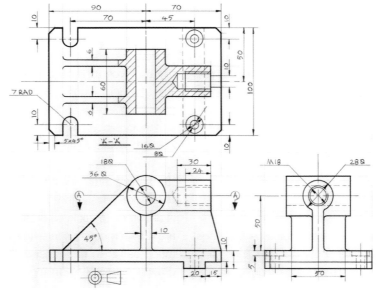

Figs 132 and 133 The same engineering drawings comparing the
effect of different line thicknesses.

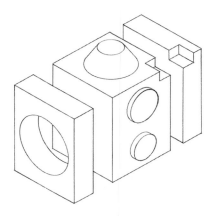

Fig 134 All line thicknesses identical.

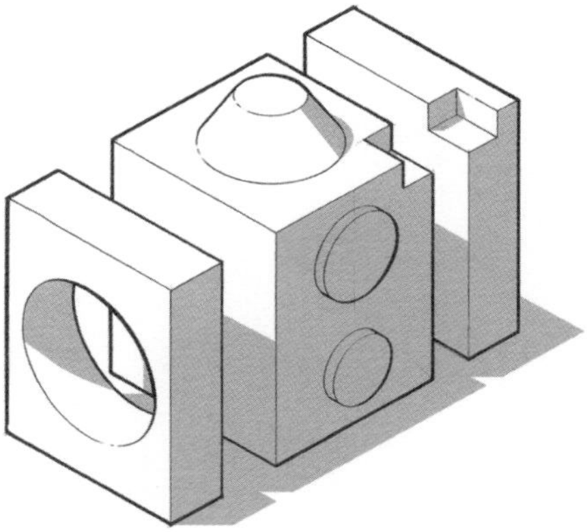

Fig 135 Thicker lines around individual components emphasize individual objects. Also the addition of shadows increase 3D impact.

ment drawing). Often just two or three views are needed for simple objects.

Figure 134 shows an isometric (no tapering perspective) exploded view of components, where all line weightings are identical. It is difficult to 'read' the drawing. Where does one component end and another begin? Figure 135 shows the same drawing with the outlines of each component drawn thicker than the rest. This helps to visibly separate each component. As well as making the drawing easier to understand, this technique gives it an added graphic impact. When drawing this type of view, designers use a convention that involves an imaginary spider. If the spider crawling over the surface of a component goes around an edge and disappears from view, then this line should be thicker than another edge, or line, that the spider crosses but can still be seen. Sometimes this thickening of silhouette is taken to extremes: designers often use a broad black line to emphasize and embolden certain important items in the designer's visual. This sometimes helps to bring the client's attention to a particular part of a drawing.

The addition of shadow further enhances the 3D aspect of the object. If you look closely at this drawing you will also see small gaps in those edge lines facing toward the light. These suggest highlights on the edges that lend the drawing a little more vibrancy.

Varying the thickness of line along its length can also be used to better express form and movement. Figure 136 shows a sketch of a horse by Leonardo da Vinci, in which the line varies in emphasis; for example, the thickened line that describes the rear leg muscles suggests deepening shadow and strengthens the illusion of three dimensions. This local thickening of a line can also help to suggest the weight of an object. For example, the line describing the underside of an object can be thickened and, as well as suggesting shadow, this can help to express the roundness or 'heaviness' of the object. Drawing a particular part of an object with greater emphasis and detail than the rest helps to focus the observer's attention on that particular aspect. This is frequently seen in portrait drawings and paintings where the all-important head and face are drawn in more carefully than the rest of the body, which is often left quite sketchy.

Drawing is a process of trial and error; you will probably never get it right at the first attempt. It is a

Fig 136 Study for the Sforza Monument. An exploratory sketch of a horse and rider by Leonardo da Vinci. c.1488

process of making mistakes, explorations, corrections and improvements carried out over time. So don't worry about your initial mistakes. Even Leonardo wasn't happy with his first attempts – his drawing of a horse shows limbs drawn in several different positions until he was happy with the result. This of course is also an exploration of how a horse moves in space. Evidence of mistakes, experiments and changes even add to a drawing's beauty, showing the workings of the artist's mind over time.

Tonal qualities in a drawing (areas of lighter or darker tones) can be used to further express three dimensions, as shown in the exploded view in Figure 135. The top areas of the object reflect more light as they face the sun and, obviously, those areas facing away from the sun are in shadow and are therefore shaded a darker tone. Curved or rounded forms will show smoother gradations of tone from light to dark as the surfaces turn away from the light source. This type of shading

in drawing is called 'chiaroscuro' – from the Italian for light and dark. It is usually a good idea (though there are of course exceptions) to use a range of tones in a drawing, from the darkest black pencil or marker through to the white of the paper. This will give the drawing more contrast and visual 'power' compared to a drawing in a greys or mid-tones only, especially if you are in a room presenting the drawing to an audience sat some distance away.

Although daunting to the novice, a clean sheet of paper offers the opportunity to flex the imagination, create new things and even change the world. A clean sheet of paper is wonderfully attractive as a sensual and infinite 'space' full of promise to the practised and creative person. Even seasoned artists and designers never lose that childlike thrill of making marks on paper. Indeed as adults we can still appreciate children's art as something special. Children's drawings and paintings have an honest response to the world untainted by the cunning visual trickery and artifice of adult art. For this reason child art on the classroom wall is often much more stimulating to look at than the paintings in an art gallery (see Figure 73 in Chapter 3).

In the process of learning to draw and becoming proficient you will inevitably fall in love with making lines and playing with shapes in the pursuit of producing beautiful objects. Thus drawing becomes a pleasurable and sensual experience and is also a skill that will last you a lifetime. A typographer or car designer will produce dozens, or even hundreds of drawings, each slightly different from the others, in search of that perfect shape or form. As noted elsewhere in this book, extremely small differences in line or shape can make a massive difference to the feel or beauty of an object. For this reason it is usually a good idea to use semi-transparent layout or marker paper on which to start designing things. For example the creation of a typeface or a family of cutlery will require many slight changes from the original sketch, and translucent paper allows you to trace over previous sketches without destroying the originals. Sometimes you might prefer a previous shape produced a few sheets back anyway, thus you can easily retrace your steps and start again from there. Drawing is a 'performance' requiring the integration of hand, eye and brain skills. You could say that the act of drawing a line is akin to ice-skating – a physically graceful 'drawing' of lines in the ice by an expert skater. Although computers can produce lines of infinite variety, designers still prefer to draw with the hand even on digitizing tablets – as Antony Grade, Head of Design at Renault Automobiles, said in 2006: 'it is the hand that leads'.

drawing and construction

Humans, animals and plant forms are probably the most difficult things to draw with any degree of accuracy. There are few straight lines in nature, but the artist can still use imaginary straight lines to help construct what he sees in front of him – stretch an arm out in front of you and hold a ruler up vertically (like a plumb line) to see where the sitter's nose intersects with their foot (or any other body part). You can then draw a vertical line on the page and mark approximately where the nose and foot occur on this line. You can even 'measure' roughly how far apart the nose and foot are from each other using the same ruler and, scaling up or down depending how big you want the drawing to be, measure off this distance on your drawing. This is what artists are doing when they stretch out an arm holding a thumb up in front of them – they're measuring how, for example, the size of someone's head compares with the size of the rest of the body. It is obviously important that the

arm is stretched out the same distance from the eye each time you measure something, otherwise big errors will be made.

For designers and artists dealing with buildings, interiors or manufactured objects, drawing or *constructing* something is somewhat simpler. Things made by machines, and assemblies of such objects – be they made of bricks, steel tubes or machined parts – are usually made up of straight lines, circles or other geometric shapes. Obviously computers are superbly accurate at constructing and drawing geometric shapes or assemblies. However, as mentioned above, the *speed* of sketching out ideas is often crucial in communicating and discussing rapidly changing concepts, perhaps during a conversation with a colleague. A 'sketch' can be drawn quickly and with reasonable accuracy so that it is understandable to someone else, even without resorting to rulers and other drawing aids.

One of the first things a budding artist or designer needs to understand is perspective and its importance in setting the scale of something – be it a table or a skyscraper. Also choosing a suitable viewpoint can give a strong clue as to how big or small a particular object on the paper is in relation to ourselves. If we can see onto the top of something, for example a table, this usually means the object is smaller or lower down than us. Conversely, if we cannot see onto the top surface of something, for example the flat roof of a building, then this must be taller than we are. However, this normality of human viewpoint five or six feet off the ground is often reversed by artists and photographers wishing to create an unusual composition – for example by taking pictures from ground level looking up, or looking down on something bigger than ourselves, often employing lenses wider or longer than our normal vision to enhance or distort the scene. At least one

Fig 137 A 'perspective' Fresco Painting of a Stage Set at Herculaneum c.AD50.

definition of an artist is someone who deliberately distorts reality in order to make us see and think about the world in a new way.

The fact that people and objects appear smaller the further away they are should seem obvious. However, people and objects don't actually get smaller with distance and to portray distance on a flat surface required a considerable conceptual leap. Early attempts at perspective can be seen in frescoes made around 2,000 years ago at Pompeii and Herculaneum, two Roman towns near Naples. The Romans had invented a sort of 'oblique' perspective (Figure 137), where lines of buildings in the same plane appear to head towards several vanishing points rather than a single point on the horizon. The Romans may have

learnt some of these techniques from the Ancient Greeks. In his famous treatise on architecture, the Roman architect and engineer Vitruvius credits the Greeks with important discoveries in the application of shading and perspective. Vitruvius describes two philosophers, Democritus and Anaxagoras, discussing an essay on pictorial illusion by Agatharcus (a fifth-century BC Greek painter of scenery for Athenian plays) where he explains how centre points of sight and distance positioned on a flat surface can guide the lines of buildings, making them appear to advance and recede – although examples of these apparently no longer exist. The Greeks certainly understood about foreshortening, as can be seen by the portrayal of circular shields and chariot wheels as ellipses in their paintings and designs on ceramics, as well as shading to suggest volume (Figure 138). For the Egyptians, however, their strict rules about drawing ruled out any likelihood of them ever discovering perspective for themselves. Other civilizations also attempted to create the third dimension in their drawings and paintings. For example, the Chinese had come up with a similar method to the Romans' oblique perspective by about the Middle Ages, although the buildings and figures do not decrease in size with distance.

Some eastern cultures regarded physical existence as a kind of 'floating' through nature and the universe, and this influence can be seen in many Chinese and Japanese drawings. According to Philip Rawson this: '… had its roots in a mixture of adapted Chinese Taoism and Buddhism, which denied any permanence, solidity, or absolute value to separate objects'.

The invention of modern linear perspective methods only really took off during the Italian Renaissance of the fifteenth and sixteenth centuries. Filippo Brunelleschi – the architect of Florence Cathedral's famous dome – discovered mathematical rules for linear perspective using the concept of parallel lines and planes converging at a vanishing point, or points, on the horizon line (the viewer's eye level). His contemporary Leon Battista Alberti invented a method of drawing through a 'window' in which the scene beyond the window is drawn on the transparent window pane by the artist who's eye position is fixed in space by a small ring attached to the apparatus. Figure 139 shows an engraving of Albrecht Dürer's drawing of a similar device. Sometimes the glass window had a grid superimposed on it – and these squares of the grid were also drawn lightly onto a piece of paper on the table top upon which the view was transferred and drawn directly. The *camera obscura* also aided the construction of perspective views and it is thought that this trick of producing an image in an enclosed box – on the inside face opposite a pin hole or lens – was widely used by artists of the Italian Renaissance and elsewhere.

As noted above, the idea that we should draw things smaller if they are further away seems straightforward to us now, but sometimes other priorities demand a different point of view. For example, in pre-Renaissance Italy, people's status in society could determine the size that they were painted in a scene: the more important they were, the bigger they would be drawn, regardless of where they appeared in space. So there is no correct way of drawing – it all depends on your priorities and what you want to express. The Cubists thought that drawing or painting an object (or scene) from only one viewpoint was too limiting – we know that there is more to a real object than just what we see from one particular standpoint – for example Picasso's cubist drawings of a violins and other instruments were attempts (among other things) to analyse and express the 'essence' of these objects seen through a number of

Fig 138 Foreshortening of circular wheels and use of shading. Greek c.340BC (from a royal tomb at Vergina – the God Pluto abducts Persephone to the underworld).

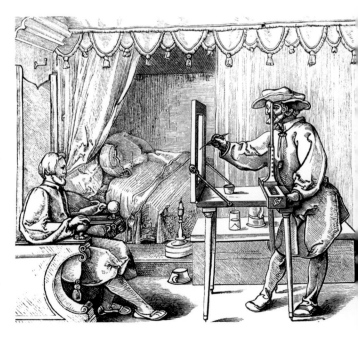

Fig 139 Drawing machine. Nineteenth-century engraving by Paul Lacroix, after Albrecht Dürer's original woodcut of 1527.

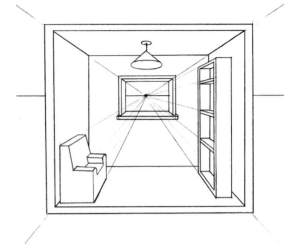

Fig 140 Single point perspective drawing.

audience responses belonging to other senses than the visual – kinetic, olfactory, tactile, even auditory – provided the objective associations are strong enough … a good work of sophisticated art may very well suggest the smell and feel of a woman through its evocative forms – and many other sensuous aspects as well.

To return to perspective drawing, there are three main types of perspective methods that can be employed to suit a particular scene or object. These all involve vanishing points – normally using single-point, two-point and three-point perspective. The vanishing point is where two parallel lines meet, or disappear, at a distance from the observer. For example for an observer standing between the rails of a railway track sees the two rails going off in the distance and appearing to merge at a point on the horizon. Figure 140 shows a view of the interior of a room in single point perspective. Like any drawing method, however, perspective drawing systems are illusions of reality and distortions are inevitable. The world is three dimensional and a drawing is produced on a flat surface. Straight lines and circles in perspective become distorted the nearer they come to the edges of a reasonably comfortable cone of vision – around 60° in humans (Figure 141). This distortion is sometimes exploited for effect by photographers using wide-angle lenses on their cameras. A building photographed using a fish-eye lens from a position half way up its height would produce many vanishing points, which, by a stretch of the imagination, could be reduced to just four – one at the centre of the earth, one in the sky and two on the horizon. The building or object would be way outside our normal cone of vision. Unusual perspective views can be fun but need to be handled with care. So don't expect all your perspective drawings to work perfectly; you

different viewpoints simultaneously on the canvas. This also includes the notion of the time taken to look at the object in the round, even including a painterly lyricism to suggest the musical sound these instruments make (a sort of visual/aural synaesthesia), as well as their surface textures to suggest the 'feel' of the wood. It could be argued that these paintings tell us more about the objects depicted than a conventional view or photograph would ever give us.

Artists have always attempted to suggest things other than the visual in their work – for example Edvard Munch's attempts to portray a person's inner turmoil or psychological state, or the suggestion of the invisible wind in Figure 131, causing the dynamic movement of the leaves. To quote Philip Rawson:

Sir Russell Brain has pointed out that the world of perceptions a man gains through the sense of sight is not limited to purely visual apprehension. The types which suggest a thorough-going objectivity in a work of visual art can arouse in a relatively wide

may well have to use considerable artistic licence in some part of a drawing to make it look right.

In all three perspective methods, one or two of the vanishing points occur on the horizon. A matchbox on a table easily fits within our normal cone of vision when looking down on it. This view, however, means that we can't usually see the distant horizon at the same time as the matchbox. Therefore, the vanishing points will be well outside any drawing of a small object and the sides of the box will appear almost parallel to each other as in Figure 142. Even if the horizon could be seen behind a low-level view of the matchbox, the vanishing points would still be well outside the frame. The key factors in determining the scale of an object in a perspective drawing are the size of the object, its distance from us and its resulting fit in our normal cone of vision. Even a large building can appear small when looking down from an aeroplane. The building will have the same degree of perspective taper as the matchbox because the relationship between the size of the object and the greater distance away of the observer's position in the sky, will result in a similar ratio.

When near a building, however, our cone of vision may be completely filled with the object (Figure 143). The resulting drawing may include some of the horizon, even sometimes include the vanishing points as in Figures 144–147. These illustrations show examples of two- and three-point perspective drawings of large buildings.

The horizon line is sometimes called the 'eye line'. This is because we can assume that the horizon is always at the same 'height' as our eyes – anything below the horizon is beneath us and anything above the horizon is higher than us. This still holds true if you are standing at the top of a high hill. If you can see the horizon (preferably across the sea), any other hill or object between you and the horizon with its highest point coinciding

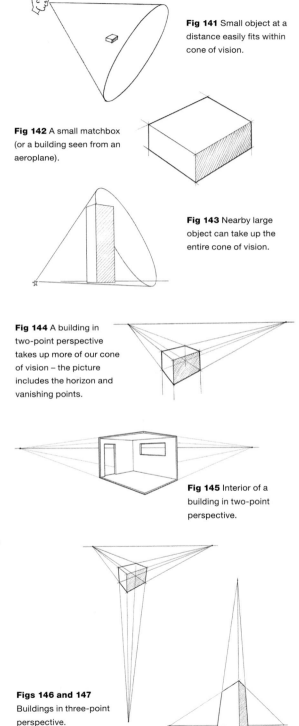

Fig 141 Small object at a distance easily fits within cone of vision.

Fig 142 A small matchbox (or a building seen from an aeroplane).

Fig 143 Nearby large object can take up the entire cone of vision.

Fig 144 A building in two-point perspective takes up more of our cone of vision – the picture includes the horizon and vanishing points.

Fig 145 Interior of a building in two-point perspective.

Figs 146 and 147 Buildings in three-point perspective.

Fig 148 Relationship between eye level and the horizon.

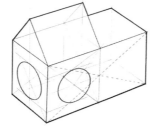

Fig 149 Major axis of the ellipse is always at right angles to the main axis of the cylinder.

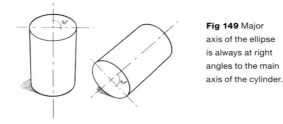

Fig 150 Different 'fatness' of ellipses. This drawing also shows a method of doubling the length of a box or building in perspective using diagonals.

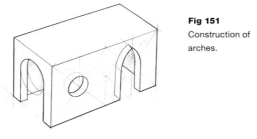

Fig 151 Construction of arches.

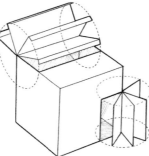

Fig 152 Arc of travel for hinged doors and lids.

with the horizon is exactly the same height above sea level as you are. If we imagined a cylindrical lighthouse (made up of a vertical stack of circles) with a halfway height that intersected the horizon, the circle or ellipse that coincided with the horizon would be seen exactly edge on.

In the example shown in Figure 148 the roof of the caravan is higher than the observer, so (on perfectly flat ground stretching from the observer to the horizon) the roof is above the horizon. The caravan's wheel is below eye level and is therefore below the horizon. The drawing shows a line of people, of exactly your height, standing at various distances between you and the horizon, this demonstrates the significance of the relationship with the observer's eye level and the far horizon.

The ability to draw reasonably accurate boxes in perspective is a very powerful tool in the construction of more complicated shapes. Drawing boxes is fairly straight forward but many newcomers find drawing circles in perspective much more difficult. There is just one important rule to remember – a circle in perspective is an ellipse – that is, it has a widest dimension (the major axis) and a narrowest dimension (the minor axis). Most people can have a good stab at drawing a tin of beans stood upright on a surface – as shown in the left-hand drawing in Figure 149. It is easy to see that the widest dimension of the top ellipse is horizontal, that is, the major axis of the ellipse is at 90° to the vertical axis of the tin (or cylinder). When the tin is laid on its side at an angle to the viewer, as in the right-hand drawing, *the same rule applies*.

This is true no matter from what angle the tin is viewed. The difficult part is deciding how 'fat' the ellipse should be. Figure 150 shows a box with sides at different angles to the viewer – the right side is more 'square on' to the viewer than the left side. Therefore, we need a fatter ellipse on the right side compared with the left. This involves judgement and experience – *so practise*. It is always useful to think of circles as the ends of imaginary cylinders. Note also the construction of the arched doorway in Figure 151 – this uses an ellipse in exactly the same way as above but only the top half of it needs to be drawn in. The lid and door in Figure 152 have been constructed using ellipses to determine the arc of travel and this determines the outer edge-point of the lid and door in various opening positions drawn in perspective. One way for the newcomer to produce accurate boxes with accurate ellipses is to use isometric drawing. Examples of this type of drawing are shown in the exploded views earlier. There is no tapering perspective involved and all the sloping lines are drawn parallel (at 30° to the horizontal) either side of the bottom front corner of a box. This makes the resulting boxes look somewhat distorted, but nevertheless still results in a particularly strong graphic image. You can produce good results with this method quite easily using a 30/60 degrees setsquare and an isometric ellipse template (35° 16'). The ellipse template can be used on any face of the cuboid (remember the same rule about the relationship between the ellipse's major axis and the cylinder's axis still prevails) and is therefore a cheap and easy way of producing visuals – especially when producing exploded views.

To take construction a little further we can introduce the important role of the diagonal line. You often need to find the mid-way point of a wall or surface in perspective. On the face of it this would seem to be a difficult judgement, as the wall appears to become smaller with increasing distance. However, we know that if we draw two diagonals joining the opposite corners of a square or rectangle, then they must cross in the middle. This is a simple but very powerful device. Thus we can apply this method to any rectangle or square

drawn in perspective and automatically discover the centre. You can carry on subdividing each half into quarters, eighths and so on, by this method. The central ridge of the pitched roof in Figure 150 was determined by extending a vertical line upwards from the central cross in the front wall of the house, and the extension added to the right hand end of the house (of exactly the same width of the original house) was calculated graphically by projecting a diagonal line from the bottom left corner to the mid-height of the original right hand vertical edge of the house. This diagonal line is then projected further until it intersects with the extended horizontal line of the original 'eaves' line.

These construction methods using boxes, diagonals and ellipses can also be applied in the construction of more organically shaped objects such as soft shaped cameras and cars. The loose sketch of a car in Figure 153 shows how its construction was made easier by first drawing a box in perspective. This helped to position the wheels at the corners. The longitudinal centre lines of the car were found by using diagonal crosses as above. After roughly drawing in the curves of the car freehand, the drawing can be tightened up further by using the nearest ellipse template to hand for the wheels and French curves for the main body curves. Sets of French curves can be found in most good stationery or graphic arts shops, as can isometric ellipse templates. Sets of other angles of ellipse templates can also be found here but are usually more expensive. Many car designers use 'ships curves' – templates originally designed for use by naval architects but also extremely useful for drawing those long gentle curves for anything else. These templates are very expensive but it is possible to make them for yourself in a workshop from sheets of PVC or Acrylic plastic (PVC is to be preferred as the chemicals in dry markers can attack the surface of Acrylic).

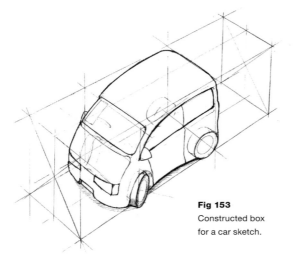

Fig 153
Constructed box
for a car sketch.

The angle of a particular ellipse template is written on its surface. For sets of templates these angles can start at around 5°, stepping up in 5° intervals up to 85° – the higher the number, the fatter the ellipse. These angles represent a circle drawn or cut into a flat cardboard sheet with the viewer's eye looking directly at the circle; therefore, at 90°, the viewer would see a perfect circle. If the sheet is leaned away from the viewer at any angle, then the circle would appear elliptical. So at an angle of say 15° the ellipse appears quite thin. In true perspective drawings, a circle would be slightly distorted, as we would see more of the half circle nearest to us than the half furthest away. However, the eye does not notice this and we can 'cheat' by using ordinary ellipse templates, as shown in Figure 154.

light and shadow

We depend of course on sunlight to enable us to see things and make sense of the 3D world. Sunshine and shadow together provide enough information about everyday objects to prevent us from bumping into them. However, those

people who depend more on light and shadow than the average person – such as a photographer, sculptor or designer – like to manipulate light (either sunlight or artificial light) in order to enhance a particular subject. Landscape photographers often choose early mornings or late afternoons to capture images – trees and buildings stand out much more in three dimensions when lit by a low-level sun, as one side is strongly lit and the other lies in deep shadow – increasing the contrast and accentuating their forms. Further, surface textures are better seen in a low-level raking light – sometimes used to bring out the brushstrokes when analysing a painting, for example, or photographing the texture of woven materials. In 3D art and design, lighting is crucial to both the seeing and presentation of artefacts.

Art schools were traditionally equipped with movable light sources in the life drawing studios. Figure 155 shows a studio in the Glasgow School of Art c.1910, where the drawing of plaster casts was practised. Note the moveable hanging electric light bulbs – moving one or two of these around a plaster cast allowed the student to create changing highlights and shadows on the casting, enabling him or her to choose the most suitable arrangement which best showed off the form and detail – just as anyone would do before taking a photograph of the same object. This technique seems to have been largely forgotten

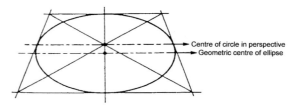

Centre of circle in perspective
Geometric centre of ellipse

Fig 154 Centre of ellipse in perspective.

Fig 155 Glasgow School of Art drawing studio showing moveable light sources. c.1910.

in many of today's art schools, where the objects and figures to be drawn are artificially flattened by the surrounding ambient light produced by many fluorescent strip lamps covering the ceiling.

The 3D qualities of drawn objects can be emphasized by the use of simple shadows. Usually the shadow is just a supporting element in the drawing – it's the actual object we are most interested in. For this reason we can often get away with a simple approximate shape of a shadow quickly sketched in – the observer does not notice inaccuracies as long as it is a believable shape. Sometimes, however, you may want to increase the dramatic element of a drawing

– this can be achieved by lighting objects from unusual angles, or through creating unusually large shadows by placing the light source close to the object – a technique often used in animations. Another unusual lighting effect occurs in the theatre where footlights illuminate the actors or performers from below – the dramatic appearances created by these unnatural lighting angles were used to particularly good effect in paintings by the French artists Toulouse Lautrec and Edgar Degas. As well as using this technique in drawings, you may want to use unusual lighting angles when photographing your models to enhance their visual impact.

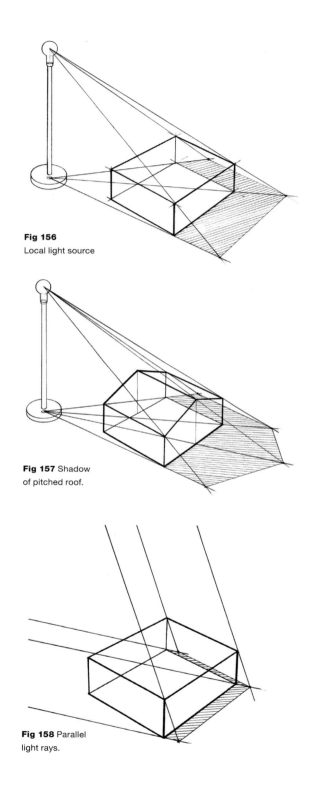

Fig 156
Local light source

Fig 157 Shadow
of pitched roof.

Fig 158 Parallel
light rays.

The basic principles of constructing shadows are shown in Figure 156 using a local light source. This method can be also be used for interiors lit from within as well as objects lit from without. In addition to drawing lines representing the rays of light – the lines drawn through the top corners of the cube in the drawings – you will need to draw 'ground lines' from a point directly below the light source on the ground (for example the base of a table lamp) through the corresponding bottom corners of the cube. Where these two lines meet is where the shadow point of a cube's top corner hits the ground. This needs to be repeated for all the corners and the points then joined up. This is the shape of your shadow on the ground. Of course the front face of the actual cube would also be in the shade but this has been left unshaded for clarity. If the object has a pitched roof, or other higher or lower feature, you will still need to find its equivalent point on the ground directly beneath it and draw the ground line through that point (Figure 157). A large shadow is created if the light source is near the object, to achieve small shadows we need to move the light source further away and

higher up at a steeper angle. We can assume that the rays from a distant sun high above in the sky are parallel to each other when falling upon relatively small objects – though if the sun is low in the sky, and you can see it just above the horizon in your drawing, then the rays will not be parallel and you will of course create large shadows again. Figure 158 shows the same object lit by a far away sun. This allows the use of parallel rays of light and also parallel ground lines. The rays and ground lines can be of any angle to suit the desired size of shadow but they must come from the same side of the object.

Some tapering objects, like a cones or pyramids with a low height but wide base, will not cast a shadow on the ground next to them – if the light source is above a certain height the shadow of the tip of a pyramid will fall within its base. Interestingly the ancient Egyptians regarded this as a symbol of eternity – the moving shadows cast on the ground by sundials and obelisks marking the passage of time were absent from the pyramid tombs of pharaohs when the sun was at a certain altitude.

case studies

Development Sketch of a Car Styling Concept

This concept sketch demonstrates how the looseness of pencil, pen, marker and pastel on paper, having reached a reasonably satisfactory stage, can be firmed up with the use of ellipse and curved templates. A manufactured object like a car needs to be drawn with smooth fast lines; a wobbly line would detract from its sleekness and could even suggest that the object is itself made from a soft material. The lines help to describe the surface directions of the car (rather like a Henry Moore's drawing of a figure) and the use of pastel, first scraped into a pile of blue dust with a scalpel and applied with cotton wool on marker paper, also helps to express the 3D form of the car through light and shade

Fig 159 Car styling concept sketch, lit by light reflected from below.

(chiaroscuro).

In this example the car is lit from below with reflected light, reversing the natural effect of overhead sunshine or street lighting and thereby increasing the drama of the drawing. A sketch such as this may appear unfinished; however, it contains enough information for us to get a good grasp of the form of the proposed design and also some idea of the sort of harmonious detail with which to delight the eye. The 'colour' of the rear lamp clusters has been suggested with areas of dark tones that contrast with the light colour of the bodywork. Similarly the darker tones of the side windows suggest tinted glass.

Although the drawing is sketchy, the loose-and-fast treatment adds a dynamic excitement and can even suggest forward motion. Our brain automatically fills in the missing (or hinted at) parts of the car and this, rather like the very powerful effect of a caricature sketch that only concentrates on essentials, enables the brain to focus more of its limited visual resources on the outlines rather than sharing these resources for processing other information or distractions. The weight of the lines has been varied, suggesting where parts of the surface might disappear round a curve or perhaps just indicating a slight change of direction in the surface. Also heavier lines serve to emphasise the door shut lines – these are 'linear shadows' where the edges of a door meet the adjacent body panel. The overall effect is a quick sketch that allows the designer to show his or her ideas to colleagues without investing too much time on a proposal that might be soon discarded. Also it is human nature to become over-protective (or too precious) towards a work that you have put a lot of time and energy into, therefore in the early stages of the design process all you need is a quick technique that sufficiently expresses your ideas in an exciting (and even beautiful) way.

A Sketch for the New Design Museum in Holon, Israel, by Ron Arad using a Digital Drawing Tablet

Fig 160 Ron Arad sketch using a digitizing tablet. c.2007.

Pencils and paper will always be with us as simple and speedy tools to aid our thinking processes and to help us communicate our ideas to others. However, developments in flat digital drawing tablets have enabled the simplicity and speed of sketching by hand to be combined with the many advantages of computer power. The sketch appears directly under the stylus you are wielding, similar to pen and paper – although lacking that certain 'resistive' feedback that the paper gives you on the feel and control of drawing a line. Many design tutors still prefer traditional blackboard and chalk over 'slippery' whiteboards and markers for this very reason, especially when it comes to drawing over large areas. The advantages of the drawing tablet, however, lie in its access to virtual colours and graphics programs, as well as 3D programs that enable you to view objects from any point of view in 3D space. You can also save (and print) a drawing at various stages throughout its development, thus keeping a record but also allowing you to retrace your steps if necessary, something not always easy with traditional sketching methods. The digital drawing tablet also allows you to import computer files, scans of existing artwork, photographs, plans and elevations, and other drawings that you can sketch or scribble over by hand without harming the original.

The digital sketching tablet may yet develop into something that actually betters drawing with pen and paper and may eventually become something you can roll up and carry in your pocket. You will still need to learn to draw reasonably well in the first place, however, as a bad drawing will be just as difficult to understand (and lack beauty) whether you are using a digital tablet or pencil and paper. The tablet drawing in Figure 160 shows a sketch by Ron Arad, a quick rendering combining lines, tone, colour, solids and spaces, and it could be argued that this is more stimulating to the creative mind than simple pencil drawings (and is also a colourful something you can produce whilst travelling on the train).

theory box

Japanese and Chinese Aesthetics

Classical Japanese philosophy proposes that reality is in a constant state of change – or in the Buddhist sense, one of fundamental impermanence. Living things lose their beauty and die and therefore beauty is a transitory, fleeting thing. Even inanimate rocks and land-scapes change or disappear over time. Unlike Greek philosophy there are no permanent ideals of beauty in the Platonic sense – perfect models that exist beyond human reach to which all earthly forms aspire. The eastern practice of Buddhism tells us, however, that an awareness of this fleeting nature of existence and beauty should not lead us to despair; on the contrary it should make us grateful for any remaining time left – time in which to value each precious hour and fill it with useful and vigorous life. This philosophy runs somewhat parallel with the views of the nineteenth-century German philosopher Friedrich Nietzsche, who agreed that life is indeed tragic, but that this should not preclude the joys of living life to the full – the highest realization of which is art. In Japan this philosophy of valuing existence and leading a useful life also goes hand-in-hand with the arts. Traditional Japanese arts have always been closely linked with Confucian ideas of self-cultivation and 'ways of living' – for example the way of tea making and the way of writing (calligraphy). As in China, the cultivated person was expected to be skilled in many of the arts; ceremonial ritual, music, poetry and even self-defence or archery. Thus the arts were more closely woven into everyday life compared with Western traditions.

The more fleeting the existence of a beautiful object, the greater is its value and there-fore sense of loss when it is gone (pathos). The short duration of cherry blossom in the spring is cause for national celebration in Japan where crowds of people turn out to view the beautiful blossom and picnic under its branches. Although pear and apple blossom may be just as beautiful a sight as the cherry tree in full bloom, the cherry is more highly valued because of the shorter duration of its blossom – which can be as little as a week. This pathos or empathy with living things can also be expressed through inanimate objects, for example the significant rock carefully placed in the garden can represent a friend who has died, or the beautiful vase in a room can be a symbol or reminder of the daughter who has left home. This 'pity' for the transience of life is expressed in the phrase *mono no aware* – the pathos (awareness) of things (mono) – thus the Japanese idea of beauty is intimately bound up with a profound sense of the emotional aspects of existence and loss.

Simplicity or an understated austere beauty (*wabi*) is a Japanese ideal, perhaps the simple raked pebble garden being the most obvious example to Western eyes, being 'cut off' (*kire*) from its natural and chaotic surroundings. This austere beauty was first admired in poetry but is also expressed through the apparent simplicity of everyday things – for example cultivating the garden or pruning trees in a way that removes superfluous elements to better encourage and express a tree's essential beauty. This is simplicity in a sophisticated sense – an elegant resolution of competing or confusing elements – and a philosophy that also applies to the design of the traditional Japanese house and other everyday objects. The tea ceremony especially expresses this simplicity through ritual and the austerity of the tea house design and its utensils. This austerity even applies to damaged utensils, providing they have been well repaired, and these imperfect utensils are often valued more highly than brand new ones and as such are symbols of moderation. Objects that have acquired a patina over time through use (sabi) – the cracks, stains and rusting of objects that have aged well – are also highly valued in traditional Japanese culture. Even in times of insufficiency and hardship, getting by with very little in an elegant way is considered a beautiful and noble aim. The term *sabi* also carries meanings of tranquillity and deep solitude. Thus beauty does not lie in opulence and extravagance but is to be found in an elegant simplicity, an ideal not unnoticed by twentieth century modernists in the West.

conclusion

Hopefully these chapters will have encouraged you to think more deeply about the relationships between design and beauty. The first and most important attribute in learning more about beauty and its creation, is your own sensual joy in experiencing beauty itself. Without this no amount of education and training will make up for it.

Santayana spoke of the sense of beauty, suggesting a sixth sense in addition to our existing five – each of us can detect beauty even though we might have difficulty in explaining it. We must all develop our own attitudes and skills towards appreciating and successfully creating beautiful pieces of work, whether in two, three or even four dimensions (the fourth dimension of time). It is useful to study good examples. There is no one right answer to a particular design problem. There are potentially as many bad solutions as there are good ones and notions of beauty are not static. We must constantly reappraise our judgements in the light of cultural and technological evolution. Figure 161 shows a twenty-first century Deconstructivist's proposal for the new extension the London's Victoria and Albert Museum. Such examples may seem strange to conventional ways of thinking, but should we accept them as beautiful? The history of art and design is full of works that were ridiculed at the time of their production, for example the Eiffel Tower in Paris, but today many of these works are widely accepted as both beautiful and meaningful. On a shorter time scale, changing fashions in contemporary design such as clothing or car styling, which may at first appear strange, can soon become accepted and admired by most of us, often in the space of weeks.

The purpose of much contemporary work in the visual arts has nothing to do with visual beauty in any case and this is the cause of a lot of

Fig 161. Proposed Extension to London's Victoria and Albert Museum for 2006 by Daniel Libeskind.

Fig 162 'Zoomorphism' – Quadraci
Pavilion at the Milwaukee Art Museum
by Santiago Calatrava, 2001. The 'wings'
are a sunscreen that can be raised or
lowered, creating a moving sculpture.

misunderstanding among the general public. For example virtual reality, electronic and conceptual art can pursue alternative aims to beauty, offering the observer/participant new ways of thinking and looking at the world – or even creating 'new worlds'. To many observers, computer, video or screen art remains soulless, however, as there is no tangible material such as paint or other surface texture to delight our sensual expectations of touch – the visceral beauty of traditional art. The beauty of these works, however, lay more in the ideas behind them, analogous perhaps to the beauty or elegance of mathematical formulae. Conceptual art, whether putting a meteorite back into orbit via the space shuttle to continue its interrupted voyage, or recreating an exploding shed frozen in space and time a split second after detonation, can provoke the audience into new ways of thinking or experiencing the world.[1]

Ernst Gombrich tells us that conceptual art is historically much more ancient than figurative art in any case – that the African mask, Egyptian hieroglyph or ancient cave painting are metaphors for the supernatural, and precede the 'revolutionary' figurative art of Classical Greece, art that was concerned mainly (or merely) with reproducing the physical appearance of people and things (mimetic art).[2] Conceptual art can make us think about issues deeper and more meaningful than simply trying to create the illusion of physical reality and appearances, whether in the form of a sculpture, painting or photograph, however well crafted these things may be.

In the field of design, the expressive forms of much new architecture in the early twenty-first century are becoming more organic and dynamic, such as Herzog and de Meuron's 'bird's nest' stadium for the Beijing Olympic games and Zaha Hadid's Central Factory Building for BMW in Leipzig. In some cases the architecture even adopts zoomorphic (animal-like) designs, as shown in Figure 162 – an echo perhaps of Hogarth's eighteenth-century serpentine ideals – replacing the strictly rectilinear and geometric forms of twentieth-century modernism. These new buildings, belonging mainly to the romantic tradition, are as much pieces of public sculpture as they are architecture and have been dubbed 'sculpitecture' by Anthony Caro. Where does fine art end and applied art begin? Today's buildings are blurring the line. There is however a significant difference between meaningful sculpture and mere decoration or entertainment. Are Gehry's, Libeskind's and Calatrava's buildings a serious blend of architecture and sculpture or mere overblown ornament?

There is much debate on whether new architecture should try to blend in or at least acknowledge their surrounding buildings, or alternatively make a statement of their own time. Analogous to this is the choice of colour in architecture, the American architect Cesar Pelli believes that: '… in a town or neighbourhood of buildings coloured only by natural materials a brightly coloured structure … could do great harm to the total ensemble, and I believe the whole is always more important than one of its parts even if that part happens to be one of my buildings.'[3]

Should this argument about colour also apply to the size, form and detailing of buildings? Many would argue that good quality buildings from any age should, within limits (for example scale), sit happily next to each other. We often see a jumble of different buildings in old towns and cities, which

Fig 163 The Great Court at the British Museum, London. 2000. Norman Foster's geodesic roof.

Fig 164 Yamaha 'Deinonychus' electric
concept motorcycle. c.2004.

most of us now consider charming, but we should not be slaves to bygone styles unless there is some important overriding factor.

Often new and complex shapes in architecture and product design owe much to the power of the computer, whether helping to determine the compound curves in car surfaces, the interlocking curves of Frank Gehry's architecture, or the shapes and sizes of individual flat triangles used to construct complex geodesic structures, for example Norman Foster's roof structure for the British Museum shown in Figure 163 (these complex computer generated architectural forms have been dubbed 'computer baroque'). The computer's ability to simulate physical objects, as well as their performance, has already had a huge influence in engineering and product design – for example the design of car engines and the analysis of forces in chassis designs before they

are even built, has led to new forms for vehicles as well as reducing manufacturing lead times.

At the start of the twenty-first century improvements in hydrogen fuel-cell technology have led to a reappraisal of electrically powered vehicles. This is also good news for the planet as long as the hydrogen is produced from renewable sources at the outset. Electric motors have several advantages over the internal combustion engine (besides being non-polluting in operation), they do not use any motive energy when the vehicle is stood still – unlike stationary cars in traffic with their engines idling. Electric motors have a high starting torque and low torque at high speed – as demonstrated by rapidly accelerating underground trains – and because of these characteristics electric vehicles do not need a gearbox or clutch – another reason why old diesel locomotives used an electric motor for the transmission of power to the wheels (the diesel engine was merely used to generate electricity). Developments in fuel cell and battery technologies will mean new and unusual possibilities for vehicle design. Figure 164 shows a picture of Yamaha's concept electric motorcycle with a motor mounted in the hub of each wheel, the batteries or fuel cell being located under the seat. This has implications for the proportion of unsprung weight of the vehicle, however, but it is probable that these problems will be overcome with developments in material science.

It is self-evident that the progress in materials science and electronics over the twentieth century has had a profound effect on the way we live and has also effected the change in the shapes and shrinkage of product designs. As recently as the 1990s most of us would have considered miraculous the sorts of things we can now do every day using a desktop PC. Advances in nano-materials science involve manipulating materials at the near atomic level (nano = one thousand millionth of a metre) and will provide opportunities for new ways of interacting with products and the environ-ment. Bonding together of different materials at the atomic level will enable you to wear your computer as an item of clothing – the circuitry, components and active displays will become an inseparable part of your shirt, and this shirt will be washable too. The computer as we know it will become virtually invisible. Smart clothes will also have adjustable thermal properties. Our buildings, the home and environment will become 'intelli-gent' – your home will know your state of physical and mental health at any given instant, running a hot bath and altering the mood of your lighting and sound system to welcome you home. It could also, in an instant, change the interior colour scheme and wallpaper patterns. Body implants could automatically release medication into your system without you even being aware of the need. Dr Ray Oliver of the Scientific Futures Group calls this 'the advance of the soft machines – where materials science crashes with art and design'. These developments have profound implications for designs of the future, but how beautiful they are will depend on you.

glossary

Abstract – Existing only as a mental concept or something taken out of context.

Additive colours – Mixing coloured light to make a new colour.

Aesthetics – Pertaining to beauty. The philosophy of beauty.

After-image – The reversed tone and colours of an image remaining on the retina after the original image has been removed (or replaced with a white surface).

Ascenders – The top parts of letter forms that stick up above the lower case 'x' height, such as in the letters b, h, d and k.

Asymmetry – Not symmetrical about a central point or axis. Off balance

Axonometric drawing – A floor plan of a building extruded up into three dimensions seen at an angle, usually from above. No perspective nor fore-shortening of objects. For example, circles remain circular and not elliptical, objects do not diminish with distance.

Balance – Elements in a composition or object have approximate equal visual 'weight'.

Bauhaus – German school of art, design and architecture, originally founded at Weimar in 1913 but moved to Dessau in 1925. The Bauhaus modernistic ideals were seen as decadent by the Nazis and the school was shut down in 1933. Bauhaus teachers included the architects Walter Gropius, Mies van der Rohe and painters Wassily Kandinsky and Paul Klee.

Baroque – Expressive or exuberant styles in architecture and design, originating in the late Renaissance period, c.1500.

Blend line – The 'line' created when two curved surfaces meet.

Brightness – The level of intensity, **luminosity** or **chroma** of a colour.

Calligraphy – Expressive hand-written letterforms with a broad nibbed pen or brush.

Capital – The 'cushion' on the top of a column where it meets the architrave (beam).

Chroma – Sometimes referred to as **saturation**, **brightness** or **luminosity** of a colour.

Chiaroscuro – From the Italian 'light and shade', used in drawings to suggest three-dimensional form.

Classical – (With a capital 'C'.) A particular period in history between about 550 and 450BC. Especially refers to the Greek Hellenistic period in art and architecture.

classical – (With a small 'c') A significant standard of work that stands the test of time.

CMYK – Cyan, Magenta, Yellow, Key (black) – Process primary colours for printing purposes.

Colour circle – The arrangement of the visible colour spectrum into a circle.

Colour constancy – The perceived colour of an object remains the same to a human observer under changing lighting conditions.

Colour modification – Colours in a composition are perceived as changing when other colours are placed next to them.

Complementary colours – Colours opposite each other on the colour circle intensify each other when placed next to each other. For example, red and green.

Composition – To design or put together elements artistically.

Contrasting colours – Similar to complementary colours but also contrasting in other ways, for example, a light colour placed next to a dark colour, or a warm colour placed next to a cool one.

Cool colours – The colours on the cool side of the colour circle. For example, blues and greens.

Counters – The negative internal shapes formed by the outlines of certain lower case letters, such as o, q, p and g.

Cubism – An early twentieth-century movement in art where several views of the same object are shown simultaneously. Movement founded by Pablo Picasso and George Braque, who were influenced by the earlier paintings of Paul Cezanne.

Descenders – The tails of letter forms that protrude below the 'x' height, such as in the letters y, p and q.

Design – Means different things to different people but in this context it refers to solving problems and/or creating compositions in two or three dimensions.

Discordant colours – Opposite of **harmony**. The reversal of natural tones of colour when placed together, such as pale violet against dark orange. Regarded as unpleasant.

Engaged column – A column partly built into and partly projecting from a wall. Similar to a **pilaster**. Sometimes load bearing, sometimes not.

Expressionism – A revolt against impressionism, turning away from the representation of external reality towards an expression of the artist's internal emotional experiences.

Fast line – A line dawn quickly and smoothly, straight or curving. Can indicate a hard, smooth surface like a car body, or suggest speed.

Fibonacci series – A particular sequence of numbers, named after a thirteenth-century Italian mathematician. Each number is the sum of the previous two: 1, 1, 2, 3, 5, 8. The ratio of these numbers is similar to the **Golden ratio**.

Flicker effect – The illusion of independent movement, where two colours of similar tone but otherwise extremely different in hue, are put against each other.

Focal point – A visual centre of attention.

Folly – A useless structure.

Font – A particular family of letterforms, such as Helvetica or Goudy.

Footprint – The term used mainly by product designers to describe the area a product takes up on a surface. For example a large toaster has a bigger footprint on the work surface than that of a smaller toaster, which is important if your kitchen is tiny.

Form – A three-dimensional shape.

Futurism – An early twentieth-century art movement celebrating the future – especially in relation to technology and way of life. Origins in the Italian artist Filippo Marinetti's Futurist Manifesto of 1909.

Gestalt – The recognition of an organized whole from shapes, forms and patterns, for example seeing a face in ink blots on a piece of paper. The whole is greater than the sum of its parts.

Golden ratio/Golden section – Greek origins, sometimes referred to as the Golden Mean or Golden Cut, where a line of any length is cut or divided into two to give the ratio of 1 to 1.618. The ratio of the smaller length to the longer length is the same as the ratio between the longer length and the overall length of the original line. The Golden Rectangle has sides conforming to this ratio

Gothic – A movement/invention in architecture from about AD1100 using the pointed arch to reduce the sideways thrust of the Roman semicircular arch

Gothic Revival – Nineteenth-century movement in architecture that revived the pointed arch in buildings.

Grid system – An underlying (ultimately invisible) grid for the consistent arranging of pages of type and pictures in a book. Also used in other areas of design when composing elements in two dimensions, such as the façade of a building.

Handshake – The careful handling of where two or more elements meet, a term usually referred to in an architectural context but is also used in other areas of design.

Harmonious colours – Two or more colours lying close together on the colour circle/solid are said to be harmonious.

Harmony – A successful composition of design elements in two or three dimensions. No two elements 'fight' each other.

Hue – A particular colour. For example, red as distinct from blue.

Iconic – A very significant and sometimes mould-breaking design.

Impressionism – A movement in painting in late nineteenth-century Europe, particularly France, where artists rejected the studio tradition and painted their first impressions of out-of-door scenes *in situ*. Claude Monet is generally regarded as the leading figure.

Isometric projection – A drawing using a 30° setsquare in combination with an isometric ellipse template (35° 16') to produce a three-dimensional view without diminishing perspective.

Juxtaposed – Placed next to each other, often for comparison.

Kerning – The typographic term for spacing between letter forms.

Kitsch – Sentimental or pretentious rubbish.

Line quality – Drawing with attention to different styles of line, such as fast, slow, light, heavy, soft or hard.

Logo – Trade mark design or pictorial symbol representing something, such as a company's brand

Lower case letters – Non-capital letters.

Luminance/Luminosity – Sometimes referred to as saturation, brightness or chroma of a colour.

Monotone – Composition using different tones of the same colour (or black and white).

Movement – The suggestion of motion in a static image or design.

Munsell system – A system of categorizing colours, invented by Albert Munsell in 1905.

Neo-Classical – A revival of Greek art and architecture.

Neo-Gothic – Refers to any building using the pointed arch and created more recently than AD1100 to 1300, especially the Gothic Revival in the nineteenth century.

Orthographic – Two-dimensional drawn views (elevations) of the side, top and bottom of an object.

Ostwald colour system – A system of categorizing colours invented by Wilhelm Ostwald in 1916. The 'open-ended' **Munsell system** of 1905 eventually became the accepted standard.

Part-line – The slightly proud 'witness' line left showing on the surface of a plastic injection moulding where two halves of the steel tool met to form the cavity.

Perspective – A method of drawing using vanishing points to create the illusion of the apparent decreasing size of objects with distance.

Pilaster – A square column, partly built into and partly projecting from a wall. Similar to an **engaged column**. Sometimes load bearing, sometimes not.

Plasticity – Three-dimensional sculptural form. Moulding a material into a form.

Pointillism – A method of painting using small dots of pure colour which 'mix' together when seen at a distance, rather than physically mixing paints beforehand. Said to produce brighter colours. Generally attributed to the late nineteenth-century painter Georges Seurat.

Post-modernism – A reaction against the 'less-is-more' ethos of twentieth-century Modernism, resulting in more playful architecture and design. Often borrowing elements of styles from the past, such as Classical or Egyptian motifs, and mixing them with the present day. Also a more playful approach to colour.

Primary colours – Colours that cannot be produced from mixing other colours.

Renaissance – Rebirth. A term generally given to the explosion of art and culture in the fifteenth century, particularly in Italy.

RGB – Red, Green, Blue. Primaries of additive colour mixing with light.

Rococo – A highly ornate seventeenth-century decorative style of architecture and design unrelated to structure. Developed from the more restrained style of **Baroque**.

Sans serif – Letterforms without serifs (those twiddly bits on the ends of strokes).

Saturation – Sometimes referred to as **luminosity** or **chroma** of a colour.

Secondary colours – Those colours achieved by mixing two primary colours together.

Serif – A short decorative foot (or head) at the end of a stroke on letterforms.

Shade – To use a darker tone in a drawing to suggest form. Also to add a small amount of black to darken a colour.

Shape – Usual refers to forms in two dimensions only.

Shut line – The line created where two elements come together, for example a closed car door and bodywork, or where two plastic mouldings meet.

Simultaneous contrast – A tone or colour can be made to appear different by placing other, differing tones or colours around or next to it.

Slow line – A drawn line created in such a manner as to suggest lack of movement or sometimes a soft material.

Spatial colours – Some colours appear to advance (usually warm colours), whereas others appear to recede (usually cool colours).

Subtractive colour mixing – Mixing pigments together to create other colours where some colour saturation is lost in the process.

Symmetry – Equal distribution of elements around a common axis.

Synaesthesia – A condition where different senses overlap in the brain. For instance, some individuals see colour when listening to sounds.

Tactile – Qualities derived from touch, or perceived through viewing surface detail.

Tension – Pulling apart, or the visually dynamic relationship between two or more elements in a composition.

Tertiary colours – Those colours achieved by mixing two secondary colours together.

Tint – To lighten a colour or tone by adding a small amount of white.

Tone – The lightness or darkness of a colour on a greyscale. Same as **value**.

Value – The lightness or darkness of a colour on a greyscale. Same as **tone**.

Vanishing point – The point at which converging lines meet in a perspective drawing.

Vernacular – The common style of architecture in a particular region.

Vibrancy – A particular resonance of colour or drawing, an exciting element or composition.

Warm colours – those colours on the warm side of the colour circle, such as reds, oranges and some yellows.

Wrought iron – Bashed or rolled into shape while hot (forged) – usually stronger than cast iron, although cast iron's advantage is that it can more easily produce complex shapes in large quantities.

Zing – a small patch of highly saturated colour set amidst a larger area of less saturated colours or greys.

Zoomorphism – animal like.

illustrations

Fig. 1. Bugatti Type 35. 1925. Technology dates but beauty doesn't. © Martyn Goddard Transtock/IPNSTOCK.

Fig. 2. Modernism – Mies Van Der Rohe's Illinois Institute of Technology, Chicago. Crown building, 1956. RIBA Library Photographs Collection.

Fig. 3. Japanese Zen Rock Garden. Rocks create ripples in smooth flowing waters. © Charles & Josette Lenars/CORBIS.

Fig. 4. Temple of Heaven. Beijing. c.1420. © Dean Conger/CORBIS.

Fig. 5. The expressive forms of the Nuragic and Contemporary Art Museum, Cagliari, Italy. By Zaha Hadid. Expected completion date: end of 2010.

Fig. 6. Overdecoration? Houses of Parliament, London. 1858. A. W. N. Pugin. Eric de Mare/RIBA Library Photographs Collection.

Fig. 7. 'The Country Dance' – an illustration from William Hogarth's book Analysis of Beauty of 1753, which compares the serpentine forms and movements of the 'ideal couple' on the left with the clumsy and graceless forms of the other dancers. Andrew Edmunds, London.

Fig. 8. Guggenheim Museum, New York. 1959. By Frank Lloyd Wright. © Murat Taner/zefa/CORBIS.

Fig. 9. Interior of a Japanese inn. Elegance through carefully considered simplicity. © image 100/CORBIS.

Fig. 10. Michael Graves postmodern Kettle for Alessi. 1985. Kettle with handle and small bird-shaped whistle in polyamide. Magnetic stainless steel bottom. Photo courtesy of Alessi S.p.a., Crusinallo, Italy.

Fig. 11. The Elaine Printer design expresses the flow of paper. c.1990. Courtesy of Ilmari Kostiainen.

Fig. 12. Art Nouveau – Entrance Gate to the Domaine Berenger, Paris. 1898. Hector Guimard. © Andrea Jemolo/CORBIS.

Fig. 13. 'Streamlining' – 1959 Cadillac Series 62 Tail. 1959. © Car Culture/CORBIS.

Fig. 14. The function-led Anglepoise Lamp design. 1933. Photo courtesy of Anglepoise Ltd.

Fig. 15. Walt Disney Concert Hall. Los Angeles, Frank Gehry. 2003. Its form could be interpreted as suggesting musical movement – the sweep of the conductor's baton frozen in time and space. © Richard Cummins/CORBIS.

Fig. 16. Crock-Pot with four-quart capacity. Designed in 2000 for Target Stores and manufactured by Black & Decker. Photo courtesy of Michael Graves & Associates.

Fig. 17. 'Go' furniture for indoor and/or outdoor use, by Ross Lovegrove. Photo courtesy of Bernhardt Design.

Fig. 18. Traditional House, Thailand. Achieving beauty through considered use of natural materials and sound craftsmanship. © image 100/CORBIS.

Fig. 19. Vitruvian Man – by Leonardo, c.1450 – 'Man is the measure of all things'. © Bettmann/CORBIS.

Fig. 20. Proportions in architecture and design relate to human proportions. Le Corbusier's Modulor. 1948. The Le Corbusier Foundation, Le Modulor 1945 © FLC/ADAGP, Paris and DACS, London. 2008.

Fig. 21. Roman Villa at Herculaneum. C.AD79. The inward sloping roof and opening allows rainwater to pour into the central pool. © Soprintendenza Archeologica Di Pompei.

Fig. 22. The Roman arch requires substantial buttressing to withstand sideways forces.

Fig. 23. Gothic (pointed) arch forces requires much less buttressing.

Fig. 24. Gothic design – flying buttresses of Notre Dame Cathedral, Paris. C.AD1280. (Note the upward extension of the vertical pinnacles above the stone arches.) © Adam Woolfitt/CORBIS.

Fig. 25. Intersecting Roman vaults of differing widths.

Fig. 26. Same as Figure 25, but using 'stilts' (shown in solid tone). This results in wavy groins where the two arches meet.

Fig. 27. Intersecting Gothic vaults of differing widths but of equal height.

Fig. 28. Aerial view of the Pantheon's concrete roof, Rome. ad123. © Alinari Archives/CORBIS.

Fig. 29. The pointed Dome of Santa Maria – Florence, completed ad1436. © Hans Peter Merten/zefa/CORBIS.

Fig. 30. Sloping rafters produce an outward thrust and can be considered as an arch comprising just two elements.

Fig. 31. A schematic of a roof truss design for the Banqueting House ceiling. 1622.

Fig. 32. Innovative roof truss design. David Mellor Design Museum, Hathersage. 2006. Photo courtesy of David Mellor Design.

Fig. 33. Joseph Paxton's prefabricated design of the Crystal Palace. 1851. Science & Society Picture Library.

Fig. 34. 'Undecorated' claret jug design by Christopher Dresser. c.1879. V&A Images, Victoria and Albert Museum.

Fig. 35. Ways to counteract bending forces.

Fig. 36. Compression and tensile forces under bending (F), weight reduction (G) and counteracting torsion (H).

Fig. 37. Fabricated and riveted iron girders forming a vault over the railway tracks. Tie rods across the base of each arch cancel out outward thrusts on the supporting outer walls. Darlington Railway Station, built c.1875.

Fig. 38. Norman Foster's spaceframe design for the Sainsbury Arts Centre, Norwich. 1977. Alastair Hunter/RIBA Library Photographs Collection.

Fig. 39. BMW R51/3 Motorcycle 1951–6. 'Traditional' tubular steel frame design, within which the engine is mounted. Photo courtesy of BMW Motorrad.

Fig. 40. BMW R1200 RT Motorcycle 2004. The engine provides the main frame component. Photo courtesy of BMW Motorrad.

Fig. 41. 'Cross-bracing' – Pompidou Centre, Paris. By Richard Rogers & Renzo Piano. 1977. © Julia Waterlow; Eye Ubiquitous/CORBIS.

Fig. 42. Tensile roof structures for the Munich Olympics in 1972. Otto Frei. View of the roof of the Olympic Stadium, designed by Gunther Behnisch with Frei Otto as roof consultant. Munich, Germany. Photo by Bildarchiv Steffens/The Bridgeman Art Library.

Fig. 43. Alvar Aalto plywood 'Paimio' chair. 1931. Still in production today as Artek number 41 chair. Photo Martti Kapanen, Alvar Aalto Museum.

Fig. 44. Plywood construction Mosquito aircraft. 1941. Image copyright of Michael Durning.

Fig. 45. Composite construction B-2A Stealth Bomber 1988. © Aero Graphics, Inc./CORBIS.

Fig. 46. Early tubular steel furniture – Mies Van der Rohe Chair. c.1927. Ludwig Mies van der Rohe. © DACS 2008 and Vitra Design Museum.

Fig. 47. Robin Day's polypropylene stacking chair. 1963. V&A Images, Victoria and Albert Museum.

Fig. 48. Vernor Panton's all-plastic stacking chair, first produced in 1967. Vitra Design Museum and courtesy of Verner Panton Design.

Fig. 49. 'Mannerist' or Baroque Church of St. Carlo, Rome. Borromini. c.1640. Photo courtesy of Christian Perrier www.imageimaginaire.com.

Fig. 50. Doric, Ionic, and Corinthian (and combined) Orders. Expressions of gender? The Orders of Architecture from Ordonnances des Cing Especes de Colonne by Claude Perrault. 1676. Private collection/The Bridgeman Art Library.

Fig. 51. Early 'nostrils' – BMW Roadster 328. 1936. Photo courtesy of BMW Group.

Fig. 52. Later 'nostrils' – BMW Concept M5. 2004. Neo-Baroque meets zoomorphism – headlamps as eyes? Photo courtesy of BMW Group.

Fig. 53. Ducati 998. 2002. Photo courtesy of Ducati UK Ltd.

Fig. 54. Philips Mixer Grinder for India. Courtesy of Philips Design, Hong Kong.

Fig. 55. Laser SB3-21 racing yacht, designed and built by Tony Castro. 2002. Photo courtesy of Tony Castro.

Fig. 56. Swiss Re Building (The 'Gherkin'). By Norman Foster, London. 2004. © Joey Nigh/CORBIS.

Fig. 57. Two squares symmetrically balanced left and right in a rectangle.

Fig. 58. Smaller left hand square requires leftward shift of both squares for overall composition to remain in visual balance.

Fig. 59. Ill-considered layout of displays.

Fig. 60. A better solution.

Fig. 61. We still read the 'missing' letter.

Fig. 62. Solving the triglyph problem (adapted from Gelernter).

Fig. 63. The Parthenon, Athens. c.450BC. The fluting on the columns modulates the depth of shadow to emphasize roundness. This illustration also shows the Triglyphs spaced at equal intervals above the architrave (main beam). © Craig and Marie Mauzy.

Fig. 64. The Temple of Hera at Paestum. c.550BC (detail) showing 'squashed' capitals that were prone to damage. The Temple of Neptune can be seen beyond. Edwin Smith/RIBA Library Photographs Collection.

Fig. 65. Some typeface terminology. Also note the slightly different 'x-to-Cap' height ratios between Times New Roman (top) and the Trebuchet MS font underneath.

Fig. 66. Automatic spacing of letters using Microsoft Word software.

Fig. 67. Letters equally spaced – unbalanced result.

Fig. 68. Shortened horizontal leg of 'L' – optimum result.

Fig. 69. Barclays Bank logo showing L and A actually joined together. Image courtesy of Barclays Bank plc.

Fig. 70. Curved letters slightly larger than rectilinear letters.

Fig. 71. Visual adjustment of letter starting positions.

Fig. 72. Readability without spaces between words.

Fig. 73. Centre rectangle at the visual centre of outer rectangle. Drawing courtesy of Becky Clay.

Fig. 74. The original London Underground Map of 1908. London's Transport Museum. © Transport for London.

Fig. 75. The model for today's map, first conceived by Harry Beck in 1931. London's Transport Museum. © Transport for London.

Fig. 76. Constructed Roman Capitals. Adapted from a sixteenth-century design by Albrecht Dürer.

Fig. 77. Quentin 'fun' font – used to advertise a circus, for example.

Fig. 78. David Mellor's 'Classic' cutlery set. Image courtesy of David Mellor Design.

Fig. 79. David Mellor's 'Odeon' cutlery set. Image courtesy of David Mellor Design.

Fig. 80. Golden rectangle.

Fig. 81. Golden spiral.

Fig. 82. Dialling on telephone. An example of 'massing' of elements in product design – sizing and grouping the finger buttons according to functions. © S. Oskar/zefa/CORBIS.

Fig. 83. Constantine College today – the 'stripped classical' style.

Fig. 84. Is the post penetrating or supporting the beam? (Adapted from Scruton.)

Fig. 85. Classical solution – also introduces subtle curvature in cone and column (adapted from Gauldie).

Fig. 86. Stansted Airport (detail). 1991. Sir Norman Foster. RIBA Library Photographs Collection.

Fig. 87. Control buttons nestling in dishes.

Fig. 88. Typical grid for a magazine page layout. Lines in the boxes represent type, the grey areas represent images.

Fig. 89. Deliberate use of white space and asymmetry for a more interesting layout.

Fig. 90. Example of blend lines in product design. Photo courtesy of Philips Domestic Appliances and Personal Care.

Fig. 91. Ford's StreetKa – an example of 'leaping' vectors and 'form slicing'. Photo courtesy of the Ford Motor Company Ltd.

Fig. 92. The eye jumps the gap – Andrea Del Sarto. Madonna and Child with St Elizabeth and St John the Baptist, c. 1528 (panel) by Sarto, Andrea del (1486–1530) Galleria Palatina, Palazzo Pitti, Florence, Italy/The Bridgeman Art Library.

Fig. 93. The bead profile running along the side of the van is absorbed by the light detail at the rear corner, and thereby 'introduces' it to a flat area of the rear door surface – a handshake or a reconciled 'Gauldie collision' where two elements meet. Photo courtesy of the Ford Motor Company Ltd.

Fig. 94. 'Slim' television – a useful visual trick.

Fig. 95. Peugeot 407 SW showing the dark coloured side window pillars and horizontal door bumper strip. Photo courtesy of Peugeot PLC.

Fig. 96. House with 'in-line' extension.

Fig. 97. House with stepped-back extension.

Fig. 98. The harsh forms of Gerrit Reitveld's Zig-Zag Chair. 1934. Vitra Design Museum.

Fig. 99. Water colour reproduction of a fourteenth-century Islamic pattern design from Alhambra Mosaic ornament in the south side of the Court of the Lions, Alhambra, from 'The Arabian Antiquities of Spain', published 1815 (w/c on paper) by Murphy, James Cavanagh (1760–1814). Private Collection/The Stapleton Collection/The Bridgeman Art Library.

Fig. 100. Pasadena Museum of California Art. Façade elevation. Image courtesy of MDA Johnson Favaro Architects.

Fig. 101. Photograph of actual museum. Photo courtesy of MDA Johnson Favaro Architects.

Fig. 102. Aston Martin four-door Rapide. 2008. Photo courtesy of Aston Martin Lagonda Ltd.

Fig. 103. Goudy Old Style typeface. c. 1916. Image courtesy of Identifont.

Fig. 104. R. Goudy's 'University of California Old Style' italic – one of the few sketches that survived the fire of 1939. Note the overlaid letters n and h, also i and l. (Image from Goudy's book Typologia first published in 1940 and reproduced here from the 1977 edition.) By kind permission of the University of California Press – publishers and copyright holders.

Fig. 105. Screen image from www. studioball. co. uk website showing visual design. Photo courtesy of Jamie Billing, Tracy Cordingley of Alte Design Ltd and www. studioball. co. uk.

Fig. 106. Visual music? – Kandinsky, Wassily, Composition VI. Oil on canvas. 195 × 300 cm Russia-Germany. 1913. The State Hermitage Museum, St Petersburg. Photograph © The State Hermitage Museum. © ADAGP, Paris and DACS, London. 2008.

Fig. 107. Subtractive mixing with paints.

Fig. 108. Additive mixing with light.

Fig. 109. The colour circle. Adapted from Johannes Itten – Bauhaus. c.1920.

Fig. 110. The three properties (or 'dimensions') of colour: (A) HUE – Red as distinct from blue, for example. (B) VALUE – The lightness or darkness of a colour, also referred to as TONE. The above shows the grey equivalents of the HUES on the left. (C) CHROMA – The strength or intensity of a colour – the top red is 'redder'. Also called SATURATION or LUMINOSITY.

Fig. 111. The Munsell colour tree. The Science and Society Picture Library.

Fig. 112. Complementary colours. The two reds are identical.

Fig. 113. Chevrons – An arrangement of warning colours (and striking design) – contrasting colours and tones. Photo courtesy of Brush Traction.

Fig. 114. Harmonic oranges and reds.

Fig. 115. Casa Araras: Bedroom. An example of using colour harmonies in warm muted colours where tranquil environments are required. © Alan Weintraub/Arcaid/CORBIS.

Fig. 116. 'Discordant' colour combinations. Generally regarded as unpleasant.

Fig. 117. Simultaneous contrast using greys. By Edward H. Adelson. 1995. Squares A and B are the same grey. ©1995. Edward H. Adelson.

Figures 118 and **119**. The same colour is perceived as changing when surrounded by different colours.

Fig. 120. Warm and cool versions of colours.

Figures 121 and **122**. Two rectangles of identical proportions can be made to appear different sizes.

Fig. 123. Flicker effect – the illusion of independent movement.

Fig. 124. 'Zing' – an attention-seeking colour highlight.

Fig. 125. Colour balance as applied to Great North Eastern Railways livery. Photo © Hornby Hobbies Ltd.

Fig. 126. 1980s Kenwood Chef KM300 food mixer – the application of an overall single colour in product design. Photo courtesy of Kenwood Ltd.

Fig. 127. A positively cheerful and optimistic interior design and colour scheme for the executive dining room, Team Disney – Michael D. Eisner Building, Burbank, California. 1986. Photo courtesy of Michael Graves & Associates and used by permission from Disney Enterprises, Inc.

Fig. 128. Light Red Over Black. Mark Rothko. c. 1960. © Tate, London 2007 and ©1998 Kate Rothko Prizel & Christopher Rothko ARS, NY and DACS, London 2008.

Fig. 129. Dotted horse and hand prints, Pech Merle Caves, southern France. c.23000BC. Photograph by P. Cabrol. © Centre de Préhistoire du Pech- Merle, France.

Fig. 130. Egyptian Eighteenth Dynasty Bas-Relief Painting of Horemheb. c.1348–1320BC. © Gianni Dagli Orti/CORBIS.

Fig. 131. Fast lines – Bamboo in the Wind. Chinese thirteenth-century Yuan Dynasty. Ink on paper. Artist Wu Zhen. Freer Gallery of Art, Smithsonian Institution, Washington, DC: Purchase, F1953. 85.

Figs 132 and **133**. Engineering drawings comparing effect of different line thicknesses. Drawings courtesy of Tim Platt, University of Teesside.

Fig. 134. All line thicknesses identical.

Fig. 135. Thicker lines around individual components emphasise individual objects. Also the addition of shadows increase 3D impact.

Fig. 136. Study for the Sforza Monument. An exploratory sketch of a horse and rider by Leonardo da Vinci. c.1488. © Alinari Archives/CORBIS.

Fig. 137. A 'perspective' Fresco Painting of a Stage Set at Herculaneum. c.AD50. Mimmo Jodice/ CORBIS.

Fig. 138. Foreshortening of circular wheels and use of shading. Greek. c.340BC. From a royal tomb at Vergina – the God Pluto abducts Persephone to the underworld. XVII Ephorate of Prehistoric and Classical Antiquities. Copyright of Hellenic Ministry of Culture-Archaeological Receipts Fund.

Fig. 139. Drawing machine. Nineteenth-century engraving by Paul Lacroix, after Albrecht Dürer's original woodcut of 1527. Instruments of Mathematical Precision for Executing Portraits, Illustration from 'Science and Literature in the Middle Ages and the Renaissance', written and engraved by Paul Lacroix. 1878. Engraving is after an original woodcut by Albrecht Durer (1471–1528). Private Collection/The Bridgeman Art Library.

Fig. 140. Single point perspective drawing.

Fig. 141. Small object at a distance easily fits within cone of vision.

Fig. 142. A small matchbox (or a building seen from an aeroplane).

Fig. 143. Nearby large object can take up the entire cone of vision.

Fig. 144. A building in two-point perspective takes up more of our cone of vision – the picture includes the horizon and vanishing points.

Fig. 145. Interior of a building in two-point perspective.

Figs 146 and **147.** Buildings in three-point perspective.

Fig. 148. Relationship between eye level and the horizon.

Fig. 149. Major axis of the ellipse is always at right angles to the main axis of the cylinder.

Fig. 150. Different 'fatness' of ellipses. This drawing also shows a method of doubling the length of a box or building in perspective using diagonals.

Fig. 151. Construction of arches.

Fig. 152. Arc of travel for hinged doors and lids.

Fig. 153. Constructed box for a car sketch.

Fig. 154. Centre of ellipse in perspective.

Fig. 155. Glasgow School of Art drawing studio showing moveable light sources. c.1910. Glasgow School of Art Collection.

Fig. 156. Local light source

Fig. 157. Shadow of pitched roof.

Fig. 158. Parallel light rays.

Fig. 159. Car styling concept sketch, lit by light reflected from below.

Fig. 160. A Ron Arad sketch using a digitizing tablet. 2007. Image courtesy of Ron Arad Associates.

Fig. 161. Proposed Extension to London's Victoria and Albert Museum for 2006 by Daniel Libeskind. Render©millerhare.

Fig. 162. 'Zoomorphism' – Quadraci Pavilion at the Milwaukee Art Museum by Santiago Calatrava. 2001. The 'wings' are a sunscreen that can be raised or lowered, creating a moving sculpture. © Joseph Sohm; Visions of America/CORBIS.

Fig. 163. The Great Court at the British Museum, London. 2000. Norman Foster's geodesic roof. © Pawel Libera/CORBIS.

Fig. 164. Yamaha 'Deinonychus' electric concept motorcycle. c.2004. Photo courtesy of Yamaha Motor Co.

notes

---

introduction

1. Norman, D. (2004), *Emotional Design: Why We Love (or Hate) Everyday Things*, New York: Basic Books.

2. Dudley, E. and Mealing, S. (eds) (2000), *Becoming Designers: Education and Influence*, Exeter: Intellect Books.

3. Cold, B. (ed.) (2002), *Aesthetics, Well-Being and Health: Essays Within Architecture and Environmental Aesthetics* (Ethnoscapes), Aldershot: Ashgate.

4. Scarry, E. (2006), *On Beauty and Being Just*, Princeton, NJ: Princeton University Press.

5. Gould, J. and Gould, C. (2007) *Animal Architects: Building and the Evolution of Intelligence*, New York: Basic Books.

6. Miller, G. (2001), *The Mating Mind*, New York: Anchor Books/Doubleday.

7. Mithen, S. (2005), *The Singing Neanderthals*, Cambridge, MA: Harvard University Press.

8. Dawkins, R. (1989), *The Selfish Gene*, Oxford: Oxford University Press.

9. Ramachandran, V. (1999), 'Art and the Brain', *Journal of Consciousness Studies*, 6: 15–51.

10. Rose, S. (1997), *Lifelines: Biology, Freedom, Determinism*, Harmondsworth: Penguin.

11. Blackmore, S. (2000), *The Meme Machine*, Oxford: Oxford University Press.

12. Mithen, *The Singing Neanderthals*.

13. Rawson, P. (1987), *Creative Design: A New Look at Design Principles*, London: MacDonald Orbis.

14. Ridley, B. (2001), *On Science*, London: Routledge.

15. Cold, *Aesthetics*.

chapter 1   on taste

1. Bayley, S. (1991), *Taste, The Secret Meaning of Things*, London: Faber & Faber.

2. Dondis, D. A. (1973), *A Primer of Visual Literacy*, Cambridge, MA: MIT Press.

3. Bayley, S. (1983), *Taste, An Exhibition about Values in Design*, London: Victoria and Albert Museum.

4. Clark, K. (1969), *Civilization: A Personal View*, New York: Harper & Row.

5. Santayana, G. (1955), *The Sense of Beauty*, New York: Dover Publications.

6. Feynman, R. (1988), *What Do You Care What Other People Think?* New York: W. W. Norton.

7. Burke, E. (1757), *A Philosophical Enquiry into the Origin of our Ideas of the Sublime and Beautiful*.

8. Cruikshank, D. (2005), *Around the World in 80 Treasures*, London: Orion Books.

9. Postrel, V. (2003), *The Substance of Style: How the Rise of Aesthetic Value is Remaking Commerce, Culture and Consciousness*, New York: Harper Perennial.

chapter 2   design evolution

1. Santayana, *The Sense of Beauty*.

2. Salvadori, M. (1990), *Why Buildings Stand Up; The Strength of Architecture*, New York: W. W. Norton.

3. King, R. (2000), *Brunelleschi's Dome: How a Renaissance Genius Reinvented Architecture*, New York: Walker & Co.

4. Yeomans, D. (1992), *The Trussed Roof: Its History and Development*, Aldershot: Scolar Press.

5. 'The Gender of the Universal' in Lupton, E. and Miller, J. (eds) (2001), *The ABCs of the Bauhaus and Design Theory*, London: Thames & Hudson.

6. De Botton, A. (2006), *The Architecture of Happiness*, New York: Pantheon.

chapter 3   composition

1. See 'Motorway Madness: David Kindersley and the Great Road Sign Ruckus' in S. Loxley (2004), *Type: The Secret History of Letters*, London: I. B. Tauris.

2. See the chapter 'Legibility' in R. McLean (1992) *The Thames & Hudson Manual of Typography*, London: Thames & Hudson.

3. Jeavons, T. and Beaumont, M. (1990), *An Introduction to Typography*, Secaucus, NJ: Chartwell.

4. Ibid.

5. Spiekermann, E. and Ginger, E. (2003), *Stop Stealing Sheep and Find Out How Type Works*, Mountain View, CA, Adobe Press, 2nd edn.

6. Barrow, J. D. (1995), *The Artful Universe*, Oxford: Clarendon Press.

7. Ramachandran, 'Art and the Brain'.

8. Kudielka, R. (1999), *The Eye's Mind: Bridget Riley, Collected Writings 1965–1999*, London: Thames & Hudson.

9. See Elam, K. (2001), *The Geometry of Design: Studies in Proportion and Composition*. Princeton NJ: Princeton Architectural Press.

10. Gauldie, S. (1969), *Architecture*, Oxford: Oxford University Press.

11. Scruton, R. (1979), *The Aesthetics of Architecture*, London: Methuen.

12. Wiggins, G. A. (1998),'Music, Syntax and the Meaning of "Meaning"', *Proceedings of the First Symposium on Music and Computers*, Corfu: Greece.

13. Rawson, *Creative Design*.

14. Norman, *Emotional Design*.

15. Scruton, *Aesthetics*.

16. Rawson, *Creative Design*.

17. Santayana, *The Sense of Beauty*.

18. Day, Lewis F. (1979), *Pattern Design*, London: Batsford.

19. Loxley, S. (2004), *Type: The Secret History of Letters*, London: I.B. Tauris.

chapter 4   colour

1. Adapted from Porter, T. (1996), 'Colour in the Looking Glass', *Architectural Design*, 66(3/4) – an issue solely devoted to colour in architecture.

2. Rawson, *Creative Design*.

3. Gage, J. (1995), *Colour and Culture: Practice and Meaning from Antiquity to Abstraction*, London: Thames & Hudson. Gage, J. (1999), *Colour and Meaning: Art, Science and Symbolism*, London: Thames & Hudson.

4. Clark, *Civilization*.

5. Itten, J. (1973), *The Art of Color*, New York: Van Nostrand Reinhold.

6. BBC Horizon broadcast on synaesthesia, *Derek Tastes of Earwax*, 30 September 2004.

7. Mithen, *The Singing Neanderthals*.

8. Wilcox, M. (1987), *Blue and Yellow Don't Make Green*, Perth, Western Australia: Artways.

9. Minah, G. (1996), *'Reading Form and Space'*, *Architectural Design*, 66(3/4).

chapter 5   drawing, communication and expression

1. Guthrie, R. D. (2006), *The Nature of Palaeolithic Art*, Chicago: University of Chicago Press.

2. Lewis-Williams, D. (2004), *The Mind in the Cave: Consciousness and the Origins of Art*, London: Thames & Hudson.

3. Gombrich, E. H. (1968), *Art and Illusion: A Study in the Psychology of Pictorial Representation*, London: Phaidon.

4. Seymour, R. (2005), 'Line of Sight', *Blueprint*, 230(May): 58–63.

5. Santayana, *The Sense of Beauty*.

6. Ramachandran, 'Art and the Brain'.

conclusion

1. Cornelia Parker's installation, *Cold Dark Matter*, 1991.

2. Gombrich, *Art and Illusion*.

3. From the journal *Architectural Design*, 66(3/4) – an issue solely devoted to colour in architecture, 1996.

further reading

chapter 1   on taste

Bayley, S. (1991), *Taste, The Secret Meaning of Things*, London: Faber & Faber.
Bayley discusses issues of taste primarily from a historical point of view. He argues that taste is 'not so much about what things look like, as about the ideas that give rise to them'. The book's illustrated chapters deal with notions of taste in the fields of architecture, interior design and fashion. Bayley compares the subjective values of taste with the more objective values of design, although he maintains that even modernists, who claimed that consideration of function alone would lead to elegance, were the product of a particular culture in a particular time.

Dudley, E. and Mealing, S. (eds) (2000), *Becoming Designers: Education and Influence*, Exeter: Intellect Books.
A 'reader'-type book with essays by different authors (teachers, designers and writers) on various issues that the student will need to consider. For example, new technologies, history, gender, ethics, globalization, as well as topics related to the teaching of design theory and practice.

Postrel, V. (2003), *The Substance of Style: How the Rise of Aesthetic Value is Remaking Commerce, Culture and Consciousness*, New York: Harper Perennial.
Postrel argues that the sensual beauty of the objects we purchase (or use) is a vital ingredient in the economic success or failure of the companies that produce these objects. We are by nature deeply biological, sensory creatures and make decisions as consumers based on our visual and emotional experiences. Postrel makes the case that the twenty-first century is the age of aesthetics; that for products to succeed in future they must be smart and pretty – function alone is not enough and she provides many examples of where aesthetics has been a crucial factor to success.

Gombrich, E. H. (1995), *The Story of Art*, London: Phaidon Press, 16th edn.
A classic text for all art and design students, this is a beautifully illustrated book on the history of Western art first published in 1950 and currently in its sixteenth edition. Gombrich discusses painting, sculpture and works of architecture produced from prehistoric times up to the very recent past.

chapter 2   design evolution

Sparke, P. (2004), *An Introduction to Design and Culture (1900 to the Present)*, 2 edn. London: Routledge.
Sparke deals with the impact of new materials and production processes on design, in the context of the changing nature of society. The book provides a history of the development of designs and includes many examples and illustrations of mass-produced products, buildings, interior designs and images. A useful glossary of designers and design movements is also provided.

Salvadori, M. (1990), *Why Buildings Stand Up; The Strength of Architecture*, New York: W. W. Norton.

The principles of structural design are introduced with the help of many line drawings and illustrations. These include ancient and modern structures such as cathedrals, towers, bridges, domes and tents. Salvadori manages to explain how fundamental loads and forces are resisted through intelligent design without resorting to too much mathematical theory.

Norman, D. (1999), *The Invisible Computer*, Cambridge, MA: MIT Press.

The more tasks that computers (and other modern devices) can do, the more complicated they become to understand and use. Norman argues that the personal computer will be subsumed into intuitive easy-to-use networked 'information appliances' in the future. He compares the early users of a device, who will put up with complexity for the sake of the benefits, to later users who want simplicity, ease of use and even pleasurability. A device should become an extension of the user's mind/body and one that doesn't get in the way of the task or goal (human-centred development). He proposes using computers as the hidden infrastructure for devices in our homes, cars and handheld devices, all having the versatility to automatically anticipate our needs and swap information for the benefit of the user.

Norman, D. (2004), *Emotional Design: Why We Love (or Hate) Everyday Things*, New York: Basic Books.

Norman discusses the role that emotion plays in consumer purchases, pointing out that decision-making consists of both conscious cognition and subconscious emotion. New research on cognition and emotion has demonstrated that attractive things really do work better – making tasks both

pleasurable and efficient from the point of view of the user. Norman also highlights the affects that different environments and interior designs have on our mood and sense of wellbeing.

chapter 3   composition

Dondis, D. A. (1973), *A Primer of Visual Literacy*, Cambridge, MA: MIT Press.

This book explores a variety of methods of mainly two-dimensional design that emphasize both theory and practice. It includes many illustrations and diagrams. Elements of visual literacy, such as composition, contrast, abstraction and many others are introduced to encourage a better understanding of visual communication. Chapters 1 to 7 each conclude with exercises that provide opportunities for the student to put into practice the principles outlined in the text.

Pipes, A. (2003), *Foundations of Art and Design*, London: Laurence King.

A beautifully illustrated book in colour and black and white, which concentrates mainly on two-dimensional art and design. The book draws upon many examples of historical paintings and drawings and includes chapters on design principles such as balance, unity, composition, perspective, colour, and others.

Norman, D. (2002), *The Design of Everyday Things*, New York: Basic Books.

Norman surveys the design of a variety of everyday objects such as door handles, kitchen drawers, electric clocks and screwdrivers and finds most of them poorly designed from the perspective of the user. For example, a door should not need instructions that say 'push' or 'pull'. A well-designed object should be self-explanatory. Many designers seem overly concerned with the visual style of the product and neglect what people actually do with these objects, which should really be the designer's starting point. That is user-centred design.

Spiekermann, E. and Ginger, E. (2003), *Stop Stealing Sheep and Find Out How Type Works*, Mountain View, CA, Adobe Press, 2nd edn.

This book has become a standard text on typography design and provides a good introduction to the subject as well as a useful handbook for practitioners. It includes concepts and principles of design that are useful to designers from disciplines other than typography and graphic design. Well illustrated and amusing.

Jeavons, T. and Beaumont, M. (1990), An *Introduction to Typography*, Secaucus, NJ: Chartwell.

This book introduces the basics of typographic design and provides a short history of the subject. It includes guidelines on such things as letter spacing and composition, as well as outlining common faults to be avoided. The book contains many illustrations and provides a useful glossary of terms used in typographic design.

MacDonald, N. (2003), *What is Web Design?* Hove: Rotovision.

MacDonald states that a good understanding of design and the design process is critical to successful Web design. He places these skills ahead of any understanding of the technology involved. Web design is essentially a collaborative venture between the designer, the client, the end users and others. The book looks at those elements and principles of good Web design with reference to many examples of case studies.

chapter 4   colour

Gage, J. (1995), *Colour and Culture: Practice and Meaning from Antiquity to Abstraction*, London: Thames & Hudson.

John Gage discusses the various uses and meanings associated with colour by different cultures over time, beginning with Classical Greece. Beautifully illustrated, the book looks at colour from various points of view; such as the historical, symbolic, scientific and the artistic.

Itten, J. (1973), *The Art of Color*, New York: Van Nostrand Reinhold.

A painter and teacher, Johannes Itten (1888–1967) was invited by Walter Gropius to join the Weimar Bauhaus in 1916 where he introduced an innovative course in form, colour, rhythm and contrast. Itten continued to develop his theories on colour and the colour circle. His principles influenced later generations of artists and designers.

Pipes, A. (2003), *Foundations of Art and Design*, London: Laurence King.

A beautifully illustrated book in colour and black and white, that concentrates mainly on two-dimensional art and design. The book draws upon many examples of historical paintings and drawings and includes chapters on design principles such as balance, unity, composition, perspective, colour, as well as many others.

chapter 5   drawing, communication and expression

Rawson, P. (1987), *Drawing*, Oxford: Oxford University Press, 2nd edn.

A comprehensive and fascinating introduction

to drawing, the book discusses the different approaches to drawing over time by artists from many cultures around the world. As well as providing a historical overview, Rawson describes different drawing methods from both the theoretical and practical points of view. The book includes around 100 black-and-white illustrations.

Porter, T. and Goodman, S. (2002), *Design Drawing Techniques – For Architects, Graphic Designers and Artists,* **Oxford: Architectural Press.**

A very useful source of drawing and graphic presentation methods for students from a variety of art and design disciplines. The book includes many illustrations covering orthographic drawing, perspective construction, shadows, the rendering of different surface textures, the effects of different line qualities, lettering and layouts, all produced using very simple drawing tools. Also included are useful drawings of objects such as classics of furniture design as well as natural objects, for example the shapes of different types of trees in winter and summer.

Eissen, K. and Steur, R. (2007), *Sketching: Drawing Techniques for Product Designer*s, **Amsterdam: BIS Publishers.**

A beautifully illustrated book in full colour providing hundreds of examples of drawing techniques, both hand sketching and computer-enhanced drawing. Aimed mainly at product and automotive designers, this book should nevertheless be stimulating for designers from other disciplines.

Powell, D. (1990), *Presentation Techniques,* **London: Macdonald.**

A classic textbook first published in 1985, aimed primarily at product design students, this book includes recommended tools of the trade and provides step-by-step illustrations of different rendering techniques, as well as many examples of artwork from a variety of sources.

bibliography

Barrow, J. D. (1995), *The Artful Universe*, Oxford: Clarendon Press.

Baxter, M. (1995), *Product Design* (Chapter 3), London: Chapman & Hall.

Bayley, S. (1983), *Taste, An Exhibition about Values in Design,* London: Victoria and Albert Museum.

Bayley, S. (1991), *Taste, The Secret Meaning of Things*, London: Faber & Faber.

Bayley, S. (2000), *General Knowledge*, London: Booth-Clibborn.

Bell, J. (2007), *Mirror of the World: A New History of Art*, London: Thames & Hudson.

Blackmore, S. (2000), *The Meme Machine*, Oxford: Oxford University Press.

Bürdek, B. E. (2005), *Design: History, Theory and Practice of Product Design*, Basel: Birkhäuser.

Cold, B. (ed.) (2002), *Aesthetics, Well-Being and Health: Essays Within Architecture and Environmental Aesthetics (Ethnoscapes)*, Aldershot: Ashgate.

Dawkins, R. (1989), *The Selfish Gene* (Chapter 13 – The Long Reach of the Gene). Oxford: Oxford University Press.

Day, Lewis F. (1979), *Pattern Design*, London: Batsford.

De Botton, A. (2006), *The Architecture of Happiness*, New York: Pantheon.

Dondis, D. A. (1973), *A Primer of Visual Literacy*, Cambridge MA: MIT Press.

Dudley, E. and Mealing, S. (eds) (2000), *Becoming Designers: Education and Influence*, Exeter: Intellect Books.

Eco, U. (2004), *History of Beauty*, New York: Rizzoli.

Eissen, K. and Steur, R. (2007), *Sketching: Drawing Techniques for Product Designers*, Amsterdam: BIS Publishers.

Evans, J. (ed.) (1995), *The Lamp of Beauty: Writings on Art* by John Ruskin, London: Phaidon.

Fletcher, B. and Cruickshank, D. (1996), *Banister Fletcher's A History of Architecture*, Oxford: Architectural Press, 20th edn.

Gage, J. (1995), *Colour and Culture: Practice and Meaning from Antiquity to Abstraction*, London: Thames & Hudson.

Gage, J. (1999), *Colour and Meaning: Art, Science and Symbolism*, London: Thames & Hudson.

Gauldie, S. (1969), *Architecture*, Oxford: Oxford University Press.

Gaut, B. and Lopes, D. M. (2002), *The Routledge Companion to Aesthetics*, London: Routledge.

Gelernter, M. (1995), *Sources of Architectural Form: A Critical History of Western Design Theory*, Manchester: Manchester University Press.

Glancey, J. (2000), *The Story of Architecture*, New York: Dorling Kindersley.

Gombrich, E. H. (1995), *The Story of Art*, London: Phaidon Press, 16th edn.

Goudy, F. W. (1977), *Typologia*, Berkeley, CA: University of California Press. (First published in 1940.)

Hughes, R. (1991), *The Shock of the New*, Maidenhead: McGraw-Hill.

Itten, J. (1973), *The Art of Color*, New York: Van Nostrand Reinhold.

Jeavons, T. and Beaumont, M. (1990), *An Introduction to Typography*, Secaucus, NJ: Chartwell.

Klee, P. (1961), *The Thinking Eye* (edited by Jürg Spiller, translated by Ralph Manheim), London: Lund Humphries.

Kudielka, R. (1999), *The Eye's Mind: Bridget Riley, Collected Writings 1965–1999*, London: Thames & Hudson.

Le Corbusier (1954 and 1958), *Modulor, Vols I and II*, London: Faber & Faber.

Lewis-Williams, D. (2004), *The Mind in the Cave: Consciousness and the Origins of Art*, London: Thames & Hudson.

Livingstone, K. and Parry, L. (eds) (2005), *International Arts and Crafts*, London: Victoria and Albert Museum.

Locher, J. (ed.) (1992), *M. C. Escher: His Life and Complete Graphic Work*, New York: Abrams.

Loxley, S. (2004), *Type: The Secret History of Letters*, London: I. B. Tauris.

Lupton, E. and Miller, J. (eds) (2001), *The ABCs of the Bauhaus and Design Theory*, London: Thames & Hudson.

MacDonald, N. (2003), *What is Web Design?* Hove: Rotovision.

Meggs, C. (2002), *Typographic Design: Form and Communication*, Chichester: John Wiley & Sons Ltd.

Miller, G. (2001), *The Mating Mind*, New York: Anchor Books/Doubleday.

Norman, D. (1999), *The Invisible Computer*, Cambridge, MA: MIT Press.

Norman, D. (2002), *The Design of Everyday Things*, New York: Basic Books.

Norman, D. (2004), *Emotional Design: Why We Love (or Hate) Everyday Things*, New York: Basic Books.

Paulson, R. (ed.) (1998), *The Analysis of Beauty*, by William Hogarth, New Haven, CT: Yale University Press. (First published in 1753.)

Palmer, J. and Dodson, M. (eds) (1996), *Design and Aesthetics: A Reader*, London: Routledge.

Pipes, A. (2003), *Foundations of Art and Design*, London: Laurence King.

Porter, T. and Goodman, S. (2002), *Design Drawing Techniques – For Architects, Graphic Designers and Artists*, Oxford: Architectural Press.

Postrel, V. (2003), *The Substance of Style: How the Rise of Aesthetic Value is Remaking Commerce, Culture and Consciousness*, New York: Harper Perennial.

Powell, D. (1990), *Presentation Techniques*, London: Macdonald.

Ramachandran, V. (1999), *Art and the Brain, Journal of Consciousness Studies*, 6: 15–51.

Rawson, P. (1987), *Creative Design: A New Look at Design Principles*, London: MacDonald Orbis.

Rawson, P. (1987), *Drawing*, Oxford: Oxford University Press, 2nd edn.

Rose, S. (1997), *Lifelines: Biology, Freedom, Determinism*, Harmondsworth: Penguin.

Salvadori, M. (1990), *Why Buildings Stand Up; The Strength of Architecture*, New York: W. W. Norton.

Santayana, G. (1955), *The Sense of Beauty*, New York: Dover Publications.

Scruton, R. (1979), *The Aesthetics of Architecture*, London: Methuen.

Sparke, P. (2004), *An Introduction to Design and Culture (1900 to the Present)*, 2 edn. London: Routledge.

Sparke, P. (1998), *A Century of Design: Design Pioneers of the Twentieth Century*, London: Mitchell Beazley.

Spiekermann, E. and Ginger, E. (2003), *Stop Stealing Sheep and Find Out How Type Works*, Mountain View, CA, Adobe Press, 2nd edn.

Viollet-Le-Duc, E. (1977), *The Habitations of Man in All Ages*, (translated 1876). North Stratford, NH: Ayer.

Whitford, F. (1984), *Bauhaus*, London: Thames & Hudson.

index